PSYCHOLOGY OF LEARNING DISABILITIES

Applications and Educational Practice

James A. DeRuiter
University of Northern Colorado

William L. Wansart

AN ASPEN PUBLICATION®
Aspen Systems Corporation
Rockville, Maryland
London
1982

Library of Congress Cataloging in Publication Data

DeRuiter, James A.
Psychology of learning disabilities.

Bibliography: p. 213.
Includes index.
1. Learning disabilities. 2. Learning, Psychology
of. I. Wansart, William L. II. Title.
LC4704.D47   371.92   82-4108
ISBN: 0-89443-687-2   AACR2

Publisher: John Marozsan
Editorial Director: R. Curtis Whitesel
Managing Editor: Margot Raphael
Editorial Services: Eileen Higgins
Printing and Manufacturing: Debbie Swarr

Library of Congress Catalog Card Number: 82-4108
ISBN: 0-89443-687-2

Printed in the United States of America

1 2 3 4 5

To Billie, Terri, Darla, Travis,
and my parents

J.D.R.

To Cathy, my parents,
and the intrepid learners I have known

W.L.W.

Table of Contents

Preface

Early in 1975 we first asked the question, "How do teachers really decide what to teach and how to teach when they work with learning disabled students?" We were reasonably certain, at the time, that formal and informal tests results were used to decide how to teach. But how were test results actually translated into teaching practices? We began to research the problem by searching libraries, asking teachers, and examining our own diagnostic thought processes.

We quickly found that very little was available in books. Most books about learning disabilities scarcely mentioned the topic. Often they said, if you find Problem A, try teaching approaches X, Y, or Z. However, they gave no clear indication of how to decide whether Problem A was really the problem, nor did they provide a rationale for choosing a teaching method in the first place. Certainly, no clear explanations were given for choosing one method over another.

Teachers were unable to be explicit about how they decided to teach learning disabled children. Many of them talked generally about identifying the student's learning style and teaching on that basis. In spite of their vagueness, however, we found that many teachers appeared to select reasonable approaches to teaching. Many of the students were learning. Our analysis indicated that teachers carefully observed students' behavior, used a combination of available data and intuitive knowledge about learners, learning, and teaching, and then decided what the student needed most and how to teach it. More research on this process may prove fruitful.

We examined our own thought processes when we made decisions about how to teach learning disabled individuals. We found that we regarded the way students process information as important, and we designed different teaching approaches depending on the kind of thinking students brought to the task. We found that age appeared to be very important in deciding how to teach because it usually indicated the quality of the student's thinking.

Contrary to our original expectations, we found that formal and informal tests were not the major basis for teaching. Formal test results were virtually useless unless we had given the test ourselves and knew something about *how* the tasks were completed, not just whether or not they were completed. In making teaching decisions we considered both the level at which the students were thinking and the internal processes with which they appeared to have difficulty. We found that our decisions, like those of teachers, were based on both observed behaviors and intuitions about teaching and learning.

We spent the next several years in an intensified search for information. We searched the literature for information that indicated which learning processes are significant in learning disabilities. We compared what we found with our own experiences, wrote definitions, and, piece by piece, formulated a theory about the psychology of learning disabled persons.

The results of this effort are in this book. We have emphasized the active nature of the learning process and the importance of interaction between teacher and student. We have stressed the necessity for understanding the internal mental events that enable learners to do what they do, a concept that we are happy to see has become a major point of view in the field in the last few years. Above all, we have attempted to present a theoretical basis for deciding how and what to teach learning disabled persons.

This book is written for practicing professionals, teachers in training, and others who are interested in theoretical issues in learning disabilities, especially issues involving the translation of theory into practice with learning disabled persons. The theory is comprehensive and is intended to cover the broadest possible age range—from birth through adulthood. We find it useful for all varieties of learning disabilities.

In our introductory chapter, we describe our beliefs about learning and learning disabilities. We recommend reading this chapter first to gain a basic understanding of the approach we take. Chapter 2 is a review of the learning processes we believe are the most important in learning disabilities. Those interested in the research basis for regarding learning disabled persons as having deficiencies in essential learning processes and those who seek a better understanding of those learning processes should find this chapter helpful. Chapter 3 explains why we regard learning disabled persons as responding in five qualitatively different ways, which we term levels of learning or response. Chapter 4 presents an integrative summary of the structures model, which is the core of the theory and practices we have developed. A thorough understanding of the concepts in this chapter is important for those who wish to teach learning disabled individuals in the way we suggest.

The remaining chapters are an explanation of assessment and teaching practices based on the structures model. Chapters 5 and 6 are about assessment, with the former emphasizing basic purposes and types of assessment and the latter the more specific processes that are involved in assessing internal mental structures.

Throughout these chapters, we emphasize that testing and teaching processes are intimately related. These chapters represent our major attempt to answer the question we began with—how teachers decide what and how to teach.

The last two chapters develop major ideas about teaching related to the structures model. Goals, strategies, and principles of teaching are explained in Chapter 7. In Chapter 8, general and specific practices related to teaching are described. Numerous examples of direct applications based on our theories are presented. Throughout these last two chapters, we emphasize the importance of teaching the learning disabled to select and use appropriate learning strategies. Also important are the concepts that learners must actively participate in the development of learning strategies and that teaching should take the form of an interactive dialogue between teachers and students.

Our theoretical approach is not the final answer to effective practices with the learning disabled. We anticipate extensive modifications and considerable development of new ideas as the field progresses. We are especially encouraged by the recent surge of interest in cognitive approaches to learning disabilities. Much will probably be learned about teaching practices from this perspective. Some findings will undoubtedly lead us to change our minds about components of the model. On the other hand, many new discoveries and developments will probably fit into the broad perspective the model represents. In any case, we hope our readers will find the structures model helpful in the formulation and continuing development of their own theoretical approaches.

We accept full responsibility for any misperceptions, misinterpretations of data, or other errors contained in this work, even though we relied on many others for some of the major concepts contained herein. As with learning disabled persons, we depend on our internal mental structures, which, like all structures, have important limitations. Some of these limitations may be too close for us to notice, and readers who wish to point them out to us are welcome to do so.

We wish to acknowledge the special contributions made by several people to this work. First, to Billie, Cathy, Terri, Darla, and Travis, the members of our families, goes a very special thank you for the unflagging support they gave us over the years we worked on this project. An additional round of applause goes to Billie and Darla for typing most of the manuscript.

Second, a great debt is owed to Dr. Corrine E. Kass whose exceptional abilities as a theorist in learning disabilities served as a major inspiration. Many of her ideas are so entwined in the concepts in this book that they are impossible to separate. If we sometimes misunderstood her ideas, we take the blame. But we wish to acknowledge that many of the major ideas we present may never have developed if she had not suggested them first.

We want to thank Tom Bidell for reading and evaluating several chapters and for contributing to our understanding of learning. Thanks to Dr. Claire Courtney from

LEARNING

Any discussion of learning disability would be incomplete without an examination of learning. In this section we analyze some common misconceptions about learning and their effects on the teaching/learning process. We present alternative concepts of learning and describe how they affect the teaching/learning process.

Learning: Common Misconceptions

How does learning occur? We believe there are four major incorrect assumptions about how learning takes place and that the effects of these assumptions combine to reduce the efficiency of teaching and learning. The common misconceptions are:

1. that learners are passive recipients of knowledge
2. that the acquisition of knowledge is an additive procedure
3. that learning will occur if tasks are broken down into component parts and these parts are presented sequentially
4. that the stimulus-response model explains learning.

Many teachers who accept these misconceptions do not do so explicitly. In fact, they may even say they believe the opposite. Their actions belie their words.

Learners as Passive Recipients of Knowledge

A common incorrect assumption about learners, primarily children, is that their only involvement in learning is that of receiving information. Children, it would seem, are waiting passively for us to present them with information. The action in this concept of learning is centered outside of the child. In schools, children are presented with bits of information and certain skills and are expected, because of the presentation, to acquire those skills and information bits. The emphasis here is that the child *receives* knowledge which is given by someone else. In schools, this someone else is usually the teacher. The teacher's job is to provide activities (activities centered outside of the child) that will demonstrate what is to be acquired. This acquisition often implies remembering. The child is expected to remember what has been presented. There is an understanding in this assumption that accumulation of information and learning are synonymous.

We regard this assumption as rooted in the notion that the adult has information, both cognitive and social, that the child needs to know. Further, it appears to be understood that this information can be presented to children, and they will remember it. Learning, therefore, becomes tantamount to "being instructed." Piaget (1977b) suggests that there are two aspects of education, the growing individual and the information which the adult is charged with teaching that individual. He says that adults view education from their own perspective and focus on the second of these two aspects, the finished product, the acquisition of this information. Because of this, Piaget says, the adult regards the child as a "little man to be instructed" (p. 695). Minimal emphasis is placed on the unique characteristics of children.

Learning as an Additive Procedure

The second common assumption about learning is that it involves the addition and storage of the information received. What is known at any time is the sum of what has been learned. This implies the storing up, in a passive way, of all information that has been presented to an individual. It implies that all the information a person has is grouped together unchanged. The information can be assembled into concepts or ideas, but the process involved is essentially an addition of specific experiences to one another.

Learning as the Sequential Acquisition of Component Parts

The assumptions presented above imply that a task can be broken down into what logically appear (to adults) to be its component parts. These parts, when presented to the child, can be reassembled within the child. The child will then be able to perform the given task.

Let us consider reading, for example. In the early elementary grades the focus of education is on the acquisition of the skills necessary to accomplish the reading task. This is usually called "learning to read." Typically, this means the various methods of decoding words are broken down into their component parts. Phonetic analysis, for example, requires the study of the sounds of individual letters or groups of letters. Structural analysis involves word parts such as prefixes and suffixes, word endings like -ed, -ing or -s and words within words. The assumption is that when these components are presented in a logical, sequential order of increasing complexity a child will be able to read. Of course the child does have to "learn" them all, but when the child adds all of these skills together, reading results. In this approach, reading is usually seen as synonymous with "teaching reading."

Well, quite surprisingly, many children do learn to read, and this, of course, supports the assumption. We are not convinced, however, that learning actually proceeds the way it seems to here. The interesting thing is that many children also do *not* learn to read. This fact, for some reason, does not cause many to question the assumption.

Learning as Explained by the Stimulus-Response Model

Most of us assume that learning has taken place when a response to a stimulus is reinforced and begins to be repeated. This assumption is a central concept in behavioristic theories. Educators often consider behaviorism as something to resort to in solving a problem of inappropriate classroom behavior. A teacher can change a child's behavior through various combinations of negative reinforcement, punishment, and positive reinforcement. The main thrust of this model is, of course, that reinforced behavior will be repeated. So, if a desirable behavior is reinforced, it will be repeated and may even replace an inappropriate behavior. We have digressed into this description to make the point that behaviorism is associated with behavior.

Are behavior and learning synonymous? We think not, but it appears that, in the assumption under discussion, learning and behavior are considered synonymous. At almost any grade level in school we find the following situation. Information is presented in some way. A child is expected to demonstrate some behavior that is considered impossible unless the information has been learned. When the behavior is demonstrated, the child has "learned."

Let us consider an example from the elementary grades. Information is presented about adding two numbers together. A practice paper is given to the child on which the expected behavior can be demonstrated. Correct behavior is reinforced, usually with a plus or smile symbol next to the correct answers. When the behavior in question, adding two numbers correctly, is exhibited often enough, "learning" is assumed to have occurred. Exhibiting the behavior and learning are synonymous.

As in the last assumption, it is true that children often learn this way. Of course, it is frequently discovered that a child has learned something unexpected or has not learned at all.

The main implication of this assumption is that learning is explained by the stimulus-response model. Essentially, this model says that learning occurs when appropriate rewards are given for the desired responses that an individual makes. We believe that learning is not explained by this model. The stimulus-response model does describe learning and does, in fact, present a picture of what can often be seen when learning has taken place. We can see that a behavior that was not previously possible can now be exhibited. While this is all very true, it begs the following question. Can one teach effectively with knowledge of a description of behavior only? Again, we think not. We believe a teacher must have an explanation of the learning process, an explanation of what actually takes place that results in the ability to exhibit a particular behavior.

Effects of These Common Misconceptions

These erroneous assumptions have a debilitating effect on the teaching/learning process. They tend to direct attention to materials and the behavioral response of the learner to these materials rather than to the individual learner. Interest becomes centered on the acquisition of a repertoire of behaviors rather than on the process necessary for the creation of those behaviors.

A focus on behavioral response engenders a tendency to view the response of the learner as either right or wrong in any given situation. This notion of "wrong" behavior does not take adequate account of the reason for the response. The behavior is "wrong," and a new behavior must take its place that can be viewed as "right." This perspective is unfortunate because the incorrect response often contains the very clues to the individual's thinking that are needed to teach the student effectively.

A focus on the *products* of learning rather than on the *process* of learning results from these assumptions. *What* is to be taught assumes much more importance than *how* it can be taught. Many programs exist in all the academic areas. Basal readers and mathematics and spelling series are found in abundance. Apparently, all one need do is place a student into a preexisting sequence of skills (behaviors) at the appropriate place and begin to add the subsequent skills to the student's repertoire. Learning will then take place. The problem, of course, is what to do when it does not. We are not suggesting that the question of what to teach is unimportant. We are suggesting that how to teach, or more importantly, how learning takes place, is of at least equal significance.

The major effect of these assumptions is to provide support for the notion that teaching does not require knowledge of the learning process. Knowledge of what it is that changes in a person when learning has taken place and how those changes occur is ignored. We can ask two questions. If a teacher knows what learning is, will effective teaching be guaranteed? Of course not! But is knowledge of the nature of learning important for effective teaching? We think it is essential!

Learning: Alternative Conceptions

How does learning occur? We suggest four alternative assumptions about how learning takes place:

1. that learning is an active process within the individual
2. that learning is a constructive representation of the world
3. that this constructive process creates living mental structures
4. that these structures constantly change.

Learning as an Active Process within the Individual

Learners do not passively receive knowledge. They are not empty vessels to be filled. Learning is an active process that takes place as a result of the interaction of the learner with the environment. Before children reach school age they learn a great deal on their own. They learn many social skills; they learn to speak the language; and they acquire a great deal of information. None of this is presented sequentially. Most of it is learned without the directed instruction of adults. It happens within the child, often in spite of adults. "Kids say the darnedest things!" was Art Linkletter's appraisal of children. Who taught them to say those things? They "taught" themselves!

Learning as a Constructive Representation of the World

Knowledge is not the copy of reality that the stimulus-response model suggests. "To know an object, to know an event, is not simply to look at it and make a mental copy or image of it. To know an object is to act on it" (Piaget, 1964, p. 177). We come to know a thing by acting on and interacting with the environment. We do not just take in a copy of reality. We actively reconstruct for ourselves the reality that is experienced. A child's reconstruction is not always accurate from the adult perspective. It does, however, move progressively toward a more complete representation. Therefore, a learner's response to a particular stimulus can never be "wrong." It can only demonstrate an incomplete representation or understanding of an object or event.

Constructive Process Creates Living Mental Structures

How can this constructive representation of the world be explained? What happens in our minds that makes this representation possible? This representation is explained by the creation of mental structures.

Structures are characterized by having parts that relate to a whole in a living way and by being self-regulating. A simple copy of reality in our minds would represent form but not structure. Let us look at a plant, for example. A plant has structure. It has an interrelationship of parts that compose the whole. The roots, stem, and leaves are each separate parts that interrelate to compose the whole plant. A pile of rocks, on the other hand, has form. It does have parts, but there is no required interrelationship. If some rocks are taken away, a pile of rocks still remains. Adding bits of information into the vessel-learner would be like building a pile of rocks. It would not be alive. It would not be able to act. Mental structures consist of an interrelated, ordered system of knowledge and active mental processes.

To illustrate, if a man is using a vacuum cleaner which suddenly stops, the following behavior may ensue. He glances down at the machine, gives it a kick with his heel, walks into an adjoining room where he picks up the disconnected electric cord and plugs it in, then returns to the vacuum and continues cleaning.

This sequence of behavior reveals something about operator and machine. The machine has an internal structure that goes into action when it is connected to an electrical power source. Less obvious, perhaps, is that the operator has an internal structure also. The nature of the operator's structure is, to some degree, evident in the behavior shown when the vacuum stopped. Why did the operator glance at and kick the machine? Why did he walk away from the machine, pick up the electric cord, and plug it in?

Answers to these questions might come from asking the operator. The replies would probably be that: (1) he glanced down because sometimes the cord detaches from the vacuum housing; (2) he kicked it because sometimes that makes the machine start; (3) he walked into the other room to check if the cord was out of the socket; and (4) he picked it up and plugged it in because it was, in fact, disconnected.

The operator of the vacuum has a mental structure that represents the structure of the vacuum cleaner, an internal representation of the machine. He knows the machine must be connected to its power source, and he uses that knowledge to guide such responses as glancing at the cord and carrying out the sequence that ends with plugging in the cord.

Mental structures other than the one representing the vacuum cleaner are also clearly present. Most obvious are the problem-solving structures used by our hypothetical house cleaner and the structures that relate to the physical responses he made. These mental structures need not represent reality completely or with total accuracy. We frequently operate with incomplete structures, with outcomes we accept as successful, at least temporarily.

The operator of the vacuum cleaner may not have a complete representation of the vacuum or of machines in general, for that matter. He may understand only that machines have internal parts that are connected in certain ways. Kicking the machine may have resulted from the vague notion that this would reestablish the connections. He may have had success with kicking the machine in the past, so this strategy is tried first. After this approach is unsuccessful, he evaluates his response in view of the structure upon which it was based, and with the new unsuccessful experience he creates a new strategy—checking the plug. The point is that an internal structure will always be present and that it will be the basis for the particular behavior, even if that structure does not result in a desired outcome.

Structures Constantly Change

Learning, like development in general, is accomplished by the generation and adaptation of mental structures. It is not the addition of more information to what is already known. Learning is the adaptation of the structures that represent what is known at one point in time into qualitatively different structures that can represent a more complete understanding of the world. This is actually a transformation process, not merely an additive procedure.

In our view, learning is any modification of existing mental structures that results from interaction with any aspect of the environment. As Sommerhoff (1974) states, ''In a very general sense, 'learning' may be defined as the adaptive changes which the information-handling mechanisms of the brain may undergo as the result of experience'' (p. 166). Piaget (1977c) suggests that this adaptation includes both *assimilation* (incorporating an event into an individual's current structure, i.e., experiencing or understanding the event in terms of a current way of thinking) and *accommodation* (adjusting or changing a current structure so it meets the demands of an event more accurately). Further, assimilation and accommodation are regulated by the process of *equilibration,* so that the new structures are kept in harmony with what was previously acquired.

Piaget describes equilibration as referring to ''assimilation and accommodation in a specific relation to each other. . . . An equilibrated system is a system in which all the errors have been corrected, the excesses compensated for. It isn't a static equilibrium like an immobile balance scale; it's the regulating of behavior'' (Bringuier, 1980, p. 44).

Mental structures are not static states, although at times of equilibrium they may be stable states temporarily. An individual is constantly assimilating information into his or her structures. This very process of the integration of information eventually produces a state of disequilibrium in which the excesses can no longer be compensated for. The disequilibrium generates the adjustment or adaptation of the structure by accommodation. This newly transformed structure will allow for a more accurate understanding of reality.

Effects of These Alternative Conceptions

We suggest that teaching requires knowledge of how learning takes place. Understanding learning as we describe it facilitates the teaching/learning process. These alternative assumptions direct attention to the creative problem-solving nature of the learner's responses.

All errors are based on something. Errors are always consistent with the structures that gave rise to them. The implication is that there is really no such thing as a ''wrong'' response, only an incomplete response. Young children consistently say that, when one of two clay balls of the same size is rolled into a link sausage shape, it has more clay than the ball that is not rolled out. Should such responses be regarded as wrong? Not in the usual sense. Instead they should be considered indicative of a less complete developmental stage. The child's structures have not developed enough to be able to conserve matter, to recognize that the amount of clay is constant when the shape is changed. They are incomplete structures. Classroom learning may be regarded in the same way. A response to a learning situation need not be seen as ''wrong,'' only as indicative of incomplete structures.

Teaching, then, will focus at least as much on the learner as on the materials. Teaching methods will be learner-based and will use materials only within that context. Effective teaching requires a knowledge of student structures. We define teaching as the arrangement of experiences in such a way that learning takes place.

The alternative conceptions point out the importance of both understanding mental structures and teaching based on this understanding. Let us explore these implications by looking at how structures can be analyzed and 'dent'fied ai d oy applying an analysis of structures to teaching.

Analysis of Student Structures

We assume that all structures are creative responses to the problem of dealing with reality. Structures develop to enable the individual to have a more accurate account of reality. We must look at the thinking strategies and subsequent behavior of individuals as an expression of the structures that underlie them. We also assume that specific internal mental structures can be accurately hypothesized from an analysis of behavior and that the resulting interpretations are important for teaching and learning.

Although internal mental structures can be hypothesized from an analysis of behavior, behavior is not the primary focus. Rather, emphasis is placed on the structures the learner has developed that make the behavior appear appropriate to that individual. We accept the notion that every action is consistent with the cognitive structures the person has developed to that point. The behavior observed reveals the structure upon which it is based.

The examples in Exhibits 1-1 and 1-2 emphasize analysis of the structures responsible for the problem-solving behavior. On the left is information about the situation and the child's responses. On the right are the tentative hypotheses an observer might form about the child's structures. The term *knows* is used in hypotheses on the right when the observer interprets the structure as an accurate reflection of reality. *Thinks* is used when the observer interprets the structure as incorrect or incomplete.

The hypotheses on the right obviously do not exhaust all available interpretations. They are statements about possible structures that are most directly relevant to the task and the teaching steps that may follow. Note also that the observations do not reflect a particularly profound knowledge of learning or mathematics. However, the observations do require a willingness to hypothesize about events that are not directly observable.

Refinement or modification of a hypothesis may occur as more information is gathered. In this example, the observer first thought that Karen knew which number to use as a divisor and which as dividend. When Karen said, "Five into two means two divided into five . . .," this hypothesis was changed to show that she may think divisor and dividend are exchangeable. Incidentally, Karen's use of dividend and divisor illustrates a common behavior pattern in learning disabled children. She uses them correctly at first, but within a few seconds seems to have "forgotten" how to work the problem. A lack of understanding of important concepts needed for long division is likely.

Exhibit 1-1 Sample Analysis of Mathematical Structures

The problem "2500 ÷ 5 =" is written on the chalk-board and nine-year-old Karen is asked to "Answer this problem and tell me what you are doing at each step." She rewrites the problem in the form $5\overline{)2500}$ and then says, "This is long division."

Karen knows how to copy numbers, that the division signs ÷ and $\overline{}$ are equivalent, where to place the divisor and dividend, and the name of the type of problem.

Karen says, "Five into zero (points to zero in unit's position) is zero," and places a zero as shown in parentheses.

$$\frac{(0)}{5\overline{)2500}}$$

Karen knows which number to use as divisor and which as dividend, that zero divided by five equals zero and that the quotient should be placed above the dividend. She thinks one starts the first operation on the right as in addition, subtraction, and multiplication.

Karen says, "Five into zero (points to zero in ten's position) is zero," and places a zero as shown in parentheses.

$$\frac{(0)0}{5\overline{)2500}}$$

Karen knows that the digits are divided in a sequence, but she thinks the sequence is right to left.

Karen says, "Five into five (points to five in hundred's position) is zero," and places a zero as shown in parentheses.

$$\frac{(0)0\ 0}{5\overline{)2500}}$$

Karen thinks that, when a number is divided by itself, the answer is zero.

Exhibit 1-1 continued

Karen says, "Five into
two (points to two)
means two divided into five,
which is ten, divided by
two is five," and places
a five as shown in
parentheses.

(5)0 0 0
5⟌2 5 0 0

Karen thinks that the divisor
and dividend are exchangeable
as in multiplication, that
division and multiplication
are equivalent processes,
that they may be interchanged
as needed and that she should
continue to manipulate the
numbers until she arrives
at a reasonable answer. She
also thinks it is more important to *answer* the problem
than it is to go through the
correct process.

In this example from our case files, the child verbalized about her actions in a relatively clear and complete way. In many cases, children's verbal explanations are less complete, even when they are directly asked to provide them as Karen was. When this occurs, the observer needs to hypothesize about what the child *might* say and then needs to check out these hypotheses with additional tasks. With Karen, interpretation was simplified by her verbal descriptions. For example, when she wrote the first zero in the quotient, the behavior may have been interpreted as simply copying the dividend if she had not explained.

Our second example is of "reading" behavior by a four-year-old boy. The reason for placing quotation marks around the word should become apparent as you read the example.

The above examples attempt to show how an observer might form hypotheses about internal cognitive structures. The process is not particularly difficult. Although it may be almost too easy to become overinvolved in far-fetched hypotheses about another's inner structures, we maintain that structures are hypothesized about much more than is commonly recognized and to do so in systematic ways will allow for more effective teaching.

Teaching Based on Structures

In relation to teaching, we must be aware that what we are dealing with is a process through which an individual comes to understand specific problem situations. The person's structures are the tools through which the problem is understood and by which it is operated upon. When we observe and analyze a behavior, we can hypothesize about the structure that would cause the behavior to make

Exhibit 1-2 Sample Analysis of Reading Structures

Derek sees the word *EXIT* above the door in a pizza parlor and says, "That says *exit*." When he is asked what that means, he replies, "Go out."

Derek knows how to read the word *exit*, and he knows the meaning of the word.

The next day, when looking at a high school yearbook, Derek sees a picture of students leaving school. The word *Exit* is written in large letters above the picture. He says, "I know that," and spells *E—X—I—T*. Derek is asked, "What's that word?" He replies triumphantly, "School!"

Derek knows the letters in the word *exit*.

Derek thinks that the picture context, not the letters in the word, determine which word is written down. He thinks that letters are completely exchangeable, having no relationship to particular sounds.

Derek is told, "No. You learned it on *Sesame Street*." He responds, "Oh! Sss—esss—aaa—me Stu—reet."

Derek has a vague notion about sounding out words, but he thinks that a clue contains the correct answer.

sense to the individual. The behavior will always be consistent when viewed through the structures that gave rise to it. When a six-year-old child says that a row of blocks that are spread out contains more blocks than another row in which an equal number of blocks are crowded together, this response is completely legitimate to the child. The child sees only one property, that of length. The longer row, although containing the same number of blocks, is longer and therefore contains more. The child has not yet developed the structures to coordinate the properties of both length and spacing.

As another example, suppose a nine-year-old child solves a subtraction problem this way:

$$\begin{array}{r} 33 \\ -17 \\ \hline 24 \end{array}$$

We need to understand that the solution is legitimate given the understanding the child has about numbers and mathematical operations. One always subtracts the smaller number from the larger. In this sense, the answer is not wrong. The child's understanding of the problem, based on the structure the child has developed, is simply incomplete.

The analysis of behavior in terms of cognitive structure becomes a guide to teaching. Our first teaching move would not be to tell the child that three minus seven is not four, nor that he forgot to borrow. Rather, we would provide instruction related to correcting the notion that the smaller number (three) is always subtracted from the larger (seven). Such instruction is consistent with the incomplete structures demonstrated by the child.

Once the structures upon which an individual's responses were based are hypothesized about, we can make use of the same processes of accommodation and assimilation responsible for the original development of the incomplete structures, thereby modifying them in a controlled way. We can introduce experiences for the child that will place the structures in a state of disequilibrium. Given that cognitive development naturally moves towards a state of equilibrium, we can provide further experiences that will allow for the development of more complete structures with respect to the particular task at hand.

Teaching, then, may be regarded as a process of providing the experiences from which the development of structures necessary to perform new learning tasks will proceed. This development of new structures will take place within the individual and is not directly dependent on the teacher's actions. It will be based on the level of maturation of the individual, the quality of the experience provided, its relevance to the new structural organization sought by the learner, and the equilibrium obtained. The process of teaching presupposes an understanding of the structures necessary for the tasks desired.

LEARNING DISABILITIES

New and more complex structures develop as age and interactions with the environment increase. Significant qualitative differences in thinking ability become apparent in all individuals as age increases.

No one would argue that children are exactly like adults. The differences, however, are often seen in quantitative terms. Adults possess more information than children. What is important, though, is that adults think in an entirely different way than children. Furthermore, children of different ages apparently think in very different ways.

Piaget (1977) has divided the development of cognitive processing into major stages (sensorimotor, preoperational, concrete operational, and formal operational stages) in which thinking changes qualitatively at each stage. Piaget's work in this area is extensive and has many implications for the way an individual learns at each stage.

Piaget is not alone in emphasizing the importance of qualitative changes in thinking and the effects of these changes on learning. Luria (1969) has found, for example, that language begins to regulate intellectual processes once it is learned. Extensive psychological data support the notion of qualitative differences in thinking and learning (See, in addition to Piaget and Luria, examples such as Entwisle, Forsyth, & Muuss, 1964; Gibson & Levin, 1975; Gollin & Saravo, 1970).

We presume, then, that there is a typical sequence in the development of mental structures and a continuous qualitative change in knowledge.

Learning disabled individuals pass through these same qualitatively different developmental stages. However, even though general development is the same, there appear to be significant differences between learning disabled individuals and their nonlearning-disabled peers. Even within a particular developmental stage, specific qualitative differences can be observed.

Qualitative Differences in Learning Disability

There is a good deal of literature supporting a theory that learning disabled individuals have significant qualitative differences compared to peers. Historically, Hinshelwood (1917), Hermann (1959), and Orton (1925), to cite a few, have clearly noted important qualitative differences between persons now called learning disabled and others. A similar emphasis exists in the current literature. Qualitative differences have been explicitly hypothesized in such diverse areas as verbal mediation (Meichenbaum, 1977), perceptual functioning (Obrzut, 1979), and reading (Haring & Bateman, 1977).

In our view, these qualitative differences between learning disabled individuals and their nonlearning-disabled peers are the result of the development of atypical mental structures in particular areas of learning. In many cases, qualitative differences in the structures of learning disabled persons significantly affect learning. We find, on the other hand, that these same individuals develop some structures that *are* typical, complete, and age-appropriate compared to the development of normal peers. It is this unique situation that makes the learning disabled person different, both from the nonlearning disabled and from persons with other handicaps. Learning disabled persons go through the same developmental stages as others, but they go through some aspects of them in a qualitatively different way. Their inadequate structures make many responses look like those of a younger child. In some cases, the thinking behind such responses is different from the thinking of both younger children and normal peers. To understand why this may be so, we need to study the internal mental processes of the learning disabled in more detail. Especially valuable is a study of learning processes in which this group may have deficits.

Deficient Learning Processes

Considerable research has been directed at clarifying which mental processes are especially important in the field of learning disabilities. A review of the available research indicates that the study of learning processes in the learning disabled can be organized under five major areas: attention, perception, memory, cognition, and encoding. Each of these areas of processing appears significantly related to learning and may be involved in the development of inaccurate or incomplete mental structures in the learning disabled. Attention is defined as the process by which stimuli are scanned, focused upon, sustained in focus, and shifted from focus. Perception is the process by which stimuli are discriminated, coordinated with other stimuli, and sequenced correctly. In the memory process, perceived stimuli are temporarily stored and rehearsed. Cognition involves recognizing, identifying, and associating meanings, and inferring new meanings from available information. In the process of encoding, internal meanings are recalled and organized for the purpose of thinking and communicating, and responses are monitored.

We suggest that deficits in these learning processes produce qualitatively different mental structures in the learning disabled. How do these qualitative differences in mental structures come about in the learning disabled? Structures are organized and develop in response to information received from the environment through the individual's information processing system. The system attempts to produce a reconstruction of reality. The processes through which we attend to our environment, perceive the environment and our experiences within it, remember and anticipate experiences, and think and reflect on these experiences, all have a significant effect on the adaptation of mental structures. If an individual has a dysfunction or deficit in one or more of the essential processes of the information processing system, producing inaccurate accounts of reality, what are the effects? Incorrect information is assimilated. The organism adapts internal mental structures to fit inaccurate representations of reality. Additionally, the individual has no way of knowing that the information is inaccurate. In a study of the figurative and operative processes of 40 dyslexic children, Klees and Lebrun (1972) discovered a similar interference of processing deficits. They found that ''the 'abusive preponderance' of perception hinders the arrival of their thought processes at the more evolved and more operative intellectual stages of development'' (p. 389).

The adaptive process does not stop. Over time, the learning disabled develop structures that are more and more distinct from the typical in some areas. These structures become an impediment to the assimilation of specific learning. In school, such individuals find themselves in a situation where their structures are inadequate to meet environmental demands.

Levels of Response

Deficient learning processes do not, by themselves, adequately explain learning difficulties. The level at which the individual responds is also significant. Processing problems may result in the development of inadequate structures, and these structures directly affect the responses of the person. However, at any point in time, the responses themselves are also extremely important in understanding learning disabilities and in designing effective teaching strategies.

We have emphasized the idea that normal cognitive development progresses through qualitatively different stages representative of uniquely different thinking strategies. We have also suggested that the development of a learning disabled individual may be qualitatively different from that of a nonlearning-disabled person. The notion of stages or levels at which qualitatively different types of responses occur is central in our approach to learning disabilities. In our view, five age-related, hierarchically ordered levels of responding best summarize the major differences between learning disabled and normal individuals. Each level indicates a significant change in the individual's mental structures. New ways of thinking, learning, and responding emerge. We expect both learning disabled and normal learners to go through these five levels, but the learning disabled fail to develop some of the important responses expected at each level. We will introduce the levels and briefly explain their major components in this section. In Chapter 3 these ideas are developed more completely.

Level One: Awareness

As the individual develops, the focus of learning changes. The responses of the individual represent the goals of learning at that time. From approximately birth through 18 months, the responses of a baby indicate a developing awareness of the environment, including his or her own body. The baby begins to note objects and movements in the room, the movement of hands and feet, even the relationship between movement and position.

At this level, children are increasing their *awareness* of the world. Physiological arousal of the system occurs as the organism attends to stimuli. The thinking strategy of the child is scarcely recognizable as thinking at first, but it soon becomes apparent that the child uses some exploratory strategies to seek information about the world. From the beginning, the child is more than a passive absorber of information. New information is actively sought. The major outcome of adequate development at the awareness level is the attainment of the response of sustained, goal-directed exploratory strategies. Learning disabled persons may have particular difficulty learning these strategies or may use them ineffectively.

Level Two: Differentiation

The second major response level is *differentiation*. The differentiation level refers to a basic understanding related to the use of inner language and the ability to discriminate likenesses and differences and perceptual detail. This level of responding is a focus of learning from approximately one year to four years.

Note that the age overlaps with the previous level. Later, we will see that other levels also are not totally discrete relative to age. We regard the levels as overlapping for two reasons. First, the age at which a particular individual reaches a response goal varies. Second, more than one response goal is sometimes worked on at the same time for a particular individual.

At level two, children learn much about the attributes of objects and events. They learn to distinguish between varied shapes, colors, sizes, weights, and amounts. The strategies that they learn and apply at this level reflect considerable reliance on the sensations that impinge on their sensory receptors. The child goes beyond exploratory strategies to what we call attribution strategies. Based on input through the senses, the child learns to categorize and classify the events and objects in the environment. Adequate development at this level leads to the formation of inner language or prelinguistic concepts. Children learn the major attributes or features of stimuli. Inadequate or inaccurate perception in the learning disabled may result in structures that attribute characteristics to stimuli that are not parts of those stimuli. Or the learning disabled person may overgeneralize excessively because important attributes are not noticed.

Level Three: Labeling

Performance at level three begins to be important at about age two and remains a focus of learning until about age eight. Level three is termed the *labeling* level and involves learning to attach correct names and simple or rote definitions to objects, tasks, and events. A notable change from the previous level is the addition of verbal language. Children learn that words comprise a special set of stimuli that are distinguishable from other stimuli in the environment. Language is correctly responded to when others speak, and words are used to seek information or give commands to others. As children increase in language skills, new forms of language use are taught. In particular, the children learn about written and quantitative language. They learn nursery rhymes, arithmetic combinations, sight words, and many new labels.

Most of the children's learning is still not based on logical thinking strategies. Instead, mechanical strategies are much more typical. Children in this stage have excellent rote memories. They rely on rote memory for most of their learning, often reciting something they have learned by rote with the errors included. Adults are amused and sometimes startled to find that children often include many incorrect words when they recite such things as the Pledge of Allegiance.

Frequently, children make little effort to fully understand what adults teach them at this stage, not because they are uninterested, but because they do not have the structures to understand. A major goal of level three is to learn appropriate rote rehearsal strategies that enable efficient learning of the massive amount of information adults expect children to learn at this time. Typical children spend a great amount of effort and time in practice and rehearsal of new information. They seek repetitions from adults when they are uncertain of labels. Learning disabled children may fail to use these strategies.

Level Four: Understanding

Level four, the *understanding* level, involves comprehension of concepts that is advanced enough to permit application of those concepts and rules. In this stage, logical strategies are learned and applied. This type of learning and thinking becomes particularly important at about nine years of age and remains important throughout adult life. Individuals learn to solve problems in academic and social situations. They learn to use both deductive and inductive strategies.

The term *cognition* describes the thinking process that is most important at level four. A person operating at this level has attained the goal of noting relationships between ideas and can apply logical analysis to any situation. Decisions about how to respond are based on meaningful thinking related to all the important components that are present in a situation. Language serves as a mediator, an intervening system between incoming information and responses. Careful planning is frequently used before action is taken. If problems occur at this level, the learning disabled person will have particular difficulty with applying logical thinking, with using rules appropriately, and with learning strategies that are helpful in a variety of situations.

Level Five: Habit

The fifth and last level of responding that we regard as particularly important in learning disabilities is the *habit* level. As with the previous level, the response strategies that are learned at this level remain important throughout adult life. We regard functioning at this level as becoming a major focus of learning at about 11 years of age. At the habit level, individuals are able to respond appropriately at will, and performance is relatively effortless. Attention to specific sensory input is minimal. Speed of responding is relatively rapid, and responses are consistently correct. The strenuous mental effort involved in careful reasoning and logical analysis at the previous level is not necessary at level five. With some tasks, responding becomes much more automatic. It may seem that we refer to simple rote response as the major output at this level, but such is not the case. Instead, we refer to the communication processes, the transmission of highly meaningful information from the individual to others and from others to the individual.

The learning process we call encoding is most significant at this level. The individual learns to receive and interpret meaningful information from the printed and spoken word, as well as from nonverbal stimuli. If the person is functioning at level five, comprehension occurs without the logical thinking required at level four. Similarly, when the individual encodes information for expression, the recalling, organizing and monitoring of the necessary responses are accomplished with relative ease. Whether oral, written, or gestural responses are emitted, it seems as if the individual simply decides to respond, and a complicated chain of responses occurs.

The response goal, then, is to achieve the ability to function smoothly and accurately with complex, meaningful stimuli. If learning is progressing in a typical way, integrated strategies are acquired that enable the individual to rapidly associate information, put information in sequence, and monitor responses. The learning disabled person may have extreme difficulty with expressing personal meanings, with automatically understanding the meaningful communications of others, and with monitoring and correcting errors.

Relationship of Levels and Processes

As age increases, the demands of the environment require higher levels of learning and the development of more complex structures. The goal or focus of learning changes. Children with specific learning disabilities continue to function at a lower level than is expected in some areas. At the same time, progress in other areas may be normal. A child's responses may, for example, indicate normal progress in verbal language learning but extreme difficulty in interpreting written symbols. The learning disabled person shows a unique mix of attained and unattained response goals. Some responses make it appear that an appropriate level of responding has been attained. Others indicate the opposite.

The pattern of responding described above can be traced to deficits in information processing. As indicated in our description of the levels of response, each level has one learning process with which it is closely associated. We view the presence of an information processing problem as an indicator of the level at which a person will have difficulty responding. Thus, persons with attention problems will have difficulty learning strategies that are important for responding at the awareness level. Similar associations are found between the perception process and the differentiation level, between memory and labeling, between cognition and understanding, and between encoding and responding at the habit level. At each level, a major process affects the development of internal mental structures. Over time, the learning disabled individual builds up many inaccurate or inadequate structures that make responding at age-appropriate levels more and more difficult. Responding does not stop, of course, but the responses indicate that the goals of learning are not being attained.

It is important to note that, in a sense, all of the levels of response are important at later ages. Each of us needs to be aware of information (level one), to perceive it accurately (level two), and to be able to label and define efficiently (level three). But certain kinds of learning and responding are more significant at particular ages than are other kinds. A child who does not learn to attend to important information and does not learn strategies that result in goal-directed behavior by the age of 18 months is regarded as having serious problems. Thus, the awareness level of responding is regarded as a focus of learning between the ages of birth and 18 months. Learning to accurately discriminate between stimuli (e.g., between a horse and a cow), to label stimuli accurately, and certainly to use logical rules are less important at this early age than learning to explore the world in a goal-directed way. Parents or professionals will likely be concerned about a child of 18 months who seems unaware of important stimuli in the environment. Less concern is typical if the same child is not discriminating between many stimuli or is not labeling stimuli correctly. Only when the child increases in age do these additional areas of learning become critical.

At each age certain environmental demands are placed on the growing individual. Certain types of responses begin to be expected. Thus, the focus of learning changes, and the importance of particular types of information processing also changes. Or at least the effects of processing difficulties change with age. A person with a severe perception problem may show few important behavioral difficulties at the age of six months. At the age of six, such a problem will probably have a serious impact on learning to read. In later chapters we will explain in more detail many of the important relationships between processing problems and behavioral responses.

Definition of Learning Disabilities

When the concepts described above are used as the basis for identifying learning disability, it becomes apparent that the level at which an individual responds is of primary importance. A major consideration is whether the person is responding at a level that would be expected, based on age. If the individual is responding appropriately on some tasks, but not on others, we assume a learning disability exists.

A definition of learning disability may be formulated as follows: Given that learning moves through stages that change qualitatively as age increases, a person may be said to be learning disabled when, in the presence of some behaviors that are age-appropriate, behavior in one or more important areas is significantly deviant from age-related expectations as a consequence of apparent deficits in essential learning processes. Behavior is considered significantly deviant when a person's approach to a task is at a qualitatively different level than that expected at the person's age.

The above definition does not provide a fully operational procedure through which learning disability can be identified. Rather, it provides a place to start, a conceptual basis that serves as a guide for the professional who is responsible for identification decisions.

CONCLUSION

We regard learning as an active process of constructing a representation of the world inside the individual. The internal mental structures each of us construct are always changing as we interact with any aspect of our environment. As structures change, thinking changes. As we grow and develop, we think in new ways that are qualitatively different from previous stages.

Learning disabled individuals suffer from a breakdown in the learning process. The mental structures they construct result in qualitatively different learning. Learning disabled individuals develop these unique structures as a consequence of deficiencies in internal learning processes. As professionals in the field, we must learn about the unique structures of the learning disabled if we are to teach them effectively. An understanding of learning, learning processes, and learning levels is required.

Chapter 2

Information Processing and Learning Disability

INTRODUCTION

Learning disabled persons have serious difficulty with information processing. This characteristic provides a unity to the field in the presence of considerable diversity among learning disabled individuals. Just as all persons with visual handicaps have difficulty with visual acuity, persons with hearing handicaps have difficulty with auditory acuity, and persons labeled mentally retarded have significantly limited intellectual capacity, so the unifying characteristic of the learning disabled is the presence of processing problems.

There is, however, some disagreement among professionals about the presence and importance of information processing problems in the learning disabled population. Some reject the notion that learning problems are related to internal mental events. Others may concede a possible relationship but prefer to emphasize directly observable behavior and the importance of effective teaching rather than problems located inside the learner.

To make our point of view clear, it is necessary to explain what we mean by information processing and processing problems. In this chapter we will describe the learning processes that we regard as most significant in relation to learning disabilities. We will present some of the research evidence for the existence of information processing problems in the learning disabled and will discuss major behavioral indicators of processing problems.

In our theoretical model of learning processes, we have emphasized only those aspects of information processing that are particularly important in learning disabilities. Some processes that are discussed in the professional literature have not been included. In some cases, we have used terms that are used in different ways by other authors, or we have used terms that replace those used by others. Several concepts served as guidelines as we developed this framework. First, a process was included only if research evidence indicated that deficiencies in that process had been found in learning disabled persons. Second, we selected only those processes that emphasized active internal events rather than passive storage of information, external responses, or stimulus characteristics. Finally, we sought to include only those processes that appeared most relevant to teaching the learning disabled.

We do not intend to imply in this study of learning processes that all learning problems are a consequence of internal deficiencies. We do accept the notion that differences in processing information have important educational implications. We are also convinced that learning disabled persons have serious processing problems and that not all learning problems are a result of poor teaching. On the other hand, we believe that teachers are responsible for effective teaching, whether processing problems are present or not. Our explanation of learning processes emphasizes how processing problems affect the behavior of learning disabled persons. The effects that processing problems have on teaching will be discussed in later chapters.

LEARNING PROCESSES: OVERVIEW

A significant issue in the field of learning disabilities concerns the importance and reality of information processing differences in persons with learning disability. We are among those who accept the idea that serious processing problems are present in this group. This point of view, although supported by considerable research, still leaves several questions. Some of these will be discussed in this section.

General Ability Patterns

Perhaps the broadest aspect of the information processing question relates to the concept of general ability patterns. The question is whether the learning disabled have a distinctive pattern of abilities and disabilities that supports the notion of unique processing. Although this issue has not been extensively researched and is certainly not fully resolved, Wallbrown and his colleagues (Wallbrown, Blaha, Wheery, & Counts, 1974; Wallbrown, Blaha, Huelsman, & Wallbrown, 1975) have found that in retarded readers abilities appeared to have a different overall arrangement than in normal readers. Wallbrown et al. (1975) conclude that "test performance of the reading disabled . . . is not necessarily interpretable in terms of the factor structure obtained for normals" (p. 180). These researchers suggest that persons with severe reading disabilities may have a less effective integration of abilities than average readers, as indicated by the finding that a smaller amount of subtest variance on the *Wechsler Intelligence Scale for Children* was attributable to a general factor in the disabled group. If the ability patterns of the learning disabled are distinctively different, the argument favoring a distinctive psychology in this group gains support. The possibility that information processing differences are present becomes more plausible. There may be some question, of course, about the equivalence of reading disability as used in the Wallbrown et al. studies (1974, 1975) and learning disability.

Causes of Processing Problems

A second major question about information processing problems is related to the causes of such difficulty. Why do the processing problems arise in the first place? Statements about causes for learning problems vary from straightforward behavioral statements to neurological, environmental, and genetic explanations. We regard the question of the causes of processing problems as significant because solutions to the problems may depend on discovering and correcting the causes. On the other hand, as educators, we believe we should focus our study on those causes that have educational significance. Therefore, we may decide to place relatively little emphasis on neurological explanations of processing problems, unless factors in this area can be clearly shown to have an impact on designing successful teaching strategies.

Neurological explanations of processing problems have always been a part of the learning disability field. The similarity between the behavior of persons with learning problems and others with known brain damage led to the logical conclusion that learning problems stemmed from neurological damage. When it became apparent that definitive signs of brain damage were not easy to find, the learning disabled were sometimes said to suffer from minimal brain dysfunction. Soft signs have frequently been taken as sufficient evidence that such minimal damage was, in fact, present. Peters, Romine and Dykman (1975), for example, found that children with minimal brain dysfunction and learning disabilities had more minor neurological signs than control children although they also reported that many of these signs disappear by the age of 11 years. Selz (1977) reported that learning disabled children showed reliable neuropsychological differences from both normal children and a group with definite brain damage. Learning disabled youngsters showed a pattern of normal motor, sensory, and sensori-motor functions, and impaired higher level cognitive, problem-solving, and language functions. Children with known brain damage were impaired in both of the above areas, normal children in neither. In a report on studies of brain-behavior relationships in learning disabled children, Rourke (1975) reported that children with high reading and spelling abilities but low arithmetic abilities performed in a way that indicates a relatively dysfunctional right cerebral hemisphere. Children who were low in all three areas or low in reading and spelling but average in arithmetic performed as if they had a relatively dysfunctional left cerebral hemisphere.

Even though some evidence of the sort cited above exists, much of it is scanty and debated. It is typical that learning disability specialists who study problems in the same or similar processes do not emphasize the same causes of those problems. As one example, explanations of problems in the attention process may include mention of developmental changes, stimulus variables, motivation, willingness to conform (Keogh & Margolis, 1976), the reticular activating system, and brain chemistry (Bryan & Bryan, 1978).

Perhaps the causes of processing problems are not unitary. Certainly, we have not reached consensus on the causes, and the search is likely to continue for some time. We suggest that persons who are responsible for the instruction of learning disabled individuals may regard a processing problem per se as the cause of a problem in learning. Perhaps as the search for causes continues in other disciplines, the result will be discoveries that give additional insight into effective treatment or preventative approaches.

Assessment of Learning Processes

A persisting issue related to processing problems concerns how these processes can be accurately measured. Information processing occurs inside the brain and cannot be measured directly. Even direct measurement of electrical or chemical activity in the brain during processing gives only general clues about what is actually happening to the information that is being processed. Psychological or educational measures also provide some information related to processing, but such tests only measure performance, not competence. Whether the person being tested arrives at a correct or an incorrect answer, the interpretation of the results requires the formation of hypotheses that cannot be fully verified.

Hallahan (in Cruickshank & Hallahan, 1975a, p. 52) has stated that it is not legitimate to observe a person performing poorly on a test, ascribe face validity to the test, and conclude that the person is weak in the cognitive ability named in the test. Obviously, some persons perform poorly on tests for reasons other than a disability in the area measured.

A problem that is less likely to be resolved, however, is whether the test actually measures the cognitive area it purports to measure. We face the problem of attempting to measure a construct, an idea, not an actual behavior. In addition, even if a test measures what it is supposed to and the person taking the test does perform poorly, we still cannot be certain of cause-effect relationships. With any formal or informal measurement, therefore, we must be cautious about our interpretation of the results.

How can the measurement of learning processes best be handled by the professional? Should we perhaps abandon all attempts to examine information processing? We believe this is neither necessary nor prudent. We suggest that alternatives are available which can assist the professional in a meaningful evaluation of learning processes. The specific approaches we suggest are explained in Chapters 5 and 6. It is important to take a practical approach to this problem. Careful examination of possible processing problems, based on an examination of behavioral responses, is important. To the degree that processing problems may interfere with learning, expectations, or performance, the professional in learning disabilities must consider these problems and attempt to set up learning conditions to meet any special needs. In Chapter 7 we present several implications for teaching that are related to the examination and testing of information processing.

As we present behavioral indicators of processing problems in this chapter, it is important for the reader to recognize that the direct connections between behaviors and processes are sometimes tenuous. A behavior of the sort presented may or may not indicate a processing problem of the type under discussion. Some behaviors probably relate to processing problems of more than one type. Not everyone has the same processing problem just because behaviors are similar. Some persons with a problem in one processing area will not show many of the behavioral indicators we discuss. Important also is the concept that we are talking about behavioral manifestations that are obviously extreme, not those that fall within a normal range of behavior. We are not discussing subtle differences, but obvious differences that may be subtle only in the sense that they are difficult to interpret. We regard the study of behavioral indicators of processing problems as one important aspect of the study of learning and learning disabilities. An examination of processes and behavioral indicators that relate to them is one aspect of the study of internal mental structures and therefore is important in designing appropriate teaching strategies.

SPECIFIC LEARNING PROCESSES

Some persons apparently do not learn language, reading, mathematics, or other skills in spite of adequate instruction (or at least instruction that is ordinarily adequate), intelligence, and emotional stability. Important differences in information processing abilities may account for some problems of this sort. Information processing approaches to learning and behavior vary in details but share an interest in the study of mental processes such as attention, perception, and memory. Some important concepts related to these approaches are:

1. Humans are able to take in and make sense out of information even though they never have exactly the same experience more than once.
2. Human behavior can be meaningfully separated and studied.
3. Human behavior can be meaningfully related to internal intake, organizing, and output processes.
4. Mental processes are organized in a system through which information moves and is acted upon.

5. Human information processing systems are in many ways similar to one another but may also reflect individual or group differences.
6. The efficiency and accuracy of human information processing systems may vary with diverse tasks.

Considerable research in learning disabilities has been directed at clarifying which mental processes are especially important in this field. In this chapter, we review some of these studies using a framework of five learning processes: attention, perception, memory, cognition, and encoding. We are not attempting to review all of the important studies in each area. Rather, we hope to provide the reader with evidence of the importance of each learning process in relation to the learning disabled.

Attention

Attention is a general term used in reference to several related mental processes that are inferred from observations of behavior. Studies of the relationship between learning disabilities and attention problems are numerous. These studies differ in theoretical orientation and the subcomponents they examine. Several writers have addressed the issues and reviewed the research related to attention processes (Bryan & Bryan, 1978; Hallahan, 1975a and b; Keogh & Margolis, 1976; Koppell, 1979; Messer, 1976; Rosenthal & Allen, 1978; Tarver & Hallahan, 1974). Emphasis on attention problems in learning disabilities ranges from specifying it as the most important characteristic (Dykman, Ackerman, Clements, & Peters, 1971) to naming it one of several typical characteristics (Kass, 1977).

The global nature of the attention process makes its importance in learning intuitively obvious. Apparent also is the need to specify subcomponents of the process, since the precise nature of attention problems in the learning disabled is important. Learning disabled persons apparently learn some things but not others. Therefore, if attention problems are an important factor, they must affect some tasks differently than others. However, research on learning disabilities and attention does not clearly indicate which specific aspects of attention account for difficulty with specific tasks.

Nearly every researcher and theoretician in the area has attempted to isolate subcomponents of the attention process. Learning disabled children have been said to have difficulty with focusing, scanning, vigilance, perseveration, impulse control, distractibility, alertness, arousal, span, selection, and other subprocesses. We found it convenient to specify four subcomponents that serve as a guide to the study of attention. The terms we use are scanning, focusing, sustaining focus, and shifting focus.

Scanning

Difficulty with *scanning* the available stimuli in the environment has been noted in the learning disabled (Bryan & Bryan, 1978; Messer, 1976) with visual tasks and possibly with auditory tasks (Margolis, 1977).

Lefton, Lahey, and Stagg (1978) compared the eye movements of four groups on a task which required matching groups of letters to a sample. One group of 24 fifth graders had been diagnosed as learning disabled and had reading scores at least two years below grade level. Normally achieving third-grade, fifth-grade and adult subjects comprised the remaining groups.

The learning disabled group made significantly more errors than the other groups. Although they did not fixate longer than their age peers, the learning disabled group fixated more frequently. In addition, after approximately five seconds, the disabled group began to use an unsystematic scanning procedure if no answer had been found. Thus it appears possible that some learning disabled children may discontinue systematic scanning after a certain point in time. This does not mean that scanning is always deficient or different in the learning disabled. Nor does it mean that all types of scanning (e.g., scanning the sounds in the environment) are deficient, that difficulties with scanning *cause* specific learning problems, or that training of eye movements will result in higher achievement. Nevertheless, difficulty with scanning may be one distinguishing characteristic of some learning disabled persons.

Focusing

Focusing on relevant stimuli, a second subcomponent of attention, has been researched in relation to "coming to attention" (Keogh & Margolis, 1976), distractibility, impulsivity, and field dependence. As with scanning, inappropriate focusing may be a distinguishing characteristic of some learning disabled persons. Keogh and Margolis suggested that learning disabled children may have difficulty beginning a task because their attention is disrupted by extraneous motor activity. In addition, they may have "ineffective organizational and selection strategies" (p. 280) that increase nontask-relevant activity because the child begins searching for information that will help with completion of the task. The increased activity makes it more difficult, in turn, to attend selectively to the appropriate features of the task.

Focusing also involves attending to the distinctive perceptual cues of relevant stimuli. We are not referring here to general task features where the person may be characterized as asking, "What am I supposed to do?" Rather, we are concerned with the stage where the individual is asking, "What is the exact nature of this stimulus?" Gibson and Levin (1975) have clearly shown the importance of learning to focus on the distinctive features of stimuli.

Learning disabled persons may have difficulty with this aspect of focusing with both auditory and visual stimuli (Hallahan, 1975a, 1975b; Swanson, 1980). Some researchers who traced this idea in more detail have shown that learning disabled persons are more easily distracted by irrelevant stimuli or have poorer selective attention (Tarver, Hallahan, Kauffman, & Ball, 1976). Others point to a propensity for impulsive responding as a possible reason for high error rates in some tasks (Cullinan, Epstein, Lloyd, & Noel, 1980; Epstein, Cullinan, & Sternberg, 1977; Kagan & Kogan, 1970; Messer, 1976). A third suggestion is that learning disabled persons have difficulty separating important and unimportant aspects of stimuli in context; that is, they are more field dependent (see Bryan & Bryan, 1978, p. 145). These interpretations are obviously related although they may result in somewhat different remedial strategies. We suggest that each may need to be considered in work with the learning disabled.

Sustaining Focus

A third subcomponent of attention concerns *sustaining focus* for as long as stimuli are relevant. Ability to sustain focus has often been termed vigilance. Studies of sustained focus have been reviewed by Hallahan (1975a), Keogh and Margolis (1976), and Bryan and Bryan (1978). Doyle, Anderson and Halcomb (1976) used a vigilance task to compare hyperactive, hypoactive, and normoactive eight- to twelve-year-old learning disabled children with a normal group of about the same age. Over a thirty-minute period, the learning disabled children made fewer correct responses and more "false alarm" responses. Also, they looked at distractor stimuli more frequently and for longer time periods. Additional analysis of the subgroups indicated that most of the differences between the normal and learning disabled groups could be accounted for by the responses of the hyperactive children.

A reasonable conclusion seems to be that some types of learning disabled persons may have difficulty sustaining their attention on prolonged tasks. At this point, the research has not clearly separated the possible effects of motivation, distractibility, or other factors on the ability to sustain focus, although Swanson (1980) interpreted his results as indicating that impulsive responding, distraction, and poor orientation did not explain lower correct responses and higher error rates by learning disabled youngsters in a vigilance task.

Shifting Focus

A fourth component of attention, *shifting focus,* is not frequently cited as an attention problem. Perhaps this is because it seems to have so little in common with distractibility, hyperactivity, and vigilance. A logical connection is more apparent when the ability to shift focus to new relevant stimuli is regarded as the opposite side of these components of attention.

Inability to shift attention to new relevant stimuli is often termed perseveration. Cruickshank (1977a) cites perseveration as a major characteristic of the learning disabled and defines it as "inability to shift with ease from one mental activity to another" (p. 52). Clements (1966), in a review of symptomatology in minimal brain dysfunction, specifies perseveration as a subcomponent of attention in a list of ten most frequently mentioned characteristics. Hallahan (1975a) reviewed one study that found reading disabled students less able than normal students to shift attention from one modality to another, but he cautioned that these results may be a consequence of intelligence differences. Wiig and Semel (1975) found that some learning disabled adolescents gave perseverative responses on a task where rapid labeling of pictures was required. No such responses were given by a carefully matched nonlearning-disabled comparison group. We have concluded that shifting focus is a fourth important subcomponent of attention because of this evidence that it is a characteristic found in some learning disabled persons.

Attention Process: Summary

In summary, the research related to learning disabilities and the attention process indicates this group may be deviant in at least four general areas, namely:

1. scanning the available stimuli in the environment
2. focusing on the distinctive cues of relevant stimuli
3. sustaining focus for as long as stimuli are relevant
4. shifting focus to new relevant stimuli

The tentative nature of these conclusions must be emphasized for several reasons. First, alternative explanations have been proposed for nearly every finding in this area. Koppell (1979), for example, has proposed that diminished processing capacity or specific processing deficits would account for nearly all of the findings. A second reason for cautious interpretation relates to measurement instruments. Methods for the selection of hyperactive (Poggio & Salkind, 1979) and impulsive (Becker, Bender, & Morrison, 1978) children have been seriously questioned. Reliability and validity for existing instruments have generally not been clearly established. In addition, the tasks used to measure problems with attention often are not directly related to school tasks. Thus the relationships to school learning are not clear. Bauer (1977) has pointed out that in school tasks clear, discrete stimuli are usually presented, and distracting stimuli are reduced. In contrast, in many research studies inattention is measured using tasks that include irrelevant or weak stimuli.

Rosenthal and Allen (1978) specified another reason why the information about attention disorders may be misleading. They suggested that if hyperkinetic children have a general attention dysfunction, it should produce inferior performance on all tasks. But many of these children appear normal in intelligence and other important areas of learning. On the other hand, if they have specific deficits in subcomponents of the attention process, it should be possible to establish relationships between subcomponents and particular learning tasks. Thus, failure or success on particular tasks could be predicted for children with attention problems. This issue is somewhat peripheral to the discussion of whether attention deficits are present in learning disabled persons, but it points out that if the deficit has no important consequences, it is rather futile to regard it as a deficit at all. Rosenthal and Allen stated that hyperkinetic children clearly experience difficulty in processing incoming information. To this point, however, research has not clearly established that these problems are best explained by the term *attention*.

Finally, we are concerned about methodological problems in the research on attention. Hallahan (1975a) cited difficulties with sample selection and matching procedures (or lack of them) numerous times in his review of research. Many of these problems persist in current research.

At a general level, we believe it is reasonable to conclude that attention problems may be present in learning disabled persons. It is interesting to note that nearly all of the studies of attention involve young children, and many writers seem to assume that attention problems dissipate or are overcome as age increases. At this point, we are not certain that attention has been completely or correctly defined. We proposed a definition with four subcomponents: scanning, focusing, sustaining focus, and shifting focus. These subcomponents appear to be potentially related to the behavior of learning disabled persons.

Attention: Behaviors

Many terms have been used to describe the behavior of learning disabled persons who are said to have problems with the attention process. Such persons are said to be hyperactive, hypoactive, impulsive, distractible, perseverative, or to have a short attention span. Erratic attention, daydreaming, even autism are sometimes mentioned in relation to attention problems.

A persisting difficulty in this area, however, is the establishment of a criterion level for calling a characteristic a problem. How active does one need to be to become hyperactive? Are there times or places where it is advantageous to be extremely active? Is a high level of activity necessarily indicative of attention problems? Is a high level of activity an advantage for very young children? How are high levels of activity and ability to learn related to one another? All of these questions become important when one attempts to identify the presence of an attention problem and to ascertain the effects that problem has on learning.

It quickly becomes apparent that a simple identification of a particular behavior (e.g., incessant finger tapping) does not identify an attention problem. At least two major components need to be examined: (1) the types of behaviors that indicate an attention problem or are correlated with attention problems; and (2) the severity level of the behavior. Unfortunately, little direct research has been done on either of these topics. We are dependent, for the most part, on clinical reports or on research studies that often measure tasks that are rather far removed from typical classroom activity. The types of behaviors we discuss here, therefore, may be related to attention problems in some cases and at some ages. Our intent is to present a logical analysis of possible relationships, not a definitive list of empirically validated facts.

What are the behaviors for which the professional should look if a problem with one of the subcomponents of the attention process is to be found? Although complete agreement has not been reached, considerable support can be found for saying that problems related to goal directedness, activity level, and internal control are significant.

Learning disabled persons may have difficulty with following through on a task until it is completed. We suggest that this indicates a problem with goal-directed behavior. A question arises, however, when an attempt is made to determine whether the behavior shown is entirely random and purposeless. Douglas (1976) says that the behaviors *are* goal-directed, but that they are not directed toward the goals of the teacher. Our own observations of some children indicate that the goals of such persons, if they exist, are very difficult to discern. Often, a lack of planning and organization are apparent. Other than immediate or very short-term goals, such as looking at an object or picking it up, goal-directed behavior is difficult to identify.

The next move of such persons is not easy to predict, except on a general level. We can predict that such children will soon be doing something different than they are doing at the moment and that the chances are high that the next activity will involve something we would rather they did not do, but we cannot predict what that behavior will be based on what the children are currently doing. It is possible, of course, that the behaviors are goal-directed, but that we are just not able to identify the goals. For example, perhaps the goal is to keep intensive stimulation coming into the brain, and what looks like purposeless activity to us is just the opposite. In any case, one major consequence accrues from difficulty in this area. The individual fails to sustain attention to a task for a time that is sufficient to meet all of the environmental demands. In structured learning situations, the teacher notes that an inadequate amount of time is spent on the task, that errors are numerous, and that the task is not completed. Over time, many uncompleted tasks accumulate to produce a student who is far behind the others.

Activity level may also be an area of difficulty for the person with an attention disorder. Two extremes may be found—hyperactivity and hypoactivity. The hyperactive person may be characterized as moving excessively, the hypoactive person as not moving as much as necessary. The former certainly seems to generate much more concern on the part of adults and may be much more numerous if the amount of literature on the topic has any relation to the incidence of the problem. Hypoactivity may lead to the same general consequences, however. The most serious of these are social rejection and failure to learn.

Many questions about activity level have not been answered. The popular concept of hyperactive persons seems to be that they are always overactive. Such is apparently not the case (Bryan & Bryan, 1978; Whalen & Henker, 1976). Excessive movement does not seem to be present in many situations, especially if the individual is not required to work on tasks that others set up. Even in structured, task-oriented situations, the problem may be with other characteristics of the person's behavior, not with excessive activity as such. Cruickshank (1977a) differentiates sensory hyperactivity (where the person is distracted by any sensory stimulus) from motor hyperactivity (inability to refrain from motor responses to stimuli). Even finer subcategories have been suggested by Denckla (1973) and by Solomons (1971). A major point made by these authors is that not all persons who have been identified as hyperactive have equal activity levels or even similar characteristics. Apparently, the behaviors of learning disabled persons that relate to activity level may include a lack of systematic, sequential examination procedures under conditions where sustained attention is demanded (Lefton, Lahey, & Stagg, 1978; Messer, 1976), and a tendency toward more rapid (Epstein, Cullinan, & Sternberg, 1977) and more impulsive (Cullinan, Epstein, Lloyd, & Noel, 1980; Douglas, 1976) responding. Wolf (1979) found, however, that learning disabled children were not more impulsive, but more error-prone.

Closely connected to the issue of activity level is that of internal control. The question here relates to whether we should look on the problem as primarily one of distractibility or as an inner drive that makes sustained attention extremely difficult. Tarver, Hallahan, Kauffman, & Ball (1976) suggested that learning disabled children show poorer selective attention and pay more attention to incidental information. Cruickshank (1977a) adds that the hyperactive child is likely to be distracted by any unusual sensory stimulus. Douglas (1976) and Swanson (1980) found that distractibility was not a characteristic in their studies.

Our own observation is that learning disabled persons with attention disorders always manage to find a distraction from a task, no matter what the stimulus situation. If the teacher makes an effort to drastically reduce the number of extraneous and novel stimuli in the child's environment, the child is distracted by the freckles on the back of his or her hand, the discoloration in a pencil eraser, or the string hanging from a loose button. Perhaps the problem is a combination of difficulty with knowing what to attend to and being able to ignore the unessential.

As with other behaviors we discussed, the result of the problem is that the individual makes more errors, spends less time attending to the task (Bryan, 1974; Bryan & Wheeler, 1972), and completes fewer of the tasks. In turn, the person falls further and further behind in academic areas and may become more and more socially isolated (Bryan & Bryan, 1978).

The above review indicates that the exact behaviors found in attention disorders are not clear although the end results are apparent. By its very nature, attention is a process that relates to all learning and responding. Perhaps because it is a global process, combined with the fact that the symptoms of attention disorders seem obvious to the unsophisticated, attention problems have been said to be related to learning problems in enormous numbers of children. For example, Whalen and Henker (1976) state that 3 to 20 percent of school-age children have been defined as hyperactive. Is the problem really this widespread? Or have parents, teachers, psychologists, and other professionals begun to use the term too frequently?

We believe the concept of attention disorders has been oversimplified and overgeneralized. We suggest that the criterion for identifying an attention problem needs to be much more stringent. A person who has difficulty sitting still, who fails to complete many structured tasks, who makes many errors, who seems to guess impulsively, or who is easily distracted, often does *not* have a problem with attention, in our view.

Renshaw (1974) presents a list of 22 "signs" of hyperactivity and suggests that recognition of the problem "is not difficult when, by the age of 5 years, at least half . . . are persistently and recurrently (not occasionally) present" (p. 82). The presence of many symptoms seems very important to the identification of the problem. Even a cursory examination of Renshaw's signs shows another problem, however—that of the degree to which a particular sign needs to be present. For example, one sign is that of "sleep disturbance." How serious must a sleep disturbance be to regard it as a symptom of an attention problem? The same question must be asked about many other symptoms such as "accident-prone," "speech problems," or "highly excitable."

We do not question the ability of expert clinicians to use these signs to make an appropriate diagnosis. We do believe there is a strong tendency to set criteria for identification too low, thereby including in the attention-disordered population many who do not have problems serious enough to warrant special treatment programs and many who have problems that should be assigned to other categories. We emphasize that the problem with attending must show up in many situations, over considerable time, be unresponsive to any but the most consistent, carefully planned intervention strategies, and be obviously in need of intervention before any other type of teaching can take place.

We often suggest to teachers that if they are capable of teaching a child to count, to read sight words, and to spell words, then the child's major problem should not be regarded as an attention disorder. Attention disorders are present in cases where the individual seems almost totally oblivious to important incoming stimuli, where learning is virtually at a standstill, and where the person appears to be almost uncontrollable. Perhaps it should be added that the reaction of the adult in the situation is not a very reliable indicator of the seriousness of the problem. Although it may be true that adults feel they are "at the end of their rope" in the presence of attention-disordered children, they may feel the same way in the presence of normal children under some circumstances. This criterion is simply too subjective to be reliable. Professionals must weigh their own feelings along this line very carefully and must also evaluate parental reports cautiously. We are not suggesting, of course, that parental concerns of this sort be ignored.

Perception

Perception is a function of the central nervous system. The organism must attend to stimuli, and the stimuli must be received into the brain by way of end organs such as the eyes and ears. Perception is closely related to attention, especially to the aspect we called focusing on distinctive cues. We recognize the overlap and interaction between these two processes (and others also) but believe that separating them may help clarify important factors in learning.

For our review, a distinction should be made between sensation and perception. Sensation refers to the stimulation of the end organs and the transmission of impulses from that stimulation. Perception requires the reception of sensations but also includes a basic level of understanding, interpretation, or attachment of meaning. Simply put, perception means that the perceiver recognizes the stimulus or at least some of its attributes. Obviously, if the receptors are undeveloped or malfunctioning, sensation and perception will be inaccurate or incomplete. Our interest here, however, is not acuity or end organ problems but perception problems at the central processing level. That is, we regard perception as a process through which sensations are interpreted. External responses are not required in perception. An infant who is physically incapable of pushing the correct button to obtain a reward may still be able to perceive the difference between a green and a red button.

Perception is often studied in relation to the receptive channel through which the interpreted sensation arrives. Thus, perception through auditory, visual, tactile, kinesthetic, and other modalities may be examined. The more general model we use specifies subcomponents that are not modality specific. We postulate three subcomponents, discriminating, coordinating, and recognizing sequence, that provide major divisions for the following discussion of perception. Potentially, each modality could be examined within these three areas. However, not all sensory channels have been carefully researched in learning disabilities. Our review examines selected studies that illustrate the perceptual processing differences found in the three subareas above.

Discriminating

Discriminating differences between stimuli, as we use the term, refers to noting distinctive differences within a particular sensory system. The term *sensory system* refers to visual, auditory, tactile, kinesthetic, or vestibular input systems. Other systems (e.g., olfactory, gustatory) can be included although their relationship to school learning is less apparent.

It may be important to refer to "senses" of time and space in addition to the more typical sensory channels mentioned above although end organ receivers separate from other modalities cannot be specified. Temporal and spatial discriminations have been suggested as problem areas for learning disabled children. Rudel and Denckla (1976), for example, found that seven- to twelve-year-old learning disabled children had more difficulty than nonlearning disabled with temporal-temporal tasks that required them to make "same" or "different" judgments about one pattern of light flashes followed by another. They did not have more difficulty than nonlearning disabled with patterns of dots presented on cards one after another. Since both of these tasks involved the presentation of visual stimuli, it may be that the children's time "sense" but not their space "sense" was less capable than normal of discriminating these stimuli. Kidder (1977), in a comparison of normally achieving, reading disabled and learning disabled seven- to nine-year-olds on an auditory task, concluded that the auditory systems of normal children were capable of making finer temporal discriminations than the other groups. We recognize the possibility of other interpretations but suggest the temporal and spatial aspects of discrimination need additional research.

Since we define discriminating as noting distinctive differences within a sensory system, evidence for processing problems in this subcomponent of perception comes from tasks where a visual stimulus is discriminated from (or matched with) another visual stimulus, an auditory stimulus is discriminated from another auditory stimulus, etc. That is, correctly naming a drawing of a square requires visual discriminating, but it also involves coordinating, the next subcomponent of perception. To make the task a more pure measure of discriminating, the subject might be asked to make separate "same" and "different" judgments about two visual, two auditory, or two tactile stimuli.

Hallahan (1975a) and Chalfant and Scheffelin (1969) have reviewed several studies that indicate possible discrimination problems in learning disabled persons. Dykman, Ackerman, Clements, and Peters (1971) found that six- to twelve-year-old children with "minimal brain dysfunction" were less able than normal controls to discriminate high and low tones. Wiig and Semel (1976) stated, "Phoneme discrimination errors of children with learning disabilities appear remarkably predictable and consistent" (p. 43). Bryan and Bryan (1978) have noted several studies that indicate problems with visual discrimination of relevant features in younger retarded readers. Fletcher and Satz (1979) found that disabled readers have problems with the early acquisition of visual discrimination skills.

Discrimination skills are obviously important. These skills are frequently said to be deficient in learning disabled children. Nevertheless, few recent comparative studies of this subcomponent have been reported, and some professionals have suggested the need for reevaluation of the assumption that the learning disabled have discrimination problems (Hammill & Larsen, 1971; Hammill, 1972; Vellutino, Steger, Moyer, Harding, & Niles, 1977). We consider the issue unresolved. We are not prepared to discard the hypothesis that discrimination of visual, auditory, tactile, kinesthetic, vestibular, temporal, or spatial stimuli may present a processing problem for some learning disabled persons. It may be that discrimination problems are most apparent in complex tasks (Blalock, 1977; Bryan & Bryan, 1978).

Coordinating

We have termed a second subcomponent of perceptual processing *coordinating* related stimuli from two or more information sources. Cross-modal or intersensory integration are other terms frequently used for this process. We are speaking of an internal process in which stimuli from more than one sensory channel are meaningfully associated with one another. Coordinating information varies from simple (e.g., associating the sight and smell of food) to very complex (e.g., associating written and spoken language in reading). The importance of this process in learning was noted by Ayers (1975) who suggested that interaction among sensory information may be more extensive than is commonly recognized. Ayers also stated that interaction may be critically important for academic learning. She adds, "The fact that a single neuron can and does respond to r.ore than one sensory modality, and sometimes requires input from more than one sensory source in order to discharge, points up the fact that the brain is designed to organize and utilize input from several simultaneous sources" (p. 317).

Birch and Belmont (1964) developed a method of presenting patterns of dots and dashes in visual and auditory modalities that has been frequently used to test the coordinating process. Subjects were asked to make equivalence or matching judgments between modalities. Comparisons between learning disabled (especially when reading is the major academic problem) and nonlearning-disabled children have typically led to the conclusion that the former group has considerable difficulty with coordinating stimuli of this type (Heath & Early, 1973; also see Bryan & Bryan, 1978; Chalfant & Scheffelin, 1969; and Hallahan, 1975a for reviews).

At a more advanced level, Vellutino et al. (1977) and Guthrie and Siefert (1978) suggested that a basic difficulty with coordinating visual symbols with verbal labels may be closely related to difficulties in reading. Possibly, this skill depends upon an individual's ability to coordinate information between the halves of the brain (Kerschner, 1977). Schevill (1978) found that reading disabled children had significant tactile-auditory deficits (but not tactile-visual deficits) compared to normal children in tasks that required letter naming after tactile input.

As with discriminating, some questions have been raised about the relationships between difficulties with coordinating stimuli and learning disabilities. We propose, however, that important differences may exist between learning disabled and nonlearning-disabled persons in this subcomponent of perceptual processing.

Recognizing Sequence

Recognizing sequence in temporal and spatial stimuli is a third subcomponent of perception. Although it is sometimes difficult to separate memory from sequencing tasks, our concern is with sequencing difficulties that are present when memory span is not exceeded or when a stimulus is not removed. Problems may appear in basic tasks such as visual tracking (moving the eyes along a stationary sequential stimulus), visual pursuit (following a moving target), catching a ball, or saying the syllables of a word in correct sequence. Difficulty with more advanced tasks such as spelling, sound blending, comprehending sentences, and understanding directional and temporal prepositions may also be related (Wiig & Semel, 1976). Recognizing sequence may be related to the scanning subcomponent in attention and to temporal and spatial aspects of the discrimination subcomponent of perception. Studies cited earlier in those areas (Kidder, 1977; Lefton, Lahey, & Stagg, 1978) may be interpreted to indicate processing problems with recognizing sequence as well.

McCroskey and Kidder (1980) have suggested that "auditory reversals" may occur in learning disabled persons because of differential temporal processing of various frequencies. Although this concept needs research, it raises the interesting possibility that learning disabled persons may process some sounds more rapidly than others. If a rapidly processed sound follows a slower processed sound in a word, confusion or a reversal could occur.

Poppen, Stark, Eisenson, Forrest, and Wertheim (1969) concluded that six- to twelve-year-old aphasics had significant sequencing problems when compared to a normal group on five measures of visual sequencing ability. The conclusion is tentative, however, because the effects of memory and language factors may account for the results. Similar conclusions appear warranted relative to auditory sequencing (reproducing auditory stimuli in correct sequence) in children said to have minimal cerebral dysfunction in a study by Aten and Davis (1968). Schevill (1978) concluded that normal children are more competent than reading disabled children in the processing of sequential tactile stimuli. Literature that indicates problems poor readers may have with eye movements has been reviewed by Gibson and Levin (1975). Taken as a whole, this research indicates that recognizing sequence may be an area of processing differences between disabled and nonlearning-disabled persons.

Perception Process: Summary

Difficulties with perceptual processing have long been a primary emphasis in the learning disability field. Clinical and research evidence indicates that dysfunctions may be present relative to three aspects of perception, as follows:

1. discriminating distinctive differences between stimuli within any one sensory system
2. coordinating related stimuli from two or more information sources
3. recognizing sequence in spatial and temporal stimuli

Many of the problems mentioned as we concluded a review of the attention process are of concern here also. Again, alternative explanations of the subjects' performance are possible (Margolis, 1977), and measurement and methodological questions are numerous.

Perception: Behaviors

We have defined perception somewhat narrowly to avoid regarding all problems with learning and with symbols as problems in perception. Nevertheless, the number of specific behaviors that may indicate problems with discriminating, coordinating related stimuli, and recognizing sequence is exceedingly large. The concerns we raised relative to attention are again present. First, the presence of a behavior, by itself, does not necessarily indicate a processing problem. Second, the behavior must be extreme enough to indicate that a problem exists.

In the area of discriminating distinctive differences between stimuli, we refer to the aspects of perception that involve a single sensory system. Perhaps the most typical behavioral signs of difficulty in this area are an inability to match similar or identical stimuli and an inability to distinguish between two different stimuli. The specific behavioral results are dependent on the task and the input mode. With kinesthetic input, problems with discrimination may show up in confusion about body position, balance, or awareness of movement. Tactile discrimination difficulties may lead to problems with fine motor control, which may, in turn, be related to difficulties with tasks such as handwriting. Visual discrimination is obviously demanded for a large percentage of school tasks. The comprehension of speech requires auditory discrimination.

We may find, then, that the learning disabled person who has particular problems with discriminating is unable to recognize familiar objects in the environment, is unable to imitate movement, cannot separate figure and ground, cannot relate two or more objects in space, struggles excessively with understanding simple verbal input, and fails to learn to read. Even the ability to interpret nonverbal information, such as tone of voice or body position (Bryan, 1977), may be related to this processing subcomponent.

Until recently, few in the learning disabilities field seriously questioned the preponderance of discrimination problems in this handicapping condition. It is intuitively obvious that a certain amount of discrimination ability is necessary for any kind of meaningful interaction with the environment. Studies of children showed many of the problems we cited above, and difficulties with discrimination seemed apparent from these behavioral indicators. As our study of the problem continues, however, many of the assumptions about the relationships between perception and school tasks are being reexamined. It has become apparent that the connections between discrimination and other abilities are not simple (Bryan & Bryan, 1978; Lovegrove, Bowling, Badcock & Blackwood, 1980; Vellutino et al., 1977). It does seem important to remember, however, that considerable perceptual learning apparently takes place throughout a person's life. Gibson and Levin (1975) have suggested that what is learned in perceptual learning is: (1) a set of common or distinctive features that distinguish one set from others; (2) invariant relations of events that occur over time; and (3) higher order variables that involve finding the relations between distinctive features or between events. The processes that are involved include differentiation by abstraction (a perceived contrast between stimuli is abstracted or pulled out of the context), learning to ignore irrelevant stimuli, and learning to use peripheral mechanisms such as visual scanning or exploring through touch. The close relationship to attention processes is evident. Gibson and Levin note that many of these processes are learned at very young ages, sometimes long before the child is able to talk about them. They also point out, however, that "There is a long road from perception of the meaning of an ongoing event to perception of meaning in words printed on a page that one is reading, but the beginning is here" (p. 20).

We anticipate that the importance of discrimination and of possible deficiencies in this process in the learning disabled will continue to be clarified through future research. Teachers should be alerted to the possibility that some children may show exceptional difficulty discriminating one visual stimulus from another, one auditory stimulus from another, or one tactile stimulus from another. On the other hand, many common problems with symbols (e.g., reversals, inversions, and phoneme discrimination problems) need to be examined much more carefully before processing problems with discrimination, as such, are hypothesized. Sometimes, verbal labeling, word knowledge, or memory problems provide a better explanation.

The second subcomponent of perception that we proposed was that of coordinating related stimuli from two or more information sources. The coordination of information from more than one sensory system is so much a part of human functioning that we may sometimes overlook its importance. Coordination happens so rapidly and automatically that once it is learned we scarcely notice it taking place. Assume for a moment that you have been blind from birth and have now had your sight restored. What will happen the first time you see an object, such as an orange, in your environment? Unless you can smell or touch it, you will be unlikely to recognize the orange, and you will probably not be able to name it. Information from your visual sense is not coordinated with the other sources of information in this case. Once you touch the orange, however, subsequent recognition of the object is very likely upon sighting of the object. Information from several sources, including vision, is automatically coordinated.

Distinctions are sometimes made between intrasensory and intersensory aspects of sensory integration (Chalfant & Scheffelin, 1969). The former refers to the ability to coordinate several different stimuli from the same sense. We include this type of processing under the discrimination subcomponent. As an example, intrasensory functioning is indicated by the ability to note relationships between size, shape, and movement when the stimuli related to these features are all received visually. Intersensory functioning is the ability involved in the coordinating subcomponent.

Behaviorally, the individual with coordinating problems may have difficulty with tracing, copying, or drawing, with associating sound and symbol in reading or arithmetic, with orienting visually to sources of sound (failing to look at a speaker), or with attaching labels to objects. However, as with discrimination, considerable caution is warranted before a coordinating problem is assumed when these behavioral indicators are present. Especially when verbal labeling tasks are the concern, difficulties with processes other than perception may well be more significant.

The third area of perceptual processing involves recognizing sequence in perceptual stimuli. Difficulties with visual pursuit and tracking, with sequencing sounds into words, with telling time, or with smooth, fluent physical movements may all be indicators of difficulty in this area. We hypothesize that problems with reading maps and with organizing and planning one's activities may be related as well.

Every organized human activity apparently involves temporal and spatial components in some way. When particular difficulties with sequence, spatial organization, or smooth flow of movement are found, the perceptual processing involved in this subcomponent may be related to the problem. The problems may show up in simple motor tasks, such as picking up objects, or in complex symbolic tasks, such as reading, writing, spelling, and speaking. The written work of persons with problems in recognizing sequence may be exceptionally messy or disorganized in appearance, in spite of adequate opportunity to practice and appropriate desire to be neat.

Reversals in reading and writing may occur although this is so much a part of typical development (and so commonly overused as an example of a learning disability) that we hesitate to point it out. In most cases, reversals probably reflect a failure to learn about constancy of position related to letter symbols, a failure that seems to be best treated as a memory problem, not a problem in perception. That is, the person who responds with "saw" for "was" or "d" for "b" can usually discriminate the difference between the stimuli but has not memorized the concept that in written language a specific sequence is attached to symbols or has not memorized the specific label that goes with a specific stimulus. Nevertheless, learning disabilities specialists should be aware that rare cases of perception problems may show up as reversals.

Memory

Memory is a complex internal process with many potential subcomponents. Some researchers (e.g., Atkinson & Shiffrin, 1971) have suggested that information from the environment flows through three levels of storage in memory. First, a literal copy of information is briefly held in a sensory store, then transferred into a short-term store, where it is coded in some phonemic fashion or in auditory-verbal-linguistic terms. Finally, the coded data are transferred to a more permanent long-term store. Control processes such as rehearsing (overt or covert repetition of information), coding (attaching additional information from long-term storage to the incoming stimulus), organizing the incoming stimuli, and using decision rules are given a central role in both learning and recall in Atkinson and Shiffrin's model.

Another model of memory (Craik & Lockhart, 1972) emphasized the importance of the degree and type of analysis to which incoming stimuli are submitted. These authors suggest that the persistence of a memory trace depends upon the depth of processing to which a stimulus is submitted. Greater depth implies more meaningful cognitive analysis. An incoming stimulus may be analyzed for sensory features (lines, angles, pitch, etc.), for patterns, and for semantic-associative meaning. A stimulus analyzed to the last mentioned stage is more likely to be recalled than a stimulus analyzed only in earlier stages. Baddeley (1976) presents several other models and evaluations of them.

Our inquiry into memory processes showed that many subcomponents could reasonably be specified. We decided rather arbitrarily, however, to limit our definition of the term to two aspects: (1) temporarily storing an impression of incoming stimuli; and (2) rehearsing by repeating stimuli internally. These factors have been emphasized in the literature in learning disabilities. Also, these subcomponents appeared to us to include the more active internal processes that are clearly associated with memory. We have included more complex acts such as associating meanings and classifying incoming stimuli as subcomponents in the process we call *cognition*. These subcomponents, among others, are very important in memory and are closely related to it. Long-term memory aspects related to recall are included under the process we term *encoding*.

Temporarily Storing

Temporarily storing incoming stimuli refers to the memory capacity or memory span of the learner. This subcomponent may relate to processing in either the sensory store or the short-term store (Atkinson & Shiffrin, 1971). McIntyre, Murray, Cronin, and Blackwell (1978) studied temporary sensory storage by comparing 20 learning disabled boys (6 to 11 years of age) with matched controls on a "span of apprehension" task. One of two target letters (T or F) was flashed tachistoscopically for 150 milliseconds. The letters were presented alone (matrix size 1) or in an array with eight other letters (matrix size 9). Subjects were asked to report which letter was shown.

The probability of recognition was lower overall for the learning disabled but dropped more rapidly for the learning disabled as matrix size increased. In fact, at matrix size 1, the probability of correct recognition was similar for the two groups. The span of apprehension for the learning disabled was reduced by approximately 30% at matrix size 9. The authors said their findings indicated "some underlying deficiency in the central processing mechanism that extracts, analyzes, and encodes information from brief visual displays" (p. 472). After ruling out distractibility factors in a second experiment, the authors hypothesized that either the learning disabled were slower in picking up information from an afterimage or their afterimage faded more rapidly. Either of these hypotheses could be said to indicate a problem with temporarily storing information.

Temporary storage may also refer to the number of hypothetical "slots" in memory. Chi (1976) has pointed out that the concepts of *capacity* and *slots* have been interpreted in different ways. Some who use the term *capacity* refer only to performance on memory tasks. In this sense, an increase in capacity has been clearly shown as age increases. Deficient performance by reading or learning disabled children has also been found (Badian, 1977; McSpadden & Strain, 1977; Richie & Aten, 1976; Schevill, 1978; Swanson, 1979). It is not clear, however, whether these deficiencies represent a reduction in capacity in the sense that the number of available slots is reduced.

Additionally, Chi (1976) stated, ". . . it is unclear whether . . . a change in the number of slots or, alternatively, an increase in the size (or 'capacity') of each slot" (p. 559) was hypothesized by most researchers. Chi found no firm evidence of an increase in the number of slots as age increases. She concluded that differences in processing strategies and processing speeds may account for apparent capacity limits in younger children. In learning disabilities there is some evidence of deficiencies in temporary storage, but some questions about capacity are unresolved. Whether learning disabled persons may have fewer memory slots or smaller slots is unknown. Are problems with temporary storage related to speed of processing or deficiencies in processing strategies? We will review some evidence related to these aspects as we examine the rehearsal subcomponent.

Rehearsing

Rehearsing by repeating stimuli internally can take several forms. It can, of course, include external as well as internal repetition. Internally, it may involve visual images, words, and perhaps representations of sensations from other sensory channels. Combinations of these probably occur also. Rehearsing is carried out in serial fashion and is usually said to be associated with short-term memory.

Through rehearsing, content in short-term memory is continuously attended to, and transfer into long-term memory is apparently facilitated. Chi (1976) suggested that learning to rehearse takes place in three stages: (1) assembling of the rehearsal process; (2) learning when to use rehearsal; and (3) learning correct execution of the process.

Assembling the process means the actual generation and repetition (internal or external) of images, words, tactile representations, etc. Young children (before age six) typically fail to use rehearsal spontaneously, at least in experimental situations. In a more general sense, much early learning depends on rehearsal, and even very young children use the process extensively. We are referring to the use of the term in the sense of receiving a stimulus repetitively over a period of time. For example, children learn the names of an object by hearing and repeating the name numerous times.

Even when a person has learned to use rehearsal, a decision needs to be made about when to use it. Hagen, Hargrave, and Ross (1973) found that nonrehearsers who were taught to rehearse would do so only when prompted. Finally, some children apparently have not learned to use the rehearsal process correctly. They may rehearse each item separately instead of in serial groups (Chi, 1976).

There is some evidence that learning disabled persons may have specific rehearsal deficits. Bauer (1977) compared learning disabled children with matched controls on recall tasks involving noun lists. Under one condition, rehearsal time was filled by asking the subject to count after a list of 11 words was read by the experimenter. In the second condition, the time between list presentation and recall was unfilled. Time delays of 0, 15, 30, 60 and 120 seconds were used between list presentation and the request for recall. In a second experiment, lists of 3, 6, 9 or 12 words were read followed by unfilled rehearsal times of 0 or 30 seconds.

Overall, the disabled group was lower in recall. In the first experiment, recall was similar in the two groups relative to words near the end of the list (equal recency effect), but the learning disabled showed lower recall with words near the beginning of the list (lower primacy effect). A lowered primacy effect is generally interpreted as reflecting deficiencies in rehearsal because Kingsley and Hagen (1969), among others, have shown that the primacy effect increases when rehearsal is used. In the second experiment, the groups were equal under immediate recall conditions for lists of three words. The learning disabled group was inferior in delayed recall with three word lists and for both immediate and delayed recall with lists of six or more nouns. Bauer (1977) interpreted the results as an indication of a rehearsal deficit.

Cohen and Netley (1978) reached a similar conclusion in a comparative study of ten- to eleven-year-old learning disabled and nonlearning-disabled subjects. Probable rehearsal deficits and a faster fading short-term memory trace were suggested as reasons for poorer recall performance by the learning disabled group. The authors also suggested that the learning disabled group showed an inability to cope with overload because their memory system was inflexible. Their conclusions appear related to those of McIntyre et al. (1978) cited earlier. Faster fading traces and slower pickup of information from an afterimage were hypothesized in the latter study. Tallal (1975) has suggested that auditory retention and verbal memory deficits in aphasics reflect an inability to analyze a rapid stream of acoustic information.

Memory Process: Summary

We conclude on the basis of the above studies that learning disabled persons may have processing deficits related to the following memory subcomponents:

1. temporarily storing an impression of stimuli
2. rehearsing by repeating stimuli internally

It is not clear to us whether the learning disabled have fewer or smaller slots available in short-term memory or whether speed of processing may be a major factor. Also, we do not know if the differences in rehearsal relate to problems with knowing *how* to rehearse or *when* to rehearse. Thus, even though we have removed some typical components (such as semantic organization and long-term recall) from our review of memory processing, research remains to be done on important aspects of this process in relation to learning disability.

Memory: Behaviors

As one moves through the processes we propose from attention to perception to memory and on to cognition and encoding, behavioral indicators become more complex and processing difficulties often become more difficult to sort out. In some cases, the classification of a particular behavior as an indicator of a specific processing problem may appear rather arbitrary, and, to some degree, this is true. In the area of memory, for example, we have decided to focus on the aspects of processing that are closely related to verbal language. We do so because the learning of verbal language is so closely tied to the demands of the school environment. It is with verbal labels that learning disabled children have enormous difficulty, especially in the early grades. Behaviorally, these children demonstrate an impoverishment of both verbal receptive and expressive labels and failure to learn sight words (attach verbal labels to written stimuli), arithmetic facts, sound-symbol associations, spelling words, counting, and the alphabet. The individual may describe something but be unable to name it (circumlocution), or use very general terms such as *thing* or *stuff* instead of a specific name. The emphasis on learning rote and arbitrary sequences in the early grades is apparent. The processing problems we noted with the memory subcomponents of temporarily storing and rehearsing stimuli are demonstrated by failure to learn this academic information.

Problems with the memory subcomponents may also appear behaviorally in two other major ways. First, a person may seem to forget a stimulus almost as soon as it is presented. In sound blending tasks, the first part of the word may be mispronounced because the person forgot the beginning of the word by the time the last sounds were produced. In verbal language, disjointed fragments may be uttered or directions may not be followed because the beginning of the sentence is forgotten by the time the end is approached (Sies, 1974). The individual may have difficulty visualizing a stimulus or with remembering a sound immediately after it is presented. All problems of this sort reflect the possibility of short-term memory problems.

The second behavioral indicator of memory problems relates directly to rehearsal and can be noted by observing the responses of an individual who is given a rote learning task. In some cases, it may be apparent that the person is not applying a rehearsal strategy. Verbal labeling and vocal or subvocal rehearsal of those labels is apparently not engaged in. Clinical observations of learning disabled persons, especially children, suggest that in many cases they do not engage in spontaneous rehearsal. Even if the person is capable of using rehearsal under specific encouragement or reward conditions, failure to do so spontaneously may be regarded as a problem with memory processing.

Cognition

Cognition may be even more complex than attention, perception, and memory. The term has been used to include all acts of knowing, perceiving, and thinking. We define cognition more narrowly with emphasis on deficiencies that have been found in learning disabled persons. Again, we recognize the close relationship this process has with the others.

We will define cognition as the process by which recognition, identification, and association of meanings takes place, and new meanings are inferred. Thus, four subcomponents will be examined: (1) recognizing that meanings are present in relevant stimuli; (2) identifying the meanings that are present in relevant stimuli; (3) associating the meanings that are identified with other relevant meanings; and (4) inferring new meanings that go beyond those identified in or associated with relevant stimuli. We want to emphasize processing that goes beyond the basic level of meaning present in perception or memory processing. The focus is on comprehension of spoken and written language, comprehension of mathematical concepts, and the categorization, organization, discovery, and use of relationships between concepts.

Recognizing Meanings

Direct evidence of processing problems in the first subcomponent of cognition is scarce and sometimes difficult to separate from processes such as attention. Factors such as motivation and expectation are also closely related. And yet, our experience with children indicates that sometimes they appear unaware of the presence of meaning in stimuli.

Recognizing that meaning is present appears important as a first step in cognition. Impulsive guessing is characteristic of children with problems in this area. They appear to answer without even analyzing the question or the stimuli available as an answer source. We find ourselves saying, "The answer isn't on my face. Look at the problem!" Children may behave as if they are unaware of the presence of meaning in the stimuli unless specifically told to look for meaning.

Even at a rather basic level, children with reading problems may have difficulty recognizing the presence of meaning. Guthrie and Siefert (1978), in a review of studies on orthographic regularities, noted that reading disabled fifth graders did not match their nonlearning-disabled age peers in their ability to use orthographic structure for word identification (e.g., to pick out the correct spelling of the word *discussion* from four alternatives when the verb *discuss* had just been presented in a preceding related sentence). Although memory, attention, and the association subcomponent of cognition are all related, difficulty with recognizing the presence of a meaningful clue in the related sentence they had been given may have been part of the problem for the disabled youngsters.

When young children were asked to discover sinking and floating relationships between water and plasticine, Blalock (1977) found learning disabled children just played with the clay while nonlearning-disabled children seemed to recognize that they could manipulate the materials to discover the relationships. Diaz (1976) found that learning disabled fourth and fifth graders did not generate their own strategy for remembering a series of sets of two stimuli. Perhaps they did not recognize the possibility of a meaningful connection between the stimuli. They did not differ from a nonlearning-disabled group when the experimenter provided sentences associating the stimuli. Nor did they differ when they generated their own associations after being told to do so. Thus, attention, memory, or associative ability as such were not likely causes of the problem. Liles, Shulman, and Bartlett (1977) reported language-disordered children less able to recognize grammatical errors in sentences with incorrect word order or incorrect syntax.

In sum, these findings indicate that recognizing the presence of meaning may be a problem for some learning disabled individuals. This interpretation may be more tenuous than most, however, because many alternative explanations of the research are possible and much of the research was not specifically designed to measure the subcomponent we are discussing.

Identifying Meanings

Identifying the meanings that are present in relevant stimuli is a second subcomponent in cognition. Several studies have found that learning disabled children may have difficulty in this area. Kohlers' (1975) results indicated that poor reading was associated with cognitive pattern analyzing and attaching semantic meaning to graphemes. Guyer and Friedman (1975) tested 41 learning disabled and 41 controls with a variety of tasks that were theoretically related to left or right hemisphere processing. They suggested that their group of seven- to twelve-year-old learning disabled children were right-brain oriented. They did not perform as well on long-term word recognition and word prediction tasks. The authors hypothesized that the disabled children did not clearly differentiate words with similar meanings, which could result in global rather than precise organization of the words in memory. Verbal and reading comprehension would be affected by imprecise or inaccurate identification of word meanings.

Vogel (1977) concluded that reading disabled second graders may be less able than average readers to use the semantic and syntactic clues provided in the morphology of written language. Especially when complex morphological rules were needed, the disabled group was significantly deficient. Wiig, Lapointe, and Semel (1977) suggested the presence of a language deficit syndrome in learning disabilities. They said this syndrome involved "cognitive-linguistic deficits characterized by reductions in the knowledge and use of morphology and syntax and in the comprehension of linguistic concepts . . ." (p. 298).

Learning disabled children had difficulty abstracting and applying relevant concepts according to Blalock (1977). For example, they understood the words *heavy* and *light* and could discriminate weight differences but, unlike a comparison group, failed to select weight as a criterion for deciding whether an object would float or sink. Learning disabled children may also be less capable of identifying meaning in social situations according to Bachara (1976).

In summary, cognitive factors have been found to be related to the problems learning disabled persons have with pattern recognition, words, morphemes, syntax, semantics, and social situations. The subcomponent of cognition that involves identifying meanings appears to be an area of processing differences between learning disabled and nonlearning-disabled persons.

Associating Meanings

The third subcomponent of cognition which we will examine is *associating* the meanings that are identified with other relevant meanings. In a sense, any recognition of meaning involves association of previously learned concepts with the stimulus, but we refer here to learning and problem solving through a complex association process. Organizing incoming information, analyzing it in depth, noting similarities and differences between abstract concepts, and applying several rules to a problem-solving task are important in this context, although not all of these have been researched.

Studies that have examined the associating aspect of cognition have frequently used memory tasks that can be organized by the learner. Typically, learning disabled persons do not spontaneously organize the material in these experiments. When Owen (1976), for example, compared 40 learning disabled eight- to nine-year-olds to a similar nonlearning-disabled group, the latter were superior in total recall and in organization of word lists.

Torgesen, Murphy, and Ivey (1979) studied the ability of good and poor readers to recall pictures of common objects after a three-minute free study time and after time spent sorting pictures. Under both conditions, 24 pictures that could be divided into four conceptual categories of 6 pictures each comprised a set. The disabled group was significantly low in recall under the free study condition. When asked to sort the cards, the recall of the two groups was equivalent. As in the Diaz (1976) study mentioned earlier, it appears that the learning disabled may profit from organizing strategies but that they may not use them spontaneously.

Experimental results are not all in agreement on this point, however. In one study (Wilson, 1977), learning disabled fourth and fifth grade children had subjective organization scores equal to nonlearning-disabled children. The subjects were asked to recall in sequence a list of 12 unrelated, high frequency words. Wilson suggested that previous results showing defective organization in the learning disabled involved experimenter-defined categories with which this group may have particular difficulty. We wonder why learning disabled individuals might have problems with such categories when others apparently do not. Incidentally, subjective organization appeared low for both groups in Wilson's study, which may account for the lack of differences between groups.

Associating meanings in reading comprehension has been studied by Prawat and Kerasotes (1978). Matched groups of ten poor readers and ten good readers from second grade were compared on comprehension questions after reading stories. The good readers made fewer total comprehension errors. Both groups made more errors on true sentences than false. The authors said that ". . . higher scores on reading measures are associated with a general ability to retrieve and compare linguistic information" (p. 188). In this study, the groups appeared similar in their response to comprehension sentences that were inferences from the stories. In contrast, Klein-Koningsberg (1977) found that nonlearning-disabled children could not discriminate old sentences (previously presented) from new sentences that were semantically similar. The comparison learning disabled group attended to individual sentences and lexical elements. Perhaps the study indicates that the learning disabled group saw the trees but may have overlooked the forest. The normal group automatically associated similar meanings to a degree that obscured minor differences. Depending on the task, this processing could be an advantage or a disadvantage. In any case, differences in associating abilities may be present.

In problem-solving tasks, Robson (1977) found that learning disabled children may have additional problems with associating meanings. Compared to a nonlearning-disabled group, they failed to retrieve and label conceptual categories as a strategy in some problem-solving tasks. When the experimenter ordered the task categorically, differences in problem solving were slight.

Thus it appears that, in the limited areas (input organization in memory tasks, comprehension of stories and sentences, and problem solving) where research is available, indications of problems with associating meanings have been found with groups of learning disabled children.

Inferring Meanings

We included a fourth subcomponent in the cognition process partly for the sake of completeness. We refer to the aspect of *inferring* new meanings that go beyond those identified in or associated with relevant stimuli. Factors such as ability to predict outcomes, detect causes, determine implications, and arrive at creative solutions are of interest in this area. Inferring is distinguished from the associating subcomponent by less concern with *organization* of material and more concern with *going beyond* the information given.

Gibson and Levin (1975) reviewed some research on inference in the area of reading comprehension. They said that much of the recent work on comprehension stresses the role of inferred knowledge. They also noted that inferential abilities seem to improve as age increases and that socioeconomic status and organization of the content can affect ability to infer. Gibson and Levin did not, however, cite studies indicating problems with inference among disabled readers or the learning disabled.

Divergent production abilities which relate to aspects of creativity are an area of relative strength in learning disabled children according to Wiig and Semel (1976). However, they noted clinical evidence that the learning disabled "demonstrate difficulties in formulating alternative responses to metaphors . . ., in explaining cause-effect relationships and in completing stories . . . in which the implications of actions must be verbalized" (p. 221). Argulewicz, Mealor, and Richmond (1979) found learning disabled children inferior based on test norms in elaboration (extra, pertinent detail added to the basic response) on the *Torrance Tests of Creative Thinking*. No differences were found in fluency, originality, abstract titles, or resistance to closure. Tarver, Ellsworth, and Rounds (1980) concluded that the "originality/uniqueness aspect of creativity is an ability of learning disabled children . . ." (p. 16). Shea (1977) concluded that nonlearning-disabled children used both associative and inferential forms of recall to apprehend word meanings. The comparison group of learning disabled children used associative but not inferential forms. Thus it appears that learning disabled persons may have difficulty with inferring meaning but perhaps only in some limited areas.

Cognition Process: Summary

In summary, we have concluded that processing problems in learning disabilities may be found in the following cognition subcomponents:

1. recognizing that meanings are present in relevant stimuli
2. identifying the meanings that are present in relevant stimuli
3. associating the meanings that are identified with other relevant meanings
4. inferring new meanings that go beyond those identified in or associated with relevant stimuli

The complexity of the cognition process and the limited research in this area make us especially aware of the need for continued research and refinement of the specific factors that are most important in learning disabilities.

Cognition: Behaviors

Processing problems related to cognition appear in at least four general areas—comprehension, rule application, structuring information, and problem solving. We will briefly discuss some of the major types of behaviors that may be related to processing difficulties in each of these areas.

Persons with cognition problems may fail to comprehend verbal information, printed information, quantitative information, interpersonal or social information, and incomplete stimuli. Difficulties may be especially apparent when meaning becomes complex and when words with multiple meanings are used. The most common behavioral result is that such persons present incorrect answers to comprehension questions. In some cases, answers that appear to have been learned by rote are given when a more meaningful response is required. It is quite possible that many learning disabled persons learn to give responses that make it appear that they understand, when in fact they do not. Careful probing may be needed to determine exactly what the person understands and whether that understanding is inaccurate or incomplete in a significant way. Requesting a verbal or written explanation from the individual is frequently helpful in this area.

Difficulty with the application of rules also seems to present problems for some learning disabled persons. At times, the difficulty shows up in erroneous responses that indicate incorrect application of a known rule. In spelling, for example, a person may know the rule "i before e, except after c," but still write *recieve,* apparently because the rule was not understood. Similar problems may show up in syllabication tasks, science experiments, alphabetizing tasks, in sentence construction, or in following sequential steps in any procedure.

In addition to incorrect understanding or misapplication of rules, it also appears likely that some learning disabled persons fail to generalize applicable rules and concepts to new situations. Teachers may face the frustration of spending considerable time on the study of how to write a business letter, only to find that the learning disabled student's practice letter has neither the structure nor the content as instructed.

The behavior of the person with cognition problems may also show that information has not been appropriately structured. The individual may fail to structure information in a personally meaningful way, so that memory of the material is facilitated. Outlining and organized note taking may be particularly difficult. The person may simply fail to do these tasks or may do them in a very haphazard and incomplete way. The consequence is likely to be that important information is not available for later study, or lack of organization makes the material very difficult to remember. Thus the learning disabled person may appear to be very slow to learn new concepts and to use them appropriately.

Finally, the learning disabled person may have difficulty with problem solving in both academic and nonacademic settings. Cause-effect explanations may be absent or incorrect; impulsive guessing may be frequent. Sometimes it appears that the person could solve the problem if adequate time had been taken to analyze the problem and to think through the steps for its solution. At other times, the flexibility needed for problem solving or an understanding of the problem seems to be lacking. Again, the end result is an incorrect answer, or a total absence of a response that addresses the problem.

All adults are frequently faced with the need to comprehend, apply rules, structure information, and solve problems. It is likely that everyone will make errors or fail to respond completely as they work through these tasks. As with the previously discussed processing problems, it is the extreme degree of difficulty, not commensurate with general intelligence, that leads us to conclude that the above behaviors may indicate problems with cognition processing in the learning disabled.

Encoding

We use the term *encoding* for the process by which internal meanings are recalled and organized for the purpose of communicating, and responses are monitored. The term encoding has been used in a variety of ways. For example, it may refer to the process of translating *incoming* stimuli into a representational code for memory storage. We use it to refer to the translation of internal representations to output or responses. That is, encoding requires an active search of long-term memory so that an appropriate expressive response can be formulated. Feedback from anticipated or expressed responses is monitored to determine whether it is correct. Three subcomponents, *recalling* internal stimuli, *organizing* internal stimuli, and *monitoring* responses, serve as an outline for this section.

Recalling

Nearly every response humans make involves recall of information from long-term memory to some extent. Our interest in *recalling* is in the processes related to locating words and ideas for spoken or written communication. The recall process of interest here is not the exact recall of a memorized sequence of words or events. Rather, we regard the entire encoding process as an active reconstruction that selectively draws on previous experiences. Previously learned information is reorganized and translated into an expressive code according to the demands of the task.

Neisser (1967) regards recall in a very similar way. He points out that recall is seldom an exact duplicate of an experienced event or stimulus. In fact, "long, highly motivated practice" (Neisser, 1967, p. 282) is required if an individual seeks to later recall a stimulus or event in exact detail and sequence. Neisser suggests that both primary and secondary processes are probably involved in rational thinking. Primary processes produce parallel thoughts, loosely related to one another in a rather disorganized fashion. These thoughts come to the surface and are then organized by secondary processes. "In remembering and thinking . . . the secondary process further examines and further develops the objects made available to it by the primary one" (Neisser, 1967, p. 303).

We have termed this primary process *recall* and the secondary process *organizing*. Thus we see that encoding is a very active process that brings about a new synthesis of previously stored information. Earlier learning is certainly used, and the organization and associations developed at the time of learning may have an important effect on the extent and type of associations used during encoding. The encoding itself probably is primarily a matter of selecting only parts of earlier memorized concepts from a variety of sources, however. Moreover, new associations and a new organization of the ideas are an integral part of encoding. We agree with Neisser in rejecting the "Reappearance Hypothesis, since it implies that the same 'memory,' image, or other cognitive unit can disappear and reappear over and over again" (Neisser, 1967, p. 281-282), in favor of the "Utilization Hypothesis" (Neisser, 1967, p. 285). In the latter, the individual's total cognitive structure and the demands of the task determine which parts of previously stored information are recalled and organized for expression.

The recall of movements (e.g., of the vocal apparatus) is important for speaking and writing (as well as for nonverbal communication), but we were unable to find comparison studies in this area. Schevill (1978) presented some information about tactile learning and reading. Kass (1972) noted some relationships between motor acts and semantic aspects of writing. Motor aphasia has long been one subcategory of verbal language disorders (Sies, 1974). These sources indicate a possible processing difference related to the recall of movements, but more data are obviously needed.

Some limited data exist for problems in the recall of *ideas*. Ideational fluency is a major dimension of language facility according to Carroll (1964). He reported that research indicated significant individual differences in facility for calling up ideas on a given topic. Wiig and Semel (1975), in a study of learning disabled and normal adolescents, concluded that the disabled group had a reduced ability to formulate complex grammatical sentences. With only a slight stretch of the imagination, Wiig and Semel hypothesized that retrieving an appropriate syntactic structure may be the problem. In a sense, the difficulty lies in recalling a concept or idea. In addition, Prawat and Kerasotes (1978) reported that problems with the retrieval of linguistic information was a likely correlate of the higher comprehension errors they found in poor readers.

Evidence for word recall difficulties in learning disabilities is substantial. They have been found by Blalock (1977) in four- and five-year-olds, German (1979) in eight- to eleven-year-olds, and Wiig and Semel (1975) in adolescents. The presence of processing problems related to the *recalling* subcomponent of encoding appears to have at least some support.

Organizing

A second subcomponent of encoding is *organizing* the internal stimuli in sequence. Again, we are primarily interested in communication through speech and writing. Schuell (in Sies, 1974) attributes the problems adult aphasics have in this area to a reduced verbal attention span: "The aphasic patient can retain only limited sequences of words in his mind at one time—whether they are words someone has just said, words he has just read, or words to express what he wants to say or wants to write" (p. 100). The aphasics Schuell mentioned were severely disabled people who had obvious problems with sequencing ideas and words in sentences. Wiig and Semel (1976) found clinical evidence of similar verbal difficulties with children: "At times, some learning disabled children jump from one topic to the next with total abandon when they engage in conversation. Sentences may be left incomplete, and the topics selected for discussion may lack a logical progression" (p. 195). Their comparative study (1975) of adolescents indicated deficits in sentence formation that may relate to these expressive language problems in learning disabilities. They mentioned "word finding and retrieval deficits" and deficits in "conceptualization, and verbal (motor) encoding" (1976, p. 195) as additional reasons for difficulty in this area.

Myklebust (1973) compared third and fourth grade groups of learning disabled (with moderate and severe subgroups) and nonlearning-disabled children using the *Picture Story Language Test*, a test of written language (Myklebust, 1965). The disabled groups were inferior in total words written, words per sentence, and syntax, and they received lower scores on an abstract-concrete scale. The learning disabled groups wrote just as many sentences per story. As age increased, they did not increase sentence length but did write more sentences. Possibly, deficits in constructing and ordering parts of sentences prevented them from writing sentences of increasing length.

Our clinical observations of expressive behavior strongly support the idea of problems in organizing responses among the learning disabled. Many children have considerable difficulty with writing stories in sequence and with expressing themselves verbally in an ordered fashion. Comparative research evidence, however, is rather sketchy. This ability has not been thoroughly researched.

Monitoring

The third subcomponent of encoding, *monitoring* responses to determine whether they are correct, probably takes place with all of the processes we have discussed. We place it as a subcomponent of encoding because this process covers the formulation of responses more comprehensively than the others. Monitoring, as we use the term, always involves overseeing responses that are self-generated. That is, we refer to self-monitoring as shown when a person corrects an expressive error and allows correct responses to stand. Deficiencies in this aspect of processing might show up as difficulty with noticing errors, with correcting errors, or with judging whether a correct response is correct. Deshler, Ferrell, and Kass (1978) defined monitoring as observing an element of a task, comparing it with an internal standard, and classifying it as correct or incorrect. They noted that monitoring make take place during formulation of the response, during execution, or after the response is completed.

Liles, Shulman, and Bartlett (1977) reported that nonlanguage-disordered children were significantly better than language-disordered children at correcting sentences that contained errors, but these were sentences presented by the experimenters. Wiig and Semel (1975) found that learning disabled adolescents were unable to evaluate or correct their own incomplete sentences. Even more convincing is the Deshler et al. (1978) study of monitoring in learning disabled and normal adolescents. They concluded that the groups used similar and appropriate criteria for judging externally generated material, but the disabled group was less willing to call an element an error in material they produced themselves. Generally, the learning disabled students had lower sensitivity to errors than normal students. On the basis of these studies, we concluded that the learning disabled may have problems with monitoring their own communicative responses.

Encoding Process: Summary

In summary, the encoding process may be deficient in learning disabled persons relative to three subcomponents:

1. recalling the internal stimuli (ideas, words, or movements) that will communicate the intended meaning

2. organizing the internal stimuli (ideas, words, or movements) in a sequence that will communicate the intended meaning
3. monitoring responses to determine whether they are correct

Additional research is needed to pinpoint the exact nature of these deficits.

Encoding: Behaviors

A learning disabled person's processing problems related to the recall, ordering, and monitoring of meaningful responses may show up in many diverse behaviors. Our interest here is not in simple associative responses, labeling, or definitions. Rather, we are concerned with the communication of personal meanings and the expression of highly meaningful, often abstract ideas. It will be helpful to note the differences between the processes of memory, cognition, and encoding. We will use an example taken from the area of spelling. When we refer to *memory* processing related to spelling, we think of the actual letters (letter sounds, letter names, shapes, etc.) and the sequence in which they must be placed to make up a word. A person who can spell a particular word correctly without looking at a model demonstrates adequate memory processing relative to that word. To show adequate functioning with the cognition process, the individual needs to know, understand, and apply the spelling rules and generalizations (e.g., its relationship to other spelling patterns) that are important for that word.

Encoding demands that the person be capable of correctly expressing the rules and generalizations and be capable of applying these rules and generalizations in all appropriate contexts with relatively little effort. For spelling tasks, only people who are responsible for teaching spelling are likely to develop processing of this sort.

Learning disabled persons generally show behavioral difficulties in encoding through a reduced ability to communicate effectively. The problem may appear with nonverbal stimuli such as postures or gestures, as well as in the oral or written expression of verbal, quantitative, or affective concepts. Thus, both reduced academic achievement and social conflicts or difficulties may be present.

The individual's difficulty with recalling, organizing, or monitoring expression may result in the formation of incorrect sentences or poorly sequenced paragraphs or stories. Productivity (the amount of output) may be reduced, and the rate of response may be significantly slowed. At times, the responses may not fit the situation. Inconsistency in responding is also common. If the difficulty is in monitoring, responses may be correct one time but incorrect the next.

Chapter 3

Levels of Response

INTRODUCTION

People learn differently at different ages. This assertion is supported by massive amounts of data, many theorists, and common-sense observations. A very young child does not approach learning tasks in the same manner as an adult. Differences are obvious in organization, planning, verbalization, rehearsal, and many other functions of the learner. Why is this true? Because two major types of changes take place as age increases. The individual matures, and the individual learns. These changes, separately and together, make it impossible for the individual to return to an earlier state of existence or manner of learning. These changes, once accomplished, cannot be undone. The internal mental structures of the individual have been modified and the modifications have become an automatic part of all thinking and learning.

The concept that qualitative changes in thinking and learning occur as age increases is the basis for proposing a model of learning that includes *levels of response*. The model suggests a sequence or hierarchy of qualitatively distinguishable responses that can be traced out as development and learning proceed. Each individual can be expected to show certain responses at roughly the same age as his or her peers. Ordinarily, learning and thinking proceed in more or less the same way from individual to individual. Unless severe limits in intellectual capacity are present, progression from the lowest to the highest level of response would be expected. We will use the term *level of response* to refer to the stages that we delineate. The use of the term *response* indicates our dependence on behavioral responses to determine whether a person has attained a particular level with any given task.

In the first section of this chapter we discuss hierarchical models of learning and development. The second section is about the unique characteristics of learning disabled persons, and the last section is an explanation of the five levels of response that we regard as important.

HIERARCHICAL MODELS OF LEARNING AND DEVELOPMENT

It is necessary to draw a distinction between the model we propose and other models that use the concept of levels of response or stages of development. Many models attempt to explain or describe the learning of children who are not having serious learning problems.

Probably the best known developmental hierarchy of this type is that of Jean Piaget. In Piaget's theory of the development of knowledge all individuals are regarded as developing through four qualitatively different stages in the evolution of thought processes. In each successive stage thinking increases in complexity. These are not quantitative increases but represent completely different thinking strategies. Once an individual's thought structures have been restructured in terms of the next higher level, that level becomes the basis for thinking. These levels develop as age increases and are always developed in the same sequence.

Piaget's theory explains the development of knowledge in all children but does not specifically address the area of learning problems. In contrast, we have attempted to focus on the levels of response that present particular difficulty for the learning disabled individual. We are not suggesting that these stages relate to learning *only* in learning disabled persons. Rather, the learning disabled person is unique, and therefore it becomes necessary to focus on the stages or levels that most clearly pinpoint areas of difficulty.

The concept of developmental levels as related directly to the learning disabled is not new. Kephart (1971) proposed a theory of development similar to Piaget's in that higher level thinking skills develop from prerequisite motor and perceptual stages. Without the foundation of successive stage completion the child will have difficulties with the activities and generalizations of the higher stages. Kephart (1973) suggests that an older child's "approach to activities on the lower level and learning resulting therefrom will be different than they would had he arrived at this lower level by the normal sequence" (p. 330). Kephart was referring to returning to an activity of an early developmental stage for remedial purposes. Kephart believed that development continues and that once development progressed beyond a particular stage, later learning changed the person. This prevented him or her from ever approaching a task associated with an earlier level in the manner of a younger child.

Kass (1977) also proposes a developmental hierarchy to explain the nature of learning disabilities. In an article about a suggested label for and definition of learning disability, she considers the characteristics of the handicap she calls dyssymbolia to be caused by the "interaction between significant deficits in developmental functions and environmental conditions which make the individual vulnerable to those dysfunctions" (p. 426). Kass presents five age-related developmental functions. A dysfunction in any of these areas is the reason for the child's failure to perform. The area of dysfunction depends on the age of the individual. Kass suggests that the characteristics of learning disability may "mean different things at different ages" (p. 425).

The levels of response component of our model of learning disabilities is, in some respects, developmental as in the age-related developmental hierarchies just presented. However, a distinction between our model and other levels models is important. Developmental models indicate that as individuals develop they are clearly at one level or another at any particular point in time. In some cases, a time of transition between levels may be included.

One unique aspect of learning disabled persons is that they may operate at distinctively different levels with one task than with another. In addition, the learning disabled individual may operate inaccurately or inefficiently at a level, even when that level is appropriate for the task. This sometimes occurs in the presence of indications that the person should be capable of adequate performance at that level. Problems of this sort are probably related to the particular information processing characteristics of the individual. To account for the possibility that learning disabled individuals may respond at more than one level at a time, the model we propose incorporates aspects of what we call functional hierarchies.

Functional hierarchies involve levels that are not necessarily age-related. They refer to levels of processing that may be sequentially developed but which exist as a hierarchy of alternative strategies, any of which may be used in response to any task at any time. In a functional hierarchy, an individual may use any level of strategy that has been developed even though the highest level attained may be the most appropriate level of strategy from which to respond. In a developmental hierarchy, on the other hand, individuals do not return to earlier stages once they have developed further.

A functional hierarchy was used in the development of the *Illinois Test of Psycholinguistic Abilities* (Kirk, McCarthy & Kirk, 1968). The authors of this test used Osgood's (1957b) concept "of behavior as a set of processes organized at several levels, projection, integration, and representation, at each of which selection among hierarchical systems of alternatives is involved" (p. 348). Kirk and his colleagues modified Osgood's model and included two levels of organization, the automatic and the representational, in the test. They did not consider these levels of response to be age-related. Rather they represented two types of processing necessary for learning. An individual responds with one or the other depending on the demands of the task.

Johnson and Myklebust (1967) present a model of learning disability which includes the concept of hierarchical levels. They propose five processes of learning which are viewed as hierarchies of experience. These processes develop sequentially from lower to higher intellectually. Although the model Johnson and Myklebust propose is not entirely clear (they describe the five behavioral classifications that they term sensation, perception, imagery, symbolization, and conceptualization as *types, processes, hierarchies,* and *levels*) it represents the concept of a developmental progression in which later functions are dependent on adequate development of earlier functions. These five processes are not, however, age-related as in the developmental hierarchies. An individual continues to use and, in the case of learning disability, have difficulty with lower level processes even though that person has progressed beyond it in the hierarchical sequence.

UNIQUE CHARACTERISTICS OF LEARNING DISABILITY

We have stated that the psychology of the learning disabled person is unique and that these unique characteristics require a description that focuses on the areas of development and response that present particular difficulty to the learning disabled. Let us explore these unique characteristics in more depth.

Atypical Development

Humans develop slowly compared to other species. It has become common, in the last 50 years or so, to conceptualize human development in terms of a series of developmental stages with each stage extending over a period of several years. Qualitative and quantitative changes related to physical, intellectual, psychological, and moral growth are frequently hypothesized. Concomitantly, school curricula have been designed to match developmental stages. Basic school subjects have been analyzed and placed in reasonable sequences that fit the learning needs and abilities of each developmental stage. For the child who is moving through developmental stages in a typical way, curriculum sequences can be presented, and learning progresses as expected. Considerable variation is present, of course, in the "typical" range. Learning does not proceed in a straight line for even the most able individuals. People do not attain particular developmental stages at precise chronological ages that are the same for everyone. Even in cases where there is an apparent developmental lag, however, individuals often move through the same stages, merely doing so at a slower pace or a later time.

But what about the learning disabled individual? Are the usual developmental stages arrived at in the usual way? Our psychology of learning disability suggests that they are not. As a consequence of the very nature of their disability, the development of the learning disabled is not typical. Problems with processing information result in unique structures in the learning disabled. Some areas of function may be relatively normal. Others are obviously deficient. A student may be normal in intelligence as measured by a test, but four years behind his peers in arithmetic skills. (We assume equality in opportunity to learn.) Adequate intelligence scores are likely only if the individual *thinks* in a way appropriate for his or her age. But the person's skills, in the above example, are out of phase. Arithmetic abilities do not match with age or apparent thinking ability. Such a person is not following a typical developmental pattern. The learning disabled person is not an overgrown second grader just because arithmetic skills are equivalent to the expectations of that grade. He or she is a sixth grader (or whatever), with the mind of a sixth grader, the thinking skills of a sixth grader, and the interests and needs of a sixth grader.

The learning disabled person is significantly out of developmental phase. The learning disabled sixth grade child is different from the second grader *and* different from the normal sixth grader in many ways. The child now has a unique mix of age-appropriate and nonage-appropriate structures that result in an atypical developmental pattern. This produces a unique set of qualitative and quantitative differences. The learning disabled may have less knowledge in some academic areas and may need to learn skills typical of a younger person. On the other hand, the same individual may have the ability to think like a much older student and be capable of a much more complex approach to learning those skills.

Conflict with Environmental Expectations

The demands placed upon a developing child in an academic environment increase and change with age. These demands require higher levels of learning and responding. We have shown that the learning disabled person has a unique set of abilities with which to meet these demands. It is popular in remedial settings to think in terms of the student's level of academic development and to set remedial expectations accordingly. This presents the learning disabled individual with two novel conflicts.

First, as students progress through school they are asked to perform tasks that generally appear to be appropriate given their age and grade level. A learning disabled person, however, may not have developed the structures necessary for adequate responding at the level required. The learner, using his or her available structures, responds in a way typical of an earlier age level. For example, our sixth grade child may be presented with a problem situation in a science class in which an understanding and application of the concepts concerned is expected. If the child's reading structures are not beyond what is usually considered second-grade level, it is likely that the approach to the task will be inadequate. Instead of focusing on the overall meaning of the concepts in a way that would meet the expectations, the student may focus on the immediate labels of words he or she is reading. The child's strategy will prevent use of the contextual relationships of the words, and the overall meaning of the concepts will be missed. The response may be inadequate to meet the task demands. This produces failure which may eventually translate into lower achievement in both reading and science.

Second, attempts to deal with the low level of achievement may produce conflict for the learning disabled individual. Our sixth grader has many age-appropriate abilities and can think like a sixth grader in many areas. If remediating the reading behavior means presenting the learner with methods and materials appropriate for second grade skills in second grade children, then these age-appropriate abilities are not being used. If the child has age-appropriate verbal language ability, this can be used to teach the deficient skills. Language can be used to guide perceptual (Miller & Rohr, 1980) and conceptual (Abikoff, 1979; Meichenbaum, 1977; Weithorn & Kagen, 1979) processes, and learning "earlier" material may be accomplished more rapidly. The student's language ability could be used to guide the use of context for word identification instead of teaching lower level individual word attack methods. In the science area, the child is probably capable of understanding the concepts if directed to use age-appropriate strategies, and requirements for certain deficient skills can be eliminated. Application of this concept will be discussed in more detail in Chapters 7 and 8.

Students' true developmental levels, indicated by all of their internal mental structures, must be considered. Methodology and content must be designed to match both the learner's structures and skills.

Age-Related Changes in Processes

We have said that the presence of information processing problems presents a unifying characteristic to the field of learning disability. Some theories of learning disability that emphasize deficient learning processes take this concept one step further. Not only do they indicate that specific processing deficits are present and are a *cause* of learning problems, but they conclude that remediation of the processing problem should lead to the ability (following instruction) to achieve academically. We suggest that the processing problem never goes away, but that age (moving up in levels) and task demands make the importance of processing problems change.

Deficits in processing can be observed at various ages. Diagnosticians can observe perceptual and attention deficits in 8- or 10-year-old children or memory problems in 14- or 16-year-old children. Do these deficits mean the same thing at all ages? We suggest that they do not.

It appears that there is a specific focus for behavioral responses at different ages. For example, Kershner's (1975) study of the relationship between reading achievement and perceptual and cognitive visual-spatial abilities suggests that second graders are able to compensate for poor perceptual abilities by using higher cognitive abilities. In Kershner's theory of stage-related learning strategies, conceptual abilities are considered much more significant than perceptual abilities during the concrete operational stage which begins around the age of seven or eight (second grade). In our view, a specific type of information processing is necessary at each of these levels of response, and the necessary processing changes at each level.

The major task of the very young child initially is to learn to orient toward stimuli, to respond in a way that shows awareness of the presence of an important stimulus. Children are not asked to make "correct" responses in the usual sense. They are regarded as not progressing adequately (making a wrong response) only if awareness of the stimulus appears absent. This lack of awareness typically shows up by a response that ignores the stimulus altogether. A close link with the attention process is apparent. A similar link between levels and processes is apparent elsewhere.

For the adolescent, a comprehension of concepts is the major focus of response. The individual at this level must respond in a way that permits the application of concepts and rules. The person must identify and use complex meaning to progress adequately. A close link with the cognition process is apparent. True, the processes of attention, perception, and memory are still needed but are not sufficient to guarantee appropriate responding.

Earlier processing may, in fact, be subsumed or redefined by later levels. The adolescent must continue to use the attention, perception, and memory processes. But now the individual must attend and perceive complex meanings instead of simple stimuli. Earlier processes change. They become more automatic because they are now monitored and mediated by the age-appropriate processes. The person might demonstrate (on tests perhaps) the presence of processing deficits associated with earlier levels, but the inability to use age-appropriate processes has the most serious effects on the individual's ability to respond adequately.

If a processing problem significantly affects responding at a particular level and only within a limited time span, remediation of that specific processing deficit will be ineffective, especially if the person is beyond the associated level in his or her development. Research results suggest that such process-oriented remediation is, in fact, inefficient (Hammill, 1972). We are convinced that the focus of remediation should be on getting the person to respond at an age-appropriate level rather than on remediating deficient processes. Learning disabled individuals must be taught age-appropriate strategies of response.

LEVELS OF RESPONSE

For all students, the goals of learning and the strategies for responding to learning tasks change with age. When working with learning disabled persons, an understanding of the age-related changes that present particular difficulty for them is extremely important. Identification and labeling of the learning disabled is of no consequence if it does not lead to specific instruction.

Instruction for the learning disabled must be based on an understanding of the way an individual responds to various tasks. Are the responses at an age-appropriate level? If not, what level of response is the individual using? This requires knowledge of when certain levels of responding become important and available to the individual. The levels we propose provide the basis for making decisions about the type of responding the person is presently using or should be encouraged to use at any given time.

The model we propose is not meant to be a complete description of all facets of human development. It is, as we have said, a description of the levels of responding expected by the environment that present particular difficulty for the learning disabled. In this sense, it is a system of reference points to aid in the assessment of each person's particular learning difficulties and to aid in making remedial decisions.

The levels are based upon observations of what generally appears to be the major focus of learning at various ages. In this sense it is a developmental hierarchy of learning goals. These goals develop sequentially in time. The infant does not share with the adolescent the goal of understanding complex meaning. Goals change as the individual matures and learns. The model is also based upon observations of the concomitant strategies that evolve to meet these goals. These strategies, once developed, can always be used. In this sense the model is also a functional hierarchy.

We have identified five qualitatively distinguishable, age-related levels of response. We will explain the nature of each level, identify tasks typical of this level of responding, and describe the areas of difficulty that each level presents for the learning disabled.

Level I: Awareness

The *awareness level* refers to the physiological arousal of the system that occurs as the organism attends to stimuli. This level is a focus of learning from birth to 18 months.

The environment surrounding the infant is filled with interesting and important stimuli. The infant's own hands and feet, physical objects in the room or crib, mother's body and voice are all stimuli with which the infant will need to become familiar. Without an awareness of these important stimuli the infant will not develop and learn. At the awareness level infants begin to orient toward the stimuli in their environment.

The relationship of the attention process to this level is significant. The infant is actively involved in scanning the environment and focusing on interesting aspects of it that have commanded attention. Focus must be sustained on desired stimuli such as the mobile hanging in the crib. That focus must be shifted to new stimuli like a mother's voice or physical presence when these become important. These processes and the awareness they represent are necessary for the development of goal-directed behavior. Through the appropriate attention processes the infant begins an active exploration of the environment. Sustained, goal-directed exploration of the environment is the major outcome of this level.

Observations of infant behavior do not center on the correctness of any particular response. Adequate development is usually judged by the presence of a response to stimuli. If the infant is aware of and responds to appropriate stimuli, adequate development is usually assumed. We are not, of course, implying that an awareness of the environment alone is sufficient to insure proper development. The infant soon begins to make perceptual differentiations and begins to remember various aspects of the environment. We merely suggest that awareness is the general focus of learning during this period and that exploration strategies develop from it.

The general problem associated with the awareness level for the learning disabled is the lack of goal-directed behavior. Learning disabled individuals may have difficulties with attention processes when they are infants. This may cause observable problems early in the individual's life. Autism may be related to severe problems at the awareness level. Some current treatments of autism appear to involve deliberate attempts to increase the child's awareness of particular stimuli in the environment (Frankel, Tymchuk & Simmons, 1976).

Other learning disabled individuals may continue to respond at the awareness level though their level of response should be much higher. Problems indicative of inadequate awareness include hyperactivity, impulsive guessing, distractibility or poor vigilance, short attention span, and erratic attention. These problems may indicate difficulties with focusing or sustaining focus. Problems that we view as reflecting an inability to shift focus to new relevant stimuli are autism, hypoactivity, perseveration, and excessive daydreaming. The persistent and excessive presence of these behaviors indicates that a learning disabled person is having difficulty responding at the awareness level. Note, however, that these behaviors, by themselves, do not establish the presence of a processing problem nor are they *always* indications that the major problems are at Level I.

Level II: Differentiation

By attending carefully to the stimuli surrounding them, children are soon able to begin to differentiate between similar stimuli. The focus of learning shifts to a new level. The *differentiation level* refers to a basic understanding related to the use of inner language and the ability to discriminate likenesses and differences and perceptual detail. This level is a focus of learning from one year through four years.

Children now begin to go beyond simple exploration of the environment. For adequate development to continue they must begin to attend to the distinctive features of objects and their relationships as well as to general events in their lives. They discover that their hands and feet are connected to their bodies and that they can manipulate and move objects. They begin to discriminate between different faces and voices, between their mother and others in the environment. The major task at Level II becomes one of the discrimination, categorization, and classification of the attributes of objects and events in the environment. Perceptual learning involves abstracting out essential features and relations from these objects and events (Gibson & Levin, 1975).

Children at Level II rely heavily on perceptual sensations. In the last part of the sensorimotor stage of development, children "perceive simple causality by perception alone" (Maier, 1978, p. 40). They infer causes from observing effects. These prelinguistic concepts comprise the child's inner language. The focus of the differentiation level is on these categorizations which form elementary concepts. Language labels will be attached to these basic concepts later, in Level III.

Now the interaction of the perception process becomes most important. Children still must continue to attend appropriately, but they now attend to the critical differences between objects and events. The child must discriminate the distinctive differences between stimuli and coordinate related stimuli. The sequence of spatial and temporal stimuli must be recognized and conserved. Children begin to discriminate the differences between phonemes and their sequencing in syllables and words. They practice these sounds by repeating them over and over, differentiating the motor movements required to form them. They babble with intonation. Children learn to respond differently to different words.

Physical action is very important at this level. Children discriminate perceptual sensations by manipulating the environment. Objects are handled, traced, and placed in the mouth. Once a child becomes mobile during this level, a household must be "childproofed" to prevent children from discovering the critical attributes of any precious or dangerous objects.

The general problem associated with the differentiation level for the learning disabled is the inability to gain accurate information about various stimuli in the environment. The learning disabled child with problems related to Level II responding might have body balance or body awareness difficulties which we would view as an inability to discriminate and coordinate kinesthetic or tactile stimuli. A child might say words with phonemes in the wrong order (e.g., blub for bulb) or might answer incorrectly when given same-different word discrimination tasks. In reading, a child may have difficulty with symbol-sound associations, may make letter or word reversals, or have difficulty sequencing sounds into words. If these behaviors are persistent and excessive, they indicate that a learning disabled person is having difficulty responding at the differentiation level.

Level III: Labeling

From a focus on perceptual signals, the child now makes a qualitative jump to an appreciation of messages. The *labeling level* is one at which the individual attaches correct names, labels, and simple definitions to objects and events. This level is a focus of learning from two years through eight years.

Children now begin to acquire the vast store of information needed to continue their development. Verbal language has developed, and words become a special set of stimuli to be categorized. Words are used to interact with and manipulate the environment. At this level children can use words to label their perceptions as an aid in processing and responding.

A child we know was trying to discriminate between the letters *b* and *d,* two confusing and reversible symbols. Finally she discovered a solution. She called the letter *b* her "freckle letter" because she had a freckle on one of her hands and that hand resembled the letter *b* when she made it into a fist with one finger extended.

Children expand their verbal skills to include written and quantitative language. Although the structures for understanding complex meaning will not develop until Level IV, simple concepts and facts are understood mechanically. The child learns concepts by rote. They are not logically considered. Tasks usually have definite right and wrong answers. Although the eventual purpose of learning is to understand (Level IV), memorization of these facts, collectively, is seen as a means to that end (Isaacs, 1960).

Most of the information the child must learn at this level is arbitrary. It has meaning only by convention (e.g., the names and sounds of the letters of the alphabet, the labels of objects and events in the environment, the names of numbers, and sight words in the reading process). This places great demands on the memory processes of temporarily storing impressions of stimuli and rehearsing stimuli. The early elementary grades fall within the range of Level III. Acquiring basic reading skills, for example, is a major expectation during this period. Early reading places a heavy demand on rote memory (Mackworth, 1972; Torgesen, 1978).

The major goal of the labeling level is the efficient learning of this massive amount of information. Children spend a great deal of time in rote practice at this level. The alphabet and counting sequences are repeated over and over. Simple songs about these sequences are enjoyed immensely early in this level. Children rehearse these things the way they understand them. Often the alphabet is recited with errors. Everyone has had a chance to practice that phantom letter *elameno* that comes between *k* and *p.* Math facts for addition, subtraction, and multiplication must be rehearsed repeatedly.

The general problem associated with the labeling level for the learning disabled is the inability to store and rehearse basic information from the environment. The learning disabled person with problems related to Level III responding might have difficulty recalling sight words in reading, math facts, or the correct spelling of simple words. The child might continue to sound out words that should be memorized. Difficulty with sound-symbol associations may be observed. The child may forget material that was presented the day before. By the time the student gets to the end of a word or sentence, the beginning may have been forgotten. The child may have difficulty following directions. The persistent and excessive presence of these behaviors may indicate that the learning disabled person is having difficulty responding at the labeling level.

Level IV: Understanding

While the rote memorization of the labeling level does not involve extensive modification of information, the individual soon develops the ability to reorganize the information in a personally meaningful way. The *understanding level* is the level at which the individual has a comprehension of concepts that is advanced enough to permit application of concepts and rules. This level is a focus of learning from nine years through adulthood.

At this level individuals begin to seek out and use complex meanings. They begin to see the relationships between ideas and the simple concepts of Level III. Language mediation becomes predominant. Individuals can generalize and apply concepts learned or invented. With the comprehension of complex meanings, they can use logical deductive and inductive processes in problem-solving situations.

At Level IV individuals are capable of considering the future and learning from the past. Careful planning is possible. Piaget (1977a) described the adolescent as differing from the child "above all in that he thinks beyond the present. The adolescent is the individual who commits himself to possibilities" (p. 437).

The goal of the understanding level is the development of comprehension of complex meanings. To accomplish this the individual must be able to recognize that meaning is present in any situation and identify that meaning. The person can identify words that require atypical spelling patterns and use relevant rules to spell them correctly. The individual can generalize these rules to words not previously encountered. The person must be able to associate identified meanings with other relevant meanings and infer new meanings. "In more skilled reading and comprehension, of course, the sum total of the reader's experience and previous learning in many areas may be brought to bear in understanding the meaning of a particular passage" (Torgesen, 1978-1979, p. 60).

The general problem associated with the understanding level is the inability to comprehend complex meanings in various situations. Learning disabled persons with problems related to Level IV responding may have difficulty with reading comprehension. They may not demonstrate creativity, flexibility, or adaptability in problem-solving situations. They may give rote answers with little apparent understanding. They may have difficulty understanding or gaining meaning from complex verbal conversations. They may have difficulty taking notes from a lecture. They may have problems with words or concepts with multiple meanings. The persistent and excessive presence of these behaviors indicates that the learning disabled person is having difficulty responding at the understanding level.

Level V: Habit

The *habit level* is one at which the individual is able to respond appropriately and at will. Performance is relatively effortless. Attention to specific sensory stimuli is minimal, and speed and consistency are intact. This level is a focus of learning from 11 years through adulthood.

The individual is now able to express the highest level of integrated meaning automatically. Communication with others and with one's self at a highly meaningful level is a major task of this level. The expression of ideas is still a constructive process but is now automatic. The person takes everything known, selects from it, and integrates it into a well-formed thought with a high level of meaning. Words and sentences are converted from an abstract pattern to a phonic form (Goodglass, Klein, Carey, & Jones, 1966) effortlessly and automatically.

Habitual overlearned systems of expression are formed. This is not to say that habituation of behavior is only found at Level V but that at this level habituation becomes a fully integrated way of operating with highly meaningful information. At this level we can initiate a particular thought, and it will complete itself without conscious control (Norman, 1980). Comprehension of communication from other verbal or written sources occurs without logical analysis. Information is integrated into an already well-developed understanding.

The goal of the habit level is to achieve the ability to function smoothly and accurately with complex meaningful stimuli. The person must be able to effortlessly recall and organize internal stimuli that will communicate intended meanings. Individuals at this level can express personal meanings quite easily and may find themselves generating original complex understandings without conscious effort. The information may have been analyzed beforehand at Level IV, but now it is expressed so easily that they may be hearing it for the first time themselves. The individual can compose written work about familiar topics, letter writing for example, without careful logical analysis. The individual at this level is capable of speaking extemporaneously with ease. Written and verbal expression can be monitored without effort as it is taking place, and corrections are automatic.

The general problem associated with the habit level is the inability to express or comprehend highly meaningful and complex stimuli automatically. Learning disabled persons with problems related to Level V responding might have difficulty in interpersonal relationships. They may be unable to express their personal views in written or verbal form and may demonstrate a lack of awareness of others' needs or feelings. They may not recognize when their own responses are correct or incorrect. Their rate of expression may be inappropriate for the situation or in any situation. Expressive syntax may be inadequate in written or verbal form. The individual may be unable to evaluate or see the implications of meaningful situations. The persistent and excessive presence of these behaviors indicates that the learning disabled person is having difficulty responding at the habit level.

CONCLUSION

The five levels of response we have described indicate the qualitative changes in the focus of learning and responding to tasks and situations that take place as age increases. An individual might respond to any task from any level that has been developed. In spelling, for example, individuals can respond at many levels depending on their skills and ability. Phonetic spelling would indicate heavy reliance on Level II responses. The person is focusing on the discrimination and sequencing of sound differences. Spelling typically requires a Level III response. Specific sequences of letters are memorized so recall can be automatic. Note that this is not automatic in the highly meaningful manner of Level V functioning. At Level IV the person can make use of various spelling rules needed for unfamiliar or atypical words that have not been overlearned at Level III. At Level V a person would be able to teach spelling to others and could teach all the important rules of spelling without needing to logically analyze each step.

Often older children and adults may be required to respond to a particular task or situation at each of the earlier levels temporarily before the person can respond at an age-appropriate level. When hearing or learning a foreign language a person must first become aware of and attend to important stimuli in the language (Level I). Then the person must differentiate the various sounds and sequences unique to that language (Level II). The person must remember various labels associated with the language (Level III) and then become familiar with various grammatical rules required to express complex meaning in that language (Level IV). Finally, if the language is studied long enough, the person can communicate easily in a highly meaningful and automatic way (Level V). Note, however that if a person is older and functioning primarily at a later level, the thinking at the later level influences the individual's awareness, differentiation, and labeling.

A more exotic example of using all of the levels is found in the film by Stanley Kubrick, *2001: A Space Odyssey*. An individual watching the film first becomes *aware* of a large object that shows up in various early scenes from time to time. The person must *differentiate* its color, size, shape, and relation to the environment. The object is a large black rectangle which does not appear to be natural and occasionally emits a high frequency sound. The person usually tries to *label* the object. What is it called? Is it a monolith of some kind? Finally the person begins to attempt to *understand* its meaning. What *does* it mean? The film never tells what it means directly. Those who see the film must begin to make associations with other things they understand. It may be a symbol for the film or an actual object placed there by aliens or both. The person makes hypotheses and logically discusses them with friends. If the person sticks to this task, a highly meaningful, well-formed understanding of the object and its intended purpose in the film will be formulated. The individual can then effortlessly communicate this personal meaning to others.

Chapter 4

A Model for the Study of Learning Disabilities

INTRODUCTION

In this chapter we will present and explain a model of learning disabilities that may account for many of the major variables important for the learning and thinking of this group. The model we present provides a summary of the preceding chapters and is the basis for the applications to assessment and remediation that follow in later chapters. Essentially, the chapter is a summary of the ways in which the learning disabled learn and why they often fail to learn, an understanding of which is critical for appropriate diagnosis and treatment.

We begin our explanation with a general description of the model. Following this, more detailed information is provided about stimulus variables and channels of learning, variables related to global processes, the problem of strategy selection in learning tasks, levels of learning and specific learning processes, and specific knowledge structures that are built up as a consequence of learning.

A MODEL

A visual representation of the major parts of our model is presented in Figure 4-1. The model has three principal divisions: channels, control structures, and knowledge structures. Channels are important especially in relation to stimulus variables. Note, however, that stimuli are separate from the internal system itself and therefore channels are located outside the large rectangle that encompasses the internal mental structures of the system. The arrows representing the flow of information from stimuli into the system are also mostly located outside of the system itself. Actually, of course, the sensory systems labeled on these arrows (visual, tactile, etc.) are parts of or extensions of the neurological structures of the human organism.

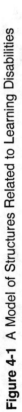

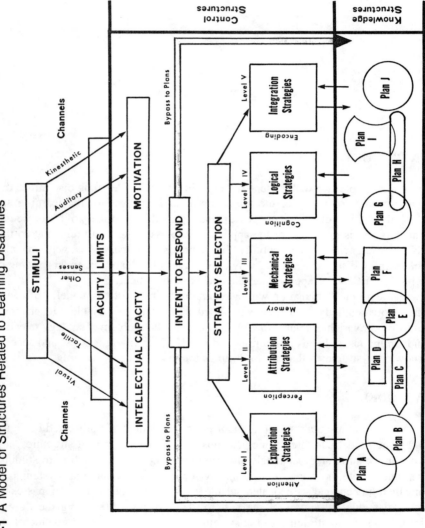

Figure 4-1 A Model of Structures Related to Learning Disabilities

Our primary interest is not in the sensory systems themselves, however, but in the flow of information after representations of stimuli have entered the central nervous system. Thus the arrows representing the channels of input are drawn in a way that shows their importance for making information available to the system but does not include them as an internal part of the system. We assume that once information has entered the brain, it is no longer "visual," "auditory," or "kinesthetic." The information can be and probably is translated into a variety of symbolic representations. Note also that the arrows that represent the flow of information enter the system but are not directed into any specific part of it. Although we know that information may initially go to particular neurological structures, this is not the focus of our model. We want to show what happens cognitively when information enters the entire system.

The control structures in the model are so named because they control both the flow of information and the responses of the organism. Four major aspects of control structures are included in our model. The first aspect involves general intellectual and affective factors, which we call *intellectual capacity* and *motivation*. These global factors are extremely important in both assessment and remediation because they set limits on the organism. We regard them as difficult to modify extensively.

Although information does not flow from capacity and motivation into the next structure, *intent to respond*, arrows are drawn to show that capacity and motivation affect what the organism does with the information. The intent to respond aspect of information processing requires a decision on the part of the individual about whether or not a response is necessary or desirable. We emphasize two major types of responses because of their importance in learning disabilities. One type is termed *bypass to plans* because it does not require effortful thinking, information seeking, or new learning. Instead, once the organism has decided to act, previously learned patterns of behavior are set into motion. For example, a person may decide to ride a bicycle and may carry out the act without additional planning or conscious thought.

The second type of internal response that an organism may make (after deciding that a response is called for) is indicated by the arrow that leads to the strategy selection structure. In many cases, the strategy the organism selects to learn new information, to gather more information, or to solve a problem is not consciously selected. In other cases, a conscious effort to select an appropriate strategy may be made. In either case, the strategy selection structures may be regarded as meta-structures or structures that oversee or control the selection and use of other structures. Strategy selection structures appear to us to be of particular interest and importance in teaching the learning disabled.

The alternative strategies an individual may select are divided into five major types that correspond to the levels of response explained in Chapter 3. The model indicates that, at different ages, qualitatively different strategies have developed and are available for use. Persons who have developed higher level strategies remain capable of also using earlier level strategies if these are appropriate. There is, however, a strong tendency to use higher level strategies whenever possible. For example, if verbal labeling (Level III) has been developed as a rehearsal strategy for learning new information, the individual will probably use verbal labels as mediators instead of or in addition to the use of visualization (Level II). As explained in Chapter 3, each level of response is closely associated with a particular learning process. To use the strategy for a particular level, the intactness of the associated process is especially important.

The third division of the model, *knowledge structures*, is made up of a variety of overlearned plans for behavior. These plans are drawn in various sizes and shapes to show that they are different from one another and may include elaborate and extended behavior patterns or very simple and short patterns, such as recognizing a single letter shape. The plans sometimes overlap to show that associations between them are typical. A major characteristic of these plans is their overlearned and automatic nature. Although it is possible for them to be inaccurate or incomplete, once they have been selected as a basis for response, virtually no conscious effort is needed for the associated response to occur. The plans are made up of the knowledge the individual has stored in long-term memory. Arrows drawn in both directions from the strategies to the plans indicate the reciprocal effects and interaction between them. Any strategy an individual may select could involve the use of information from a plan or plans. The plans an individual has available affect the particular strategy selected and the effectiveness of its use. These processes and other details about the model are explained more extensively in the following sections.

Channels of Input

In the field of learning disabilities considerable emphasis has traditionally been placed on the channel of input that is used for the intake of information. We regard this emphasis as somewhat misplaced for several reasons. First, it has led to the development of the concept that persons with learning disabilities are likely to be either auditory or visual (or possibly tactile or kinesthetic) learners and that difficulties with processing information in a particular channel account for the learning disability. This division of disabled learners on the basis of a strong channel of input seems much too simple. Only the *stimulus* dimension of learning is accounted for in such a model. Important processes, such as memory and cognition, and significant responses that depend on more than one input channel or are not directly related to an input channel are likely to be ignored or regarded as relatively insignificant. Also, learners who appear weak in several channels or who have difficulties with only some stimuli in a particular modality or modalities are not accounted for in a channel model. We are not suggesting that the channel of input or the type of stimulus used is unimportant, only that other aspects of learning are equally significant.

More potent arguments for questioning a "channel" division of disabled learners exist. Research on teaching clearly indicates that in areas such as reading a modality preference approach (e.g., using an "auditory" method such as phonics to teach "auditory" learners to read) does not result in significantly higher achievement (see Tarver & Dawson, 1978, for a review). Tarver and Dawson note that the accurate measurement of auditory or visual preferences presents a problem because tests are not highly reliable and valid. A careful examination of tests that purport to measure separate auditory and visual processes, thereby identifying auditory and visual learners, shows that performance on those tests can be dramatically affected by the use of processes typically associated with a channel that is supposedly not being measured. For example, on the *Illinois Test of Psycholinguistic Abilities* (ITPA) (Kirk, McCarthy, & Kirk, 1968), the Visual Reception subtest is designed to show preferences for or difficulties with visual processes. However, the actual items on the test seem to be significantly affected by the use of language, thus indicating that processes other than visual are involved. For example, one item shows a picture of a very wet puppy in a bathtub, which the child is asked to match with a second picture chosen from four possible responses. The correct response, a picture of a small child in wet rain clothes, does not necessarily provide a purely visual match. In fact, we often find that children ask to see the stimulus page again, and after they do so, they frequently say something like, "Oh, he's all wet." The words used indicate that some language concepts and labeling are helpful in completing the task. It may be that when meaningful thinking is required to complete a task, processes that are not related directly to channels of input are typically used. The evidence seems to show that tests such as the ITPA do not clearly separate visual and auditory processes (Newcomer, Hare, Hammill & McGettigan, 1974). Newcomer and her colleagues report that the "visual modality as measured by the ITPA is completely without substantiation as a valid dimension" (p. 510).

Other commonly used tests, such as the *Detroit Tests of Learning Aptitude* (Baker & Leland, 1959), also appear to measure more than single modality functioning. On two tests that are named *visual* memory tests, for example, the Detroit requires a *vocal* response. Although the input stimuli are received through the eyes, they must be labeled, thus demanding the recall of stimuli that came in originally through the ears. In addition, it is possible, if not likely, that subjects could rehearse the test items by repeating the names of the objects rather than by rehearsing how the objects look. Even a cursory examination of tests shows that most of them demand some sort of cross-modal functioning. In cases where such functioning is not demanded, it is often still possible to use information or processes related to more than one channel of input. Obviously, it is not possible to control the type of internal stimuli a subject uses to complete a test item.

Control of the modality a child actually uses during instruction is equally difficult (Tarver & Dawson, 1978). In a given situation, a teacher can control the type of stimuli to which a student is exposed, but not what happens inside the student. One can easily do "auditory" things with visual stimuli and "visual" things with auditory stimuli. In fact, it is questionable whether internal stimuli should be regarded as directly related to channels. Are verbal labels necessarily "auditory" or can they be thought about in other ways? Can one think about the way something looks without visualizing it? Empirical evidence is not available to answer such questions, although Ceci, Lea, and Ringstrom (1980) found that stimuli coming in through auditory or visual modalities may trigger different semantic associations and thus affect recall abilities. The limited evidence we do have indicates it may be prudent to regard the channels of input as somewhat separable but not to separate learners only on the basis of the channel of input that appears most effective for learning.

We should attempt to use effective stimuli at all times. Whether those stimuli fit a "strong" or a "weak" modality depends on what the teacher is trying to accomplish and the type of task under consideration. If a teacher has evidence that an individual must learn to use certain types of stimuli effectively in order to complete a certain task, ways to enable the learner to use those stimuli must be sought. Ceci et al. (1980) found that free recall and cued recall deficits disappeared in children with either visual or auditory memory problems when help in classifying the memory items was given during learning. Thus "visual" learners may be able to learn auditory information adequately, given effective teaching. The same may be said for "auditory" learners with visual material. The problem becomes more complex and perhaps is less solvable when both visual and auditory memory scores are low (Ceci et al., 1980). If learning is more efficient when stimuli are made available through a particular channel, those stimuli should be presented. In either case, the *stimuli* are manipulated and not the internal processes of the learner. For these reasons, the channel dimension is placed outside of the central processing parts of the model shown in Figure 4-1.

We suggest that nearly all learning tasks demand a high degree of integration of information from more than one channel of input. In assessment and remediation, the channel of input must be considered in order for learning to proceed efficiently. Evaluation of an individual's abilities might indicate, for example, that special assistance will be needed to enable the person to interpret visual symbols correctly. To argue that such a person should be regarded as an auditory (or tactile, kinesthetic, etc.) learner is a moot point. For instructional purposes, separating learners on the basis of a preferred input modality is not very useful.

The flow of information into the central processor is limited by the nature of sensory systems. Some stimuli (e.g., very high-pitched whistles) cannot be received at all, even though we know they exist and can be perceived by nonhuman species. In addition, a particular individual may have acuity limits not found in others. The more obvious senses in which these occur are vision and hearing, although similar limits may exist in other senses. Such limits may be correctable through the use of glasses or hearing aids. To the degree that correction is not possible, learning and the instructional strategies used may be affected. Generally, however, the learning disabled are regarded as not having peripheral nervous system disorders as a primary disability (Johnson & Myklebust, 1967). Thus, although evaluation of acuity limits and correction of problems in this area are important, we regard this as somewhat outside of the domain of the learning disability specialist. Difficulties with acuity demand the services of specialists in other areas and should be routinely dealt with prior to evaluation for learning disability. The concern of the learning disability professional centers on the remaining aspects of the psychology of learning disability that are shown in Figure 4-1.

Control Structures

Control structures both set limits on the ability of the organism to respond to incoming stimuli and provide the means for responding in varied and flexible ways. The four major components of control structures are described in more detail below. These four components are: (1) intellectual capacity and motivation; (2) intent to respond; (3) strategy selection; and (4) specific strategies.

Intellectual Capacity and Motivation

The global factors of intellectual capacity and motivation make up the first component of control structures. We include these factors in the model because they affect all aspects of learning and processing. We have separated them from other control structures because they are perhaps less amenable to modification through direct instruction and are therefore not a focus of instruction by the teacher of the learning disabled. Atkinson and Shiffrin (1968) have suggested that a distinction should be made between processes (in memory) that are not under conscious control and those that can be selectively used by an individual. Torgesen (1978-1979) calls the former *structural* variables and mentions length of time between the onset and decay of an iconic image and the speed with which memory may be scanned for an item as examples. The term *control* processes is reserved by Torgesen for selectively used mental activities such as verbal rehearsal of items and organization or categorization of items to be learned. We use the term *control structures* much more broadly. One reason, of course, is to avoid use of a term like structural structures.

In our model, intellectual capacity and motivation are regarded as general factors that must be taken into account in assessment and remediation. Intellectual capacity is important because it indicates the learning potential of the individual and because it may help to identify the individual as primarily learning disabled rather than primarily mentally retarded. In a rough sense, intellectual capacity may be equated with intelligence as traditionally measured on intelligence tests. We recognize the dangers in using an IQ score as an indication of intellectual capacity but suggest that the general concept is useful. In actual cases, we are interested in an individual's true ability to learn, not in performance on a test. Estimates of intellectual capacity require expert judgment that depends on a variety of evaluative measures combined with trial teaching lessons. We are not suggesting that learning disabled persons are different from nonlearning disabled in intellectual capacity, only that careful consideration of capacity is essential to thorough analysis and adequate treatment of learning disability. We concur with many others in the learning disability field who regard the typical learning disabled person as at least average in general intellectual capacity.

General intellectual capacity consists, then, of inherited potential to learn and the basic neurological and psychological structures that enable learning to take place. We are not referring to conscious thinking processes and strategy selection but to general abilities that are not greatly affected by learning and practice. Many of these factors may change with physical and neurological maturation. These factors are obviously closely related to the learning processes explained in Chapter 2, differing primarily in an emphasis on more global processes, compared to the specific processes explained earlier. We prefer to leave general intellectual capacity somewhat undefined, saying only that it includes the ability to learn and is related to factors such as speed of processing and the neurological limits of the organism. We regard intellectual capacity as related to the differential approach to the measurement of abilities cited by Sternberg (1979b). Those who have pursued a differential approach to understanding mental structures have studied "relationships between patterns of individual differences in scores on psychometric ability tests" (Sternberg, 1979b, p. 214). We assume that these patterns and differences are significant but provide only part of the information needed for appropriate teaching in learning disability. An alternative to the measurement of mental abilities and content, the information processing approach (Sternberg, 1979b), also needs to be incorporated in learning disability and is a major focus in this book.

The motivation component is somewhat similar to intellectual capacity in that it is a very general factor that probably affects learning in many important ways. In the broadest sense, motivation includes the innate urges of the organism to move, to seek information, and to grow and learn. Regarded this way, motivation is not something that is learned or easily modified. This term has frequently been used in psychology and education to refer to something quite different—the ability of a person to provide someone else with a motive or to induce action or learning in some way. In this sense and in the general sense of learning to like something, motivation can perhaps be modified. We prefer to look at it from the former perspective and emphasize that motivation is always intrinsic to the learner. Motivation comes from the innate urge to grow and learn, not from external stimulus changes or reinforcement. The task of the teacher is not to motivate but to prepare tasks, content, and rewards that meet the needs and interests, the motivations, of the students. Thus motivation is obviously an important factor in assessment and in the preparation of instruction, but it is not a direct focus of teaching.

Intent to Respond

In the broadest sense, intent to respond may be regarded as an individual's will. Consciously or unconsciously, a decision is made to respond or not to respond to every stimulus that impinges on the organism (as well as any thought that arises, even though no external stimulus is apparent). In this case, we do not regard the neurological activity of the brain that occurs during perception of the stimulus as a "response." However, any additional thinking, associating, or preparing for an external response (i.e., vocal or motor) may be regarded as part of the response. A further distinction needs to be drawn between the actual response and the decision to make a response. The latter is the focus of this part of the model. The concept of an "intent to respond" structure is similar to Norman's (1980) idea that at a conscious level we select a response, and then the corresponding action takes place at another level.

Whether an individual decides to respond to a particular stimulus is related to the person's current motivational status, experiential history, and the perceived consequences of responding or not responding. Obviously, the decision to respond is both important and complex. The individual must first decide that the stimulus contains important information before a decision to respond can be made. Hofstadter (1979) has pointed out that any message may be regarded as having at least three levels of meaning. He calls these the *frame, outer,* and *inner* messages.

According to Hofstadter, the frame message may be apparent from the shape or patterns found in the stimulus and contains the information that "I am a message; decode me if you can!" (p. 166). Hofstadter explains that "to understand the frame message is to recognize the need for a decoding-mechanism" (p. 166). In our model, this means that the person makes a decision to respond because the need to select a plan or a strategy for dealing with the message has become apparent. We are using the term *message* very broadly here, including any external stimulus and possibly internal stimuli as well.

The outer message contains the information needed to decode the inner message, i.e., "To understand the outer message is to build, or know how to build, the correct decoding mechanism for the inner message" (Hofstadter, 1979, p. 166). The outer message, then, may contain the information that "I am in English. Get someone who knows English to decode me." In our model, the individual decides which specific strategy or plan to use to decode the message.

The inner message is the exact meaning inherent in the stimulus. In the case of a message sent by someone, it is the meaning intended by the sender of the message. To get this meaning the individual must use the appropriate strategy or plan in a correct way to gain accurate meaning.

Learning disabled persons may have difficulty with frame messages in at least two ways: 1) failure to inhibit responses; and 2) failure to "activate." Both of these problems may be related to the attention process that we associate with Level I responding later in the model. That is, one could hypothesize that a dysfunction in the attention process underlies both a failure to inhibit responses and a failure to respond when a response is called for. Of course, alternative explanations are possible. Perhaps motivation, degree of effort required (and the person's desire to avoid that effort), or insufficient practice with a task are equally plausible explanations.

In any case, it appears that some children may fail to inhibit responses to messages that do not contain important information (Cruickshank, 1977a). Others may fail to "actively engage the task through the use of efficient strategies and other techniques of intelligence" (Torgesen, 1977, p. 33; also see Hallahan, Gajar, Cohen & Tarver, 1978). Perhaps the failure here is not really a matter of failing to detect the presence of a frame message, since in the Hallahan et al. study the children did make a response. They may have recalled less because they were hindered from "actively seeking appropriate learning strategies . . ." (Hallahan et al., 1978, p. 235). If the latter hypothesis is correct, the problem may be in the strategy selection component of the model in Figure 4-1. Note, however, that an individual's decision to respond may lead him or her to use the bypass to plans. The intent to respond decision is thus shown to include more than just a decision to respond. It is a metastructure in which is included a decision to respond in one of two ways—strategy selection or bypass.

A bypass decision means that the individual responds as if the incoming information matches previously overlearned or highly familiar information. A plan is selected that supposedly matches the stimulus. If the match is correct, everything goes well. If the wrong plan is selected (e.g., a d is called a b), one type of problem is indicated. In this case, the individual may have the correct plan stored. The decision to use the bypass is not the problem, although help may be needed in choosing the correct plan. Perhaps some inactive learners use the bypass when they do not have a plan stored to match the stimulus. Their response appears to be an impulsive guess. In such cases little similarity between stimulus and response is apparent. For whatever reason, then, an inactive learner may be one who chooses to use the bypass and appears to guess impulsively.

Treatment would focus on enabling the individual to go to strategy selection instead of to the bypass. Note, however, that the use of the term *inactive* to describe a learner with a problem of this sort is not entirely accurate because the learner actively selects a plan and makes a response. *Inactive* apparently does not mean that the person does *nothing* according to Torgesen (1977) but that the task is not appropriately engaged. A person who refuses or who is unable to make any response at all may be a different type of inactive learner. In such cases, the teacher may need to manipulate the variables that relate to the motivation component. For the person who does not actively engage the task, remediation may involve making the individual more aware of the strategies available for selection and use. As noted by Torgesen (1977), in memory tasks several "meta" variables appear important. Awareness that one can effectively act in the environment and awareness of one's own cognitive abilities, for example, are cited as important variables on the basis of research findings. Perhaps some learning disabled persons need remedial help in developing the needed awareness so that an active learning strategy is selected when necessary.

Strategy Selection

Outer messages also present a problem for learning disabled persons. Outer messages require the selection or construction of a decoder, activities that are subsumed under the *strategy selection* component in Figure 4-1. The learner may think, "Now that I know that this task demands the selection of a decoder (and I don't have one already built), exactly what type of decoder will work best?" Parallel statements could be presented for the completion of any task or the solution of a problem. Such a thought may be very conscious and explicit or it may be almost unconscious—the individual just "knows" that the need to select an appropriate strategy exists. Learning disabled persons may be unaware of the need to select a strategy (the problem discussed as a part of the intent to respond component) or may select the wrong strategy. A strategy may be selected from a level (referring to levels in the model) that is less effective than another level would be, or the individual may select an ineffective strategy even though it is at an appropriate level of response. To illustrate the selection of a strategy from a less effective level, consider the number series 1, 32, 63, 94, 125, 156, 187, and 218. A Level III strategy to remember this series might be to verbally rehearse them in sequence several times. Recall is likely to be much more effective with less time spent in learning, however, if a Level IV strategy is used. This strategy would require the application of a "rule" based on recognition of the pattern the numbers follow. The rule might be concisely stated as "eight numbers of increasing amounts starting with 1 and adding 31 to each successive number." The same example may be used to show how an individual may select a less effective strategy from an appropriate level by pointing out that rules more complex, difficult to remember, or complicated to apply might have been devised by the learner. One rule could be, for example, "Start with 218 and decrease the units digit one whole number for each succeeding number, at the same time decreasing the number by 10 three times until the number 1 is reached."

Strategy selection is, of course, highly complex. It requires, first of all, that the person has a repertoire of strategies available from which selections can be made. The importance of both experience and age is readily apparent. Age is particularly important because some strategies will not be available if the required type of thinking has not developed. Strategy selection is also complicated by the concept that tasks usually require the use of more than one strategy. The rule cited for remembering the number series above may need to be learned by rote, for example, thus requiring the use of a Level III strategy within a Level IV task. Another alternative is to write the rule on paper. This response (and the formulation of the rule itself, to a degree) requires Level V thinking. We see that individuals need to be flexible in strategy selection both in initial selection and in completing subcomponents of a task.

One of the major tasks of the teacher of the learning disabled, in our view, is to address the strategy selection component. The learning disabled person who has difficulty with this component may profit from instruction in how to select appropriate strategies and in how to shift flexibly to alternative strategies when they are needed. Deliberate, conscious use of appropriate strategies may need to be taught. Assessment should include an analysis of the way in which the individual selects strategies as well as the type of strategies used for important tasks. A second major task of the teacher is to develop a repertoire of strategies, as explained in the next section.

Specific Strategies

The final component of control structures, specific strategies, receives primary emphasis in teaching the learning disabled. It is here that the individual learns to use appropriate strategies to decode an inner message, and to obtain the correct, intended information from stimuli.

We propose a model with five levels from which strategy selection may take place. Each level represents a qualitatively different type of strategy as explained in earlier chapters. A particular learning process is closely associated with each level. In Figure 4-1, the major process for each level is written to the left of the box for the level. Based on our experience as well as the research reviewed in previous chapters, we hypothesize that learning disabled persons may have difficulty with using appropriate strategies in accurate ways from one or more levels. Difficulties at a particular level may be attributed to deficiencies in the use of the associated learning process.

We assume that once an individual decides upon a strategy to complete a task, something can still go wrong in the carrying out of that strategy. Some steps in the strategy may be missing or functioning improperly. Perhaps the individual does not attend to the necessary components of the task or fails to perceive them accurately. Whatever the particular explanation, the learner fails to learn; the problem is not solved; and the task is not completed.

Careful analysis of the use of strategies for important tasks must be completed as a part of appraisal of the problem. Careful probing of the ways in which an individual uses strategies helps determine remedial tasks. Sometimes important strategies are found to be missing, even though the age of the person leads the examiner to expect them to be present. Frequently, a strategy is found to be used adequately with one task but incorrectly with other similar tasks. The learning disabled person shows an inconsistent pattern. Sometimes attention, perception, memory, and other processes appear to function adequately, but at other times significant deficiencies appear. The task of the learning disability professional is to assess which processes are deficient and which levels of response have not been attained as expected. We suggest, however, that this appraisal always be carried out in the context of a particular task to which a particular strategy is applied. That is, for remedial purposes, it is much more important to identify the specific problems with strategy selection and strategy use than to identify the presence of a processing deficiency that affects every task.

The task in remediation is to build appropriate strategies for the tasks that the individual must learn to complete. What individuals must learn is determined, to a large degree, by the demands placed on them by the environment. The individual can choose which tasks to emphasize. Teachers also must make wise choices about which environmental demands should be a focus of strategy learning. No matter what the task, however, remedial instruction needs to develop the learning disabled person's ability to select and apply appropriate strategies. Strategies are selected for teaching based on three major considerations: (1) the nature of the task; (2) the age of the disabled learner; and (3) the particular characteristics of the student.

The nature of the task is important because some tasks are most efficiently dealt with using strategies from a specific level. Counting the blocks in a row, for example, demands Level III strategies. One cannot logically determine the answer to such a problem (Level IV). Neither can one know how many blocks are present by noting the attributes of the blocks (Level II). The solution can be obtained only by some kind of rote, mechanical counting of the items.

The age of the learner is particularly important because younger children may not be capable of employing strategies that typically develop at later ages and because it is important to emphasize strategies that are appropriate for the age of the learner. Children over age nine, for example, should learn to use strategies that rely on logical thinking. For many tasks expected of persons nine years and older, mechanical strategies are not adequate.

Finally, the specific characteristics of the learner are important because these inform the instructor that teaching some strategies is unnecessary (if already known) or unprofitable due to the specific processing problems of the individual. Specific characteristics may also have some effect on the way in which information is presented and the aspects of the stimuli or tasks that are emphasized.

Specific strategies for each level, as well as principles related to teaching them are presented in later chapters. Briefly, the strategies for Level I are termed *exploration strategies* because they involve learning to seek information in systematic, sustained, goal-directed ways. That is, the individual learns to attend to those stimuli that are important for the task at hand. Although the use of these strategies is obviously a subpart of strategies at later levels, our focus is on the strategies that a baby learns in the first 18 months of life. Failure to learn these strategies or to use them appropriately is a problem in young learning disabled persons. A typical strategy that a young child learns to employ to gain information is to track an important stimulus visually. Another may be to "get into everything"—to explore the environment almost continuously. The strategies at this level are very primitive, hardly recognizable as strategies at all.

At early levels, the unconscious nature of strategy selection and use is also most apparent. The child does not consciously think, "I can gain the information I need in this situation by visually tracking that moving object with my eyes." In a specific situation, the child does not process the idea that "I can tell if that dog is going to come close to me and knock me over if I keep watching to see how close it approaches." Nevertheless, the behavior of the child makes it appear that the strategy was selected and used because it accomplished the goal expressed above in quotation marks. For learning disability specialists, the important point is that we must learn to identify the strategies that young children probably use at this level so that we can teach learning disabled children to use them.

Level II strategies are termed *attribution strategies* because they emphasize ways of gaining basic information about stimuli that enable the development of inner language. We define inner language as a basic level of concept development that is prelinguistic. Later, at Level III, language labels are attached to these basic concepts. At Level II the child is learning to classify and categorize objects and events on the basis of their specific attributes, such as size, weight, color, and shape. At this level, the child expands and extends the exploration strategies of Level I to an emphasis on the distinctive features of stimuli. Much of the learning that occurs at this level may be dependent on which features of the stimulus are most salient, although the child gradually learns to pay close attention to attributes that are not obvious at first. Part of this learning takes place through the use of verbal labeling, a Level III process that begins to be particularly important around the age of two. However, the children are also learning many differences and similarities through the use of attribution strategies. Some of the important attributes that are probably important for later learning include the differences between phonemes, the differences that distinguish the direction and angle of lines, and the differences between facial expressions.

What strategies does the child use to learn and apply this information? Again, it is difficult to specify the thinking of the child, but it is possible to identify the apparent strategy that lies behind behavior. The child often uses the strategy of practicing phonemes by repeating them over and over. In doing so, some attention may be focused on the way the tongue needs to move to make the desired sound register through the ears. The child appears to be using a strategy of repetition and feedback, with corrections based on whether the feedback indicates the need for change.

Children learn about lines, angles, and directions by tracing objects with hands, fingers, even tongues, and by copying what they see. They learn to put together information about how something looks with the way it sounds and feels by dropping the object, by touching it, or by throwing it. They solve problems through trial-and-error strategies based on what they have observed or heard before or simply on the basis of manipulating the stimuli in the environment until a solution appears. Many of their solutions do not meet adult criteria, of course, but the child is unruffled. When putting together a puzzle, for example, the child will probably try several pieces in each position until a piece is found that fits reasonably well even though it is not exactly the correct piece. Over time, and with adult correction, the child will learn to fit the pieces in exactly the correct position, of course, at which time the strategy for making the puzzle changes. Instead of trial and error, the child may carefully lay out each piece and then systematically pick out pieces in some order and place them appropriately. The strategies a child may employ at Level II are more complex than those of Level I and may become more individualized for any particular task. Again, the task for the learning disability professional is to identify the essential strategies needed to complete tasks at this level and then to teach them to the learning disabled person who lacks them or uses them incorrectly.

Mechanical strategies are the focus of Level III. From about two years to eight years, children use tremendous amounts of energy to learn vocabulary, the alphabet, counting, sight words in reading, sound-symbol correspondences, nursery rhymes, simple definitions, and innumerable other things. The strategies they use appear to be "prelogical" in the sense that they do not rely first of all on logical connections between concepts or facts. Rather, they rely on rote or mechanical repetition. This is not to say that thinking and learning at this level are illogical or cannot include some elements that meet adult standards for logical thinking, but that formal thinking in a Piagetian sense is not typical at this age.

Children continue to be involved in the exploration and attribution strategies of Levels I and II as they participate in experiences. Included in these experiences are massive amounts of mechanical repetition. Learning to count, for example, usually occurs over a period of several years during which the major strategy is to imitate a model. Children repeat what the model says until the labels are learned in correct sequence. The arbitrary nature of language labels (as well as the arrangement of arbitrary sequences such as the alphabet) may be a major reason why so much mechanical learning takes place at this age. Arbitrary information cannot be learned through logical strategies. It is fortunate that children seem to respond so well to rote strategies at this age since this enables them to learn the information needed as a basis for logical thinking.

The strategies that children use at Level III, then, may include asking for repetitions of information they wish to learn (read it again, Daddy) or simply repeating the item over and over. The preschooler repeats the alphabet 30 times in an hour, perhaps inventing games to vary the repetition and make it even more interesting. The kindergartner comes home and repeats the poem she learned for each member of the family. The second grader writes his spelling words five times. In problem solving, the individual tries to recall previously memorized steps and to apply them in correct sequence. If the memorized steps are not known or have been forgotten, the child usually says, "I can't do it," instead of attempting to determine logical steps to obtain a solution. The world is made up not so much of options and possibilities, but of right and wrong answers, based on direct experience or the child's recollection of what a trusted adult or peer has said. It matters little to the child whether the answer is logical, except perhaps in a very elementary sense. Practice, rehearsal, imitative repetition, and the application of memorized sequences or steps dominate the strategies used.

The deliberate and conscious use of strategies becomes very apparent at Level IV. Although children continue to use verbal rehearsal (and, in fact, begin to use it as a deliberate strategy to make learning easier), much of their learning and problem solving reflects the use of *logical strategies*. Logical analysis is applied as appropriate to new learning tasks, problem solving, and comprehension of concepts. A major strategy at Level IV is the use of induction. The person observes particular instances and draws a general conclusion to fit the observations. The direct alternative, deduction, is a second important strategy in which specific conclusions are reached by reasoning based on a general principle or principles. Many other strategies are employed as well, including simple strategies such as careful rereading of a passage that was not fully comprehended or more complex ones such as translating the words just read into more familiar terms, summarizing content, and categorizing content on the basis of logical relationships.

Sternberg (1979b) has suggested a number of steps in problem solving that reflect strategies an individual may use. Depending on the type of problem encountered, a person follows a sequence of operations that Sternberg terms encoding, mapping, inference, application, justification, and response. Each of these steps involves the active manipulation of the terms of the problem or the response to it. Sternberg's model of mental abilities provides a good example of a way to include information processing approaches in the study of normal intelligence. With research advances along such lines, new insights will probably occur about the processing deficiencies of learning disabled persons. Currently, efforts to understand the components of mental abilities deal not only with problem solving but with Level II abilities as well (Rose & Fernandes, 1977). In our model, the four subcomponents of cognition (recognizing, identifying, associating, and inferring meanings) provide guidelines for studying the strategies that are important at Level IV. Teachers need to identify the specific strategies relative to each of these components that may need to be taught to their students.

The final set of strategies is called *integration strategies*. These strategies are used to rapidly associate, sequence, and monitor information. Through indepth understanding and extended practice over time, the person learns to express and understand meanings with relatively little effort. Strategies at Level V have a somewhat automatic nature, making the thinking that accompanies them difficult to analyze. Also, the distinction between integration strategies and the plans from the knowledge structures portion of the model is not easy to maintain.

It is important, at this point, to recall the reason for this model—to understand the psychology of learning disability and point the way to effective teaching. Since specific methods of teaching can be identified for Level V and since learning disabled persons appear to have specific problems with strategies at this level, a separate category is helpful. Strategies at Level V involve a high level of understanding and expression. At each previous level, many aspects of the strategies become automatic. The plans found in the knowledge structures category in Figure 4-1 have an automatic character. But in these cases, depth of meaning is not as great.

To illustrate, we will examine the task of learning to spell accurately. We will trace some important activities that are a part of spelling at each level. At Level I, the individual must be aware of little black marks on paper, of the presence of sound, and of the separability of sounds and words from one another. At Level II, the person must be capable of distinguishing between sounds, shapes, and directions of lines, as well as the movements needed to form written letters.

Spelling is primarily a Level III task. At this level, the individual actually memorizes the specific sequences of sounds and letters, the correspondences between letters and sounds, and the definitions of the spelling words. For most people, correct spellings of many words becomes automatic at this level. In a sense, each overlearned word becomes a *plan* or a part of the knowledge structures. When it is necessary to spell the word, the person can simply use the bypass to plans, locate the word, and write it down. Deliberate use of strategies is no longer necessary in order to use the word appropriately.

At Level IV, the person may learn to make use of a variety of spelling rules that may be useful in spelling unfamiliar words. It is possible, of course, to mechanically memorize rules and use them in a way that seems more like Level III functioning than Level IV. For the most part, however, learning and applying spelling rules (and exceptions), understanding prefixes, suffixes, and root words, and truly understanding that spelling is "sound written down" are important aspects of spelling that correspond to Level IV.

What is left for Level V? The ability to automatically use and write out the actual spelling words has already been delegated to Level III. We suggest that Level V involves the ability to teach others how to spell accurately without the need to use the logical, effortful analysis that is a part of Level IV functioning. That is, the person who has learned to operate at Level V with spelling is able to spell accurately, understands the nature and rules of spelling, and can teach this information to others in appropriate sequence with relative ease. Not only is the person able to use the rules of spelling with almost effortless accuracy, but he or she can teach others to do the same. It is not necessary for such a person to ''puzzle out'' whether a rule or an exception applies to a particular spelling word. Such information is known from previous study and experience.

Obviously, individuals will differ in the degree to which they attain Level V with this (as well as any other) task. Also, it is not important for most people to reach Level V in the spelling area. With many other tasks (e.g., reading compre- hension and verbal, gestural, and written expression) Level V functioning is very helpful, however. As with the previous levels, the teacher of the learning disabled must identify the strategies that an individual appears to lack at Level V so these strategies can be taught as needed. Although it is difficult to analyze exactly which strategies humans use to recall, sequence, and monitor highly meaningful re- sponses, it may be possible to teach learning disabled persons strategies that will enable them to respond in this way.

Deshler, Ferrell, and Kass (1978), for example, suggest that external monitor- ing by a teacher during the execution of a written language task may help learning disabled students learn to monitor their own production more effectively. Learning disabled persons may learn to recall and sequence words, sentences, and para- graphs more automatically following a study of sentence and paragraph structure. Teaching focuses on patterns and logic at Level IV. Through repeated applications of this information, the individual learns to function at Level V. Although indi- viduals continue to function at Levels IV and V throughout life, the teacher of the learning disabled may need to explicitly point out the advantage of functioning at Level V to some students with certain tasks. In cases where rapid recall, accurate sequencing, and appropriate monitoring do not develop, strategies for accomplish- ing these are developed and taught.

Arrows are drawn in both directions from each level in Figure 4-1 to the knowledge structures. These arrows illustrate that a reciprocal relationship exists between strategies and plans. Through strategies, plans are constructed and stored. When strategies are used, subparts of those strategies require the use of previously stored plans for rapid, accurate execution.

In our view, the task of the teacher of the learning disabled is to address two major components of the model in Figure 4-1, the strategy selection and level components. Some responsibility to enable the individual to make a correct decision with the intent to respond component was also pointed out. With this component, it may be necessary to teach when it is appropriate to use the bypass to plans and when to move to strategy selection. For the most part, however, the teacher of the learning disabled should concentrate on helping the student (1) select appropriate strategies in flexible ways and (2) develop efficient and effective strategies for learning and applying what is learned. If teaching is directed in this way in learning disabilities, it provides a distinct role for the specialist and an excellent complement to the task of regular education. The task of regular education is clarified in the following section on knowledge structures.

Knowledge Structures

Although knowledge structures, as we define them, play a very important role in the mental structures of humans, we will not develop this aspect of the model in detail. Our reason is simply that this area is the concern of regular education and needs to be developed in that context. Knowledge structures refer to the content of the curriculum in schools as well as all the other pieces of knowledge that have become overlearned through the experiences of the individual. They include the patterns of behavior that enable a person to ride a bicycle, follow a route from home to office, recognize a written word, recite the Preamble to the Constitution, recognize the face of a familiar person, etc. Over time, each of us builds up an almost limitless number of such plans. They vary in size, shape, and amount of association with other plans, as illustrated by the varying sizes, shapes, and amounts of overlap in Figure 4-1. The plans may be incomplete or inaccurate and still be used by the individual.

Even though an accurate, complete plan is present, an individual is not assured of errorless performance in a particular task. At least two major types of errors appear likely—selecting the wrong plan or becoming ''sidetracked'' by a closely associated plan. The first type of error can be illustrated by typing errors, word substitutions, attempting to place a manual shift lever in an automobile into the ''drive'' position of an automatic transmission, and endless other common mistakes. The second type of error appears when a selected plan goes awry during execution. For example, a call from home with a request to stop at the store for a gallon of milk, a promise to fulfill that request, and a plan that includes stopping at the store on the way home does not assure that the milk will be in the refrigerator at six o'clock. Many an individual has started on Plan A and actually executed it only until it intersected with Plan B. Perhaps a more effective strategy is required.

Regular education's task is not necessarily limited to helping students develop knowledge structures. In fact, we urge regular educators to emphasize the development of control structures as well. The close relationship between the teacher of learning disabled persons and regular education is apparent. The learning disabilities teacher uses content from the curriculum as strategy selection, and sets of strategies are emphasized. The regular educator is responsible for teaching knowledge structures but needs to develop strategies in all students. The changing nature of our knowledge about the universe appears to make the acquisition and use of strategies more critical than many knowledge structures.

Responses

Where are the arrows that indicate the action the individual takes? How does one get from internal mental events to external responses? Arrows could be drawn from the large rectangle in Figure 4-1 to the outside of the page. Certainly, the external responses of the individual are extremely important since they provide the information needed to evaluate structures and strategies, as well as the means for interaction between people and between the individual and other aspects of the environment. They are not shown in the model because we want to emphasize the internal aspects of the psychology of learning disabilities. External responses are assumed to be the eventual result of many internal mental events. We are less interested in the external responses themselves than in the internal mental events and how they relate to external responses.

Chapter 5

Assessment: Purposes and Types

INTRODUCTION

In the next two chapters we will emphasize the importance of evaluating internal mental structures. Our goal is to demonstrate how the model we have developed can be applied to the task of assessment. This chapter has two main sections. The first explains some misconceptions about assessment and presents some alternatives. The consequences of assessment practices from these two perspectives are also discussed. The second section develops several ideas about the purposes of assessment by contrasting three major types of analysis that are typical in the field of learning disabilities.

Obviously, these two chapters do not contain everything you will ever need to know about evaluating mental structures. Evaluation is, in a sense, too individualized a process to be fully explained. Accurate evaluation evolves out of direct contact between an expert clinician and an individual student. Abstract discussions about assessment provide some help, of course, but they do not replace practice of the process.

ASSESSMENT: MISCONCEPTIONS

In Chapter 1 we explained four common misconceptions about learning and noted the effects these assumptions have on teaching and learning. The assumptions were that humans are passive recipients of knowledge, that the acquisition of knowledge is an additive procedure, that learning will occur if tasks are broken down into component parts and these parts are presented sequentially, and that the stimulus-response model explains learning. These misconceptions also have an effect on assessment. Someone who accepts them is likely to regard testing as a way of finding out how much information the subject has passively received. In testing, an excessive emphasis is likely to be placed on performance rather than competence, behavior rather than learner structures, products rather than process, and materials rather than methods.

We identify four misconceptions about the testing process that are usually associated with the misconceptions about learning. All are typical of a psychometric approach to assessment. They are: (1) testing is sequential; (2) testing determines the individual's knowledge; (3) testing identifies problems; and (4) testing tells how to teach. Explanations of each follow.

Testing Is Sequential

Most tests used by educators and psychologists start with easier questions and gradually become more difficult. When we give these tests, we assume that the older someone is the more answers the person will know and the "higher" he or she will go in the test, at least until some limit is reached in the teenage or early adult years. Until these years are reached, we give harder and harder tests as age increases. We use statistical procedures to arrange test items in logical order from easier to more difficult. As a person gets older, it is more likely that the questions toward the end of the test will be answered correctly and we attach grade or age levels to the sequence. This quantitative perspective is closely associated with the concept that learning proceeds in an additive way through component parts.

Testing Determines the Individual's Knowledge

Almost invariably, tests assume that an individual either knows or does not know answers to the questions in the test. Probably most of us recognize that when we give a test we measure performance, not competence. We are aware that under other conditions the student may be able to perform in a different way. But when we use the results from tests we often persist in treating the results as a measure of competence. We say that the student is reading at the fourth-grade level when we mean that the *score* was at that level. We say that the person's instructional reading level is at third grade when we mean that a certain number of correct responses were made in a passage that purports to be at that level. Errors are regarded as undesirable indicators of lack of knowledge. We may be tempted to teach students (tell them the answer) immediately when they make an error, even when they are taking a formal test. We want them to get a higher score, as if a score really matters.

The tendency to look at scores this way seems to be insidious. Even though we know the dangers, we find ourselves entrapped. For example, a teacher recently said, "I know that IQ scores change, but right now he is performing in the retarded range." When asked how she knew this, the teacher reported that the child had received a low score on an IQ test. She regarded the score as an accurate reflection of the child's intellectual status even though she had virtually no evidence that indicated why the child received the score. General competence level was assumed from a tiny sample of behavior. It seems that if a test is constructed and normed we believe it can be trusted to measure knowledge. Scores take on their own independent meaning, separate from other considerations. Many school districts have gone so far as to demand formal test scores that "prove" how much a person knows (or does not know) if he or she is to be placed in a special program. Even though we know we cannot trust test scores, we continue to depend on them as reliable indicators of knowledge, as an objective means of evaluation (compared to informal or clinical evaluation), as an accurate way of comparing a person with peers, as indicators of where to begin instruction or additional testing, and as good predictors of future performance. Each of these uses assumes that testing accurately reflects the competence of the individual.

Testing Identifies Problems

Obviously, if testing tells us what a person knows, it also identifies problems. Often, this misconception finds a focus in academic areas. If we identify the amount an individual knows, we have also identified where that amount is deficient. Again, a quantitative point of view is apparent. The level at which a person falls in a curriculum content sequence is regarded as more important than how the person operates with the content or how new learning occurs. A student is said to have a "math problem" because of a score (from a reliable test, of course) that is two standard deviations or three years below a standard. Now we know the problem, right?

Of course, some are not satisfied with this "answer." They seek an answer to a deeper question about *why* the student has this problem. Notice, however, that they still seek an answer. They attempt to identify a specific problem through assessment procedures. They may believe that tests need improvement, but the conviction stands firm that good tests, when invented, will identify problems. Somehow, the ability structure of the individual will be determined if they ask the right questions, check out all possible problems with valid and reliable instruments, and confirm the presence of those problems through corroborating scores and observations. The questions about what the person does and does not know, what the individual's weaknesses and strengths are, and what the problems and abilities are will be answered. Diagnosis in the sense of answers to the question of "What is the problem, and what is its cause?" is regarded as the immediate outcome of assessment.

Testing Tells How to Teach

Logically, it would seem that if we can identify the problem we should be able to explore ways of solving it. Maybe the most effective ways of teaching have not been discovered, but somehow there is a direct connection between problems we identify and the teaching techniques we need to use. Or, from a behavioral point of view, we can regard the behavior we want to change as the "problem" and set up the contingencies to change that behavior. In either case, we hope that eventually we will develop a diagnostic handbook that identifies problems and tells us what to do about them. In this "cookbook" we will list a problem, show how to identify the problem, and then list 3 to 10 sure-fire ways of treating it. Presto! The problem is solved! We all know it's not that simple, but we continue to look for direct connections between problems and teaching strategies. We hope we can generalize the solutions to all learning disabled persons with similar problems.

When we assume that testing tells us how to teach, we also assume that testing and teaching are separate processes. They are related in that one leads to the other, but they are not simultaneous or reciprocal.

Consequences of These Misconceptions

If a psychometric attitude toward testing is taken, the resulting misconceptions have important consequences. One result may be that mental structures become inflexible. Pirsig (1974) calls this problem "stuckness" (p. 274), a term that vividly describes what happens when unexpected obstacles appear. Pirsig defines stuckness in the context of motorcycle repair. A screw that must be removed to repair the machine is stripped and cannot be removed. The mechanic is thinking about the more important problem, repairing the motorcycle after the screw is removed. The unexpected physical stuckness of the screw results in "stuck" mental structures. The mechanic is stymied in his or her attempts to get at the more significant problem and can think of no alternatives to solve the less important problem. In a similar way, examiners expect to use tests to identify significant problems in learning. When the tests fail to do so, the examiner may attempt to find better tests rather than seeking alternatives to a psychometric approach. Learning disabled individuals may have a similar problem when they are asked to solve problems. The old way of thinking does not work, but they persist in using it. Pirsig suggests that becoming stuck leads to "gumption traps" (p. 296), which are defined as an inability to continue with the task because of the discouragement that results from becoming stuck. Energy is drained away from the most important task. Teachers give up trying to find alternatives in testing and may become discouraged with teaching. Learning disabled students give up trying to learn.

In assessment, use of the psychometric model leads to stuckness that emphasizes reliability and validity questions, adapting people to tests, discerning causes of problems, convergent testing, and remediation lists. Each of these concerns is discussed in the following sections.

Reliability and Validity Questions

The psychometric model is justifiably concerned with questions of reliability and validity. The entire approach depends on the concept that reliable and valid measurement of psychoeducational characteristics is possible through tests. Tests are tested, often repeatedly, to determine whether they meet minimum criteria in these areas. The problem in learning disability is that we seldom find tests that meet the criteria. Further, we despair of ever really building acceptable tests because of past failures and we conclude that learning disabilities cannot really be measured with certainty. We may even decide that they do not exist because the psychometric model has been unable to identify them at a scientifically acceptable level of certainty.

Often, we switch to strict academic-behavioral models that leave many unanswered questions but appear to provide a meaningful way of changing behavior without worrying about validity and reliability. After all, how can you be wrong if all you do is report exactly what you see, repeat the observations several times, and check occasionally by having a second observer verify them? Surely all of the important behaviors will be observed if we do this. Surely we can assume that appropriate learning has taken place if the student behaves in the way we desire after we teach based on the academic-behavioral model. If children say "two plus two equals four" they certainly know this fact. We need worry about nothing else. In this way, we trap ourselves in a way of thinking that leaves us stuck with inadequate models.

We can consider the problem from another direction. Let us assume that the psychometric approach is a response to the need for reliability and validity. That is, we did not become concerned about reliability and validity because we were trying to construct good tests, but we tried to construct good tests because we were concerned about reliable and valid measurement. Is this why models that depend on clinical judgment are often rejected? Are they too subjective and unscientific? We suggest that the psychometric approach may lead to exactly this conclusion. The result is that the clinical model may be rejected, on the surface at least, and ways of making it work effectively are not sought. Why do we say "on the surface?" Because we believe that the clinical model is always used to some degree by teachers who consider themselves to be following another model. The unfortunate concomitant, however, is that they use it less consciously, deliberately, and effectively than they might because they may not realize they are using it. They fail to clearly recognize that they *always* interpret test results. Measurement can be quantified by a test, but subjective humans quantify it and apply it through subjective interpretation.

Adapting People to Tests

The common misconceptions about assessment frequently result in one of two approaches to testing. First and least desirable is the "battery" approach. In the closet that contains all of our tests we place little labels that classify each instrument. At least three major classifications are typical in learning disabilities: tests of intelligence, tests of academic achievement, and tests of psychological processes. In addition, we may subdivide the tests on the basis of age, affective variables, whether or not they are surveys or true tests, formal or informal, projective or nonprojective, or some other classification. The battery approach requires that, when a child is referred for testing, the examiner select certain tests from the closet based on the age and reason for referral. The same set of tests is given to every person who fits the age level and the general characteristics that have previously been identified. From this test battery, the psychometrician diagnoses the problem and makes recommendations.

The second approach, which might be called hypothesis testing, attempts to be more flexible and requires that tests be selected to fit more detailed information about the person being tested. The psychometrist enters the testing situation with a large repertoire of testing instruments and techniques and draws selectively from them depending on the responses the subject makes. Thus, the results of one test lead to a hypothesis about the problem, and the next test is selected to check out that hypothesis. Again, the examiner is perceived as diagnosing the problem, this time by gradually narrowing down the possibilities until the problem is identified.

Both of these approaches have components that are worthy of consideration. The first suggests that very similar tasks can be given to a variety of subjects. The second selects tasks based on individual characteristics. Note, however, that the battery approach tends to describe results in terms of constructs taken from the test. The hypothesis testing approach defines characteristics in terms of the answers or errors on the test. Both assume that a diagnosis will result from the assessment. The usual outcome is a description of a problem that fits a test or constructs from tests but may have little to do with the individual. The subject is said to suffer from "acute situational schizophrenia," "learning disabilities," or "visual-motor integration" problems. The person is adapted to the test model, to norms, or to the curriculum. Little or nothing is reported about the mental structure of the individual, how the person seems to think, learn, and interact. Thus we come to think of learning disabled persons as having a visual memory problem, and the problem takes on an existence of its own. Assessment is something we do to the subject. We attempt to remediate the problem, which may turn out to be remediating the test. We continue our endless search for tests that will carry out the identification of the problem more quickly and accurately. Surely someone will soon advertise a new test that will answer every possible question in 20 minutes or less.

An additional consequence of adapting people to tests and norms should also be mentioned. We assume from correlational studies based on the test norms that we can predict future performance. Of course, prediction may be important, and it is often done accurately. A problem arises, however, in predicting from group norms to individual cases. The argument that we should use formal tests so we can be assured of more accurate predictions should be regarded cautiously. Prediction of this sort must not overlook the individual exceptions in correlational data. The reasons why a person received a certain score must be carefully considered before predictions are made. Even more important, prediction of future learning must not take the place of careful examination of the thinking of the individual.

Discerning Causes of Problems

The psychometric approach tends to search for causes in an abstract and more distant way than we believe appropriate. The emphasis on finding answers and identifying problems often distracts from the analysis of the current mental structures of the individual. More time than necessary is spent trying to decide whether the problem is caused by some sort of general processing problem inside the subject or whether it is caused by lack of experience, bad experiences, or some combination thereof (Quay, 1973). Or we may spin our wheels trying to decide whether the lack of learning is really due to a learning disability or to an emotional problem. These questions are regarded as important in making appropriate placement or treatment decisions, but we see them as much less important than deciding whether the individual needs help, who can best provide that help, and exactly how to teach.

The emphasis on discerning causes has led to the use of a model that forces us to make decisions in a less than desirable way. The model, mandated by federal and state laws in the United States, requires that a problem be identified before a student is placed in a special program. Thorough assessment is presumed, again, to identify the problem and its cause, thus leading to appropriate placement. Specific tests may be designated by school districts, and only these tests are considered acceptable as diagnostic instruments. If a deficit cannot be identified by the use of these tests, the need for special services is presumed not to exist. To the frustration of the teacher who knows the student is not learning but does not know how to teach him or her, no significant help is provided.

In our view, this model needs to be changed from the local to the federal level. Instead of going from problem identification to placement to teaching, we need to start with teaching and end with decisions about placement, based on teaching needs. The model now commonly used requires early labeling of an individual as learning disabled, the most general, abstract, and hypothetical level of analysis. Until we discard the psychometric model, an extensive change in procedures is unlikely.

Convergent Testing

The psychometric model need not emphasize convergent questions in tests, but nearly all of the tests related to learning disability seem to do so. Obviously, this is partly a result of the test builder's concept of learning as an inactive sequential process made up of component parts. Tests should be constructed to follow the sequence of learning, they assume. Even more predominant is the concept that all we need to know is whether or not a student knows an answer. How that answer was arrived at, the meaning of errors, and how responses fit with the mental structures of the individual are presumed to be unimportant or unmeasurable.

We encourage test builders, if they must persist in designing more instruments, to construct tests that allow for great divergence in response. They may even come up with handy little tasks that allow the examination of how an individual thinks.

Remediation Lists

We mentioned remediation lists when we discussed the misconception that testing tells how to teach. This common consequence probably occurs, in part, because when teachers are provided with test results they still ask, "But how do I teach this student?" Hardhearted diagnosticians may tell teachers that teaching is *their* job, but most want to help. We write down some suggestions of what and how to teach if a particular problem has been identified. Once written, the suggestions take on the power of being the correct things to do. Seldom do we ask for the supporting rationale for the teaching technique. We find the place in the book that names a student's problem and select a technique that sounds interesting and appropriate from the available list. If the technique does not work, we go back to the list. If nothing works, we search for a new problem, which also provides us with a new list.

This entire process presumes that our diagnostic procedures accurately identify problems and specify "where the child is." Grade or age scores are taken to mean the same thing for each student who achieves them. A second-grade child and a fifth-grade child with identical grade level scores on a reading test are regarded as having identical reading skill. The fifth grader is presumed to think about reading in the same way as the second grader, and therefore teaching for the two should also be very similar. In this way, we begin to believe that scores tell us something about instruction, and that remediation lists are accurate.

We regard this kind of thinking as diametrically opposed to the attitude needed for effective teaching. We must abandon it if we are to switch our emphasis to *how* tasks were done and *why* they were done that way. Test scores yield some information about performance compared to other persons, but they do not tell *why* that performance occurred. Unless the reason for the performance is known, a score is meaningless in individual assessment. Compare the case where a person fails a driving test because he or she has no legs with the case where failure is due to falling asleep during the driving test. Identical scores may result, but the scores do not tell why failure occurred or what to do about it. In a particular case we may have obtained a reliable and valid test score. That is, we may have concluded that we are truly measuring what we want to measure (validity) and that the individual knows no more or less than his or her actual score reflects (reliability). What does this score tell us? If necessary, it may tell us something about how to classify the subject. It may inform us that the person has the mental structure essential for completing the task, but scores alone say very little about those structures. Usually we cannot even tell which items were correct, which ones were not answered at all, or which were answered incorrectly. More importantly, we cannot determine from the score how each task was approached.

Herndon (1971) reports as follows on an experience in giving a test to students and evaluating the grade scores:

> With all, it was now clear that among say eight kids all supposed to be reading at 4.5-4.8 reading level, making errors A, B and D (but not C), there were in fact eight kids some of whom were reading all kinds of stuff, some who would only read the newspaper, some who would only read *Mad* magazine (or look at it anyway) and some who wouldn't read anything at all. Thus the test could only mean something if you never looked at the kids themselves. Once you did, you had to abandon it. It was a good lesson and I recommend it (p. 139).

The evaluator must obviously go beyond the scores to interpret structures and to design teaching.

Teachers often feel they really do not know what or how to teach even when they have numerous test scores, long lists of remedial suggestions, a specific diagnostic hypothesis, and a master's degree. They return to school, seek more expert consultants, and read more lists in books on remediation. They request courses that will *really* tell them how to interpret test results. All of this is based on a false premise—the belief that the answer lies elsewhere than in their own creative solutions to learner's needs, solutions which evolve out of the interaction between teacher and student.

ASSESSMENT: ALTERNATIVE CONCEPTIONS

Partial revisions of current approaches to assessment are not enough. We need a revolution! Before we are accused of being too radical, let us explain that a revolution means a qualitative rather than a quantitative change. We do not need a better application of the psychometric or behavioral models. We need a new model.

Our approach attempts to do things that the psychometric model seeks to avoid. Four alternative conceptions, each corresponding to an opposite misconception, summarize the assumptions that are a basis for the approach. They are: (1) testing is holistic; (2) testing is an analysis of mental structures; (3) testing forms hypotheses; and (4) teaching tells how to teach.

Testing Is Holistic

Most advice about assessment, we believe, tries to be too systematic and sequential. We are given an almost endless list of areas to be checked out. When we study tests of a particular area such as reading, we see minute breakdowns of literally hundreds of subskills. For many of the thousands of tests on the market, publishers make extravagant claims such as "Identify children with potential learning problems quickly and easily," "It will work, no changes necessary," or "Can he cope? Find out in 20 minutes." New methods for task analysis, cluster analysis, and criterion-referenced analysis are numerous. We doubt whether most of these efforts result in any real advances in the ability of teachers to teach effectively. Teachers usually tell us that after all the sophisticated formal and informal analyses are finished, they still have very little information about what and how to teach, especially if they did not do the testing personally. What is to be done?

We find that teachers frequently ask how tests can be used to identify, for sure, whether or not a student has a learning disability. Administrators ask if we have any graduate students interested in helping them develop local norms for tests because the national norms do not apply. Should we cooperate? Should we attempt to answer these questions? We frequently are asked which specific tests go with each level in our model. Is there an honest answer? To help you understand the attitudes we have toward assessment, note that we see these questions as unanswerable, at least in the way the questioners expect. Administrators' requests for help in developing norms leave us with the feeling they are asking the wrong people. The great concerns among those who work on the assessment process seem to be reliability and validity, careful breakdown and sequencing of tasks, and thorough analysis of the problem. We see the need for a more holistic approach in which the emphasis is on effective teaching and changing the hypotheses derived from testing to fit with new information and new learning the student acquires.

How can assessment be holistic and still emphasize an individual's specific mental structures? Resolution of the problem is possible through careful definition of the term *holistic*. Holistic assessment is both systematic and intuitive, both hierarchical and heterarchical, both particular and general. In addition, we explain later that assessment is really both teaching and testing. Appropriate testing, we believe, requires an integration of these paired concepts. We do not suggest that one first be systematic then intuitive, but systematic and intuitive at the same time. The pairs above do not reflect a continuum or a dichotomy, but an integrative set. How is this so?

Testing that is both systematic and intuitive requires that the person who tests knows curriculum, environmental demands, and the nature of learning. It demands an organized theory upon which testing procedures are based. This knowledge provides a systematic base that translates into an intuitive mode of operation. The translation does not necessarily happen easily. Professionals must study extensively, try out the procedures deliberately, and practice them diligently if they wish to reach this level. Only then are they likely to analyze mental structures, form hypotheses, and integrate teaching and testing in the way we propose. They will learn to rely on and trust their intuition as well as a logically structured system. Their own creatively integrated systems will make it possible to individualize in a holistic way.

The terms hierarchical and heterarchical refer to relationships between components of a system. Hierarchical means that components are arranged in a sequence from lowest to highest or from less inclusive to more inclusive. Each successive component is in some way superseded by or encompassed by the next. Heterarchical implies that the system is made up of a network of interrelated components, all of which have reciprocal effects. Human thinking and learning, we believe, can be regarded as functioning in both of these ways simultaneously. Testing becomes a system that both uses this human ability and tries to assess the individual in terms of it. The mental structures of the individual being tested are evaluated in terms of both hierarchical and heterarchical functioning.

The particular and the general are both important in assessment. This generalization holds at several levels. The particular mental structures of the individual are significant, but they gain more significance when understood in relation to the structures that are generally developed in humans. Individual structures greatly affect how learning will proceed, but learning generally proceeds in similar ways for everyone. The particular structures of the individual need evaluation for effective teaching, but the general structures that control them must also be understood. The part and the whole are both important, but equally important is the recognition of their interrelationship.

In this section we want to emphasize that assessment cannot be reduced to a simple system with specific sequential steps that can always be followed. The human mind is complex. Effective teaching demands that we try to understand the complexities of the student. At the same time, we must recognize the beautiful simplicity and wholeness of the human mind. We can grasp the total picture and its parts, simply because we are human. We can use our own abilities to analyze and integrate information, to derive coherent hypotheses, and to use the hypotheses effectively. We need not be at a loss because the learning disabled person is a complex creature. Our own minds are equally complex and we believe it is entirely possible for teachers to know enough about the mental structures of learning disabled persons to help them learn effectively.

Testing Is Analysis of Mental Structures

Whether an individual is "right" or "wrong" (by adult standards) on a test item is relatively unimportant. Does that statement startle you? It should, if you are either a behaviorist or a supporter of the psychometric model. However, it ties in closely with the concepts of learning and learning disability we have expressed.

We are not interested, first of all, in what a person knows and does not know or what the person does and does not do. We are interested in performance only insofar as it helps us "understand how the child [or adult] constructs his or her reasoning" (Bovet, 1981, p. 2). We want to know about the individual's mental structures, the underlying principles that guide thinking and behaving. What are the structures that led to a right or wrong answer? Why does the answer seem reasonable to the student? How stable are the structures that are the basis for the response? How are different structures interrelated?

Testing Forms Hypotheses

Thinking of assessment as problem solving is attractive. It supports the idea that the components of the problem are known (or at least knowable) and that a solution is likely if careful analysis and logic are used. Assessment is given a scientific aura. But thinking of assessment as problem solving may result in conclusions that are difficult to support. For one thing, it presumes that a single answer is correct and that everyone will agree on that answer. A quick perusal of case study files and the comments of different professionals shows that this conclusion is overly optimistic. It also presumes that an answer (or pattern of answers) given by a subject reveals the solution to the problem. We conclude, given this perspective, that we know the problem of the student because we know how he or she responded on a test.

We propose that instead of regarding testing as a problem-solving venture, it be regarded as a means of forming reasonable hypotheses. The advantages of this view include less emphasis on proving that we are right or wrong and less concern about reliability and validity. Also, it more closely reflects the way teachers actually operate, whether they know it or not. Notice we are not suggesting that hypotheses are formed so they can be tested to see whether they are correct (an approach we criticized earlier). Rather, they are formed so the teacher can use them as a basis for instruction. If instruction is successful, the accuracy of the hypothesis is not proven, nor is accuracy necessarily important in this regard. As Pirsig (1974) points out, the concept that the scientific method narrows choices and isolates an answer is erroneous. Instead, the generation and testing of hypotheses leads to more hypotheses and on to infinity. We must accept a hypothesis as temporarily accurate, teach on the basis of it, and see what happens. We must avoid becoming so invested in our "answers" to a student's problem that we cannot evaluate the situation with fairness. If the hypotheses we form are of the "this student thinks . . . " variety, we believe that either learning will occur through teaching based on the hypotheses or the teacher will recognize the need for alternative hypotheses. In either case, the chances for effective instruction are good. The teaching is based as directly as possible on the thinking of the student, and the teacher is willing to change instruction as new evidence about the thinking of the student becomes available.

Teaching Tells How To Teach

Once we have formed a hypothesis about how a student thinks, we can attempt to change or develop that thinking. Again, note the emphasis here. We are not attempting to solve a problem but to develop mental structures. How do we know how to teach? Does our hypothesis tell us? In a sense it does, and certainly it contributes to what we do as teachers. But the hypothesis tells us more about *what* to teach than *how* to teach it. Our general knowledge of how to teach comes from an understanding of the learning process. Specific knowledge of how to teach a particular student comes from the teaching process as it is applied with that student.

What does the term *teaching process* mean? In our view, it means much more than imparting information. It means the total set of interactions between student and teacher, and it includes testing. In fact, when we state that teaching tells how to teach we are assuming that teaching and testing are inseparable. They should be regarded as phases of the same process. The teacher does not know whether learning has occurred unless testing is carried out. On the other side, testing without teaching is fruitless. Therefore, we regard the two processes as intimately and essentially linked. Specific teaching methods come from teaching with this perspective as a guide. Since each person's structures are different, it is only by teaching and noting the results that specific next steps in teaching can be generated.

Consequences of These Alternative Conceptions

The second part of this chapter emphasizes the idea that the purpose of testing is to be able to teach effectively. Therefore, the consequences of our assumptions about testing may be stated in terms of how teaching is affected. As we discuss these consequences, we define testing as holistic analysis of mental structures from which hypotheses about teaching are formed. Remember, however, that testing and teaching are regarded as a single process, and this integrated process leads to the formation and revision of hypotheses. This perspective results in four major consequences: (1) teaching matches the nature of learning; (2) teaching matches human thinking; (3) teaching is truly developmental; and (4) teaching results in learning. Let us explore each of these consequences.

Teaching Matches the Nature of Learning

Our description of learning was that it is an active, constructive process of representing the world. In our view, learning, like development, depends on the equilibration process. If modification of existing mental structures is to occur as a result of interaction with the environment, disequilibrium must be present. Our view of assessment takes this description of learning into account. Assessment is the study of internal mental structures and their modification. Assessment is a continuous process, inextricably linked with teaching, and the entire operation is constantly changing. As the teacher interacts with the student, the student's structures change. Necessarily, teaching also changes if it is to remain effective. Modified structures require a new kind of disequilibrium, or learning ceases.

With this perspective, a teacher is less likely to become ensnared in a curriculum-based set of sequential objectives. Objectives are modified based on the structures the student demonstrates. If a student is not making progress, forgets the material "learned" the day before, or does not seem to be learning at an age-appropriate level, the teacher reexamines the hypotheses on which teaching is based. The teacher knows that learning has not actually occurred. More of the same methods and materials will not be persistently presented to the student in the hope that learning will eventually result. At the same time, the teacher knows that learning does require persistent effort—on the part of both teacher and student. The difference is that the effort is aimed at creating disequilibrium relative to the current structures of the student, not at the teaching of a sequenced curriculum or a test-related problem.

Testing and teaching, then, are based on a systematic theory that takes account of the nature of learning. It is on this basis that the teacher knows what to look for during the testing phases of teaching. Assessment always presupposes theory (Sommerhoff, 1974). Only if we have some expectations for performance would we want to take a measurement. Implied in our measurement procedures are our theories about the outcome we anticipate. We would never give a test of written language to a cat or test people for the ability to fly unaided. Our knowledge of the world obviously controls the type of questions we ask. We presume that an explicit theory that organizes this knowledge will result in more acceptable practices in the assessment of learning disabilities. From a theory of learning, we derive the structures model, which provides the framework for the teaching/testing process.

Assessment, in this perspective, becomes a matter of asking the right questions. Errors by a student are regarded as being constructed out of active mental structures, rather than as imperfect imitations of correct models. In learning disability, errors may show how the structures of the learning disabled are qualitatively different from those of nonlearning-disabled persons. Errors reveal the structure of thought.

Assessment emphasizes the processes people go through, not just the products of thinking. Many varied aspects of thought, such as simultaneous and successive processing, verbal mediation and cognitive levels, are regarded as significant in relation to assessment (Merluzzi, Glass & Genest, 1981). All of the mental structures that relate to important tasks are presumed to be important in assessment, because each structure affects how teaching proceeds.

Teaching Matches Human Thinking

One of the concerns that led to this book was that teaching and testing, as currently practiced, often do not match. What teachers do in the classroom with learning disabled individuals does not appear to have a direct relationship to results from tests. We are convinced that the way teachers think is often not consistent with the way tests are constructed. Specifically, tests are much more structured and much less intuitive than teachers. Tests are limited to tiny samples of behavior. They cannot ask, "What is it that this child really needs?" Psychometric models are extremely limited in their ability to account for all of the important data that are available. Problems identified through tests may be significant only in terms of the constructs that the test builder used to make the test. They may have little to do with the real needs of the child.

Teachers, on the other hand, function on the basis of mental structures that are as complex and interrelated as the structures of the students they teach. Teachers can use the holistic, integrated, hypothesis-forming thinking typical of humans. If they are encouraged to do so as a part of the teaching/testing process, the real needs of students are more likely to be met. Teaching becomes a sophisticated, creative act, which requires teachers to call upon all of their available mental resources. It requires them to analyze the nature of thinking and learning and demands teaching strategies that match the characteristics of the individual learner.

Teaching Is Truly Developmental

When we think of developmental teaching, we often think of a curriculum sequence that matches the physical and mental changes involved in human growth. We recognize that people will not all move through the sequence at the same rate, but we assume that everyone moves through it in approximately the same way. To be truly developmental, we must recognize that the thinking of a 14-year-old is likely to be significantly different from the thinking of a 7-year-old, even if they apparently have exactly the same skills in a particular academic area. This concept is central in understanding our approach to the teaching/testing process.

The mental age of the student makes a critical difference in the way teaching proceeds. If we are to teach effectively, we must know how the student thinks. We must recognize that thinking changes as the individual develops. To be truly developmental, we must ask how the student thinks about the content we wish to teach, not just how much the student knows. Development must be understood in terms of the internal mental structures of the individual, not the external curriculum sequence.

Especially in learning disabled persons, we can expect to find qualitative differences between thinking ability and skill development in academic areas. By our definition, some of their thinking abilities will be at age-appropriate levels while other performances indicate lower level thinking. Developmental teaching requires that teaching strategies focus on the use of the highest possible level of thinking. Assessment phases of the teaching/testing process should concentrate on the analysis of age-related mental structures so that appropriate developmental teaching can be designed.

Teaching Results in Learning

While our approach to assessment may not always result in learning, our point is that learning will take place only if and when teaching matches the nature of learning, thinking, and development. Students may ''forget'' what they learned a day or a week earlier if our efforts to teach are directed toward obtaining better test scores rather than toward the modification of mental structures through the stimulation of disequilibrium.

We can expect an emphasis on curing processing problems if we maintain a psychometric approach. Teachers will continue to seek answers from sources other than their own creative teaching abilities if we continue to pretend that tests identify problems accurately and that remediation lists really tell teachers what to do. Although we have much to learn and new discoveries to make, we suggest that effective teaching in the learning disabilities field requires a focus on the close ties between testing and teaching, on a holistic approach to assessment, on the analysis of internal mental structures, and on the formation of creative, flexible hypotheses about how to teach a particular learning disabled person.

When teachers state the hypotheses they derive from the teaching/testing process in terms of ''This student thinks . . . ,'' the goals of teaching become apparent. They know exactly what they wish to change in the student's thinking. For example, a student who thinks that context should not or cannot be used to identify an unknown word in reading needs to be taught in relation to this idea. Teaching better word attack skills does not solve the problem.

If teachers understand that learning is the modification of internal mental structures, they are likely to recognize that methods of teaching are much more important than the materials used. They will emphasize the importance of the equilibration process. They will have less difficulty knowing how to teach because they have formed a reasonable hypothesis about the thinking of the student. Teaching becomes a creative dialogue between student and teacher. Testing becomes a matter of selecting tasks that allow for the analysis of mental structures through careful observation and interpretation.

PURPOSES OF ASSESSMENT

Appropriate teaching is the goal of evaluation for educators of the learning disabled. By definition, the usual educational procedures have in some way failed to provide for adequate learning with this group. Evaluation of the reasons for failure and the current status of the learning disabled individual are presumed necessary to determine changes needed in instruction.

Of course, not everyone who has extreme difficulty in school is learning disabled by our definition. Inadequate teaching, a lack of opportunity to learn, and negative environmental influences are other factors that may lead to school failure. When information processing deficits are present, the factors above often compound the problem. Although these factors are important, our emphasis is on the person who shows some behaviors at an age-appropriate level but not others because of apparent deficits in essential learning processes.

When we decide that appropriate teaching is the ultimate goal of evaluation, we also recognize that labeling, diagnosis, screening, identifying causes of problems, obtaining test scores, or placing a person into or out of a special program are, at most, subgoals. Each subgoal may be important in certain contexts, but all must be subsumed under and directed toward the goal of effective teaching. With this goal in mind we can specify the type of analysis that might be needed to reach the goal.

Types of Analysis

What do we mean by types of analysis? Doesn't a reasonably comprehensive theoretical model provide all that is needed for assessment? We believe the type of analysis still needs to be specified. One of the remarkable capacities of the human mind is that it is capable of analysis of many types. The type of analysis or level of description engaged in makes a difference. For example, Hofstadter (1979) says that if someone describes a novel at the letter level (describing the letters or concepts associated with any particular letter in a word) the description would have no meaning relative to the book. Description must go beyond the word level to the level of concepts (e.g., plot and characters) and their relationship with the real world.

What type of analysis and level of description is needed in learning disabilities? We have stated that effective teaching is the goal, so obviously we want to design our analysis to accomplish this. But how are individual characteristics and instructional techniques related? Some authors state that there is little empirical support for differentiating instruction on the basis of specific student aptitudes or for prescribing intervention on the basis of performance on aptitude measures (Salvia & Ysseldyke, 1981; Ysseldyke, 1978).

We suggest, however, that to ignore individual characteristics is to ignore one of the major components of the educational process. We teach *active* learners who always bring particular mental structures to the learning task. The precise nature of mental structures is, in our view, the most important factor of all. Efforts must be directed at understanding mental structures and how they relate to the activity of the teacher. Teachers of the learning disabled cannot wait until all answers about testing and teaching are available. In spite of the limitations, they must use the resources they have. Let us examine the types of analysis that may help accomplish the teaching/testing tasks for which teachers are responsible.

Academic-Behavioral Approaches

Academic-behavioral approaches to assessment emphasize the direct study of academic problems or skill deficits. The goal of this type of analysis is not only to identify the general academic area of difficulty, but to specify the skills that the individual has. Two closely related approaches to assessment, task analysis and criterion referencing, frequently focus on the evaluation of specific skill deficits. Both task analysis and criterion referencing emphasize the study of specific individual performance. Comparison with others is not a major concern. Instead, the student is compared with a criterion to determine which parts of a task are performed and which are not. In both approaches, the subskills necessary for reading, writing, spelling, speaking, mathematics, and so on are carefully analyzed and placed in sequence. This sequence should reflect the order in which the subskills are typically learned. In assessment, the place in the sequence where the student lacks a skill is identified and teaching begins there. An example of this process is shown in Exhibit 5-1.

In the area of mathematics, a person who fails to provide correct answers to some long division problems may be asked to work a problem to see whether the steps in the process are understood and carried out correctly. Prior to the test, the examiner has analyzed the steps in the long division operation so the exact point of breakdown can be pinpointed. As shown in Exhibit 5-1, we assume the student carried out the entire process correctly except for steps that involve subtraction. This operation is examined in more detail. The specific performance of the student is illustrated in Exhibit 5-1. Correct performance is shown in the column on the right.

The student shows some knowledge of long division but borrows unnecessarily. This error leads to an attempt to carry and, of course, an incorrect answer. The student goes on to the next problem without completing this one because of confusion. Additional assessment of the difficulty may be needed to determine whether the student borrows in this way only under certain circumstances (e.g., when the subtrahend contains a zero). When the exact nature of the student's problem is identified, teaching may begin with direct instruction in the precise area of difficulty. If an academic-behavioral approach is followed with the example in Exhibit 5-1, instruction would be given about when to borrow.

Task analysis has been described in different ways. In some cases, the academic prerequisites and skill sequences are emphasized (Haring & Bateman, 1977). In others, information processing prerequisites needed to accomplish an academic task are also regarded as important (Stellern & Vasa, 1973).

Exhibit 5-1 An Example of a Student's Approach to Long Division

The problem:　　　$134\overline{)7065}$

Student's Work　　　　　　*Correct Performance*

First step:
1. Divide 134 into 706.
   Write 5 above tens
   column.
2. Multiply 5 × 134.
   Write product—670.

1. Divide 134 into 706.
   Write 5 above tens
   column.
2. Multiply 5 × 134.
   Write product—670.

$$\begin{array}{r} 5 \\ 134\overline{)7065} \\ -670 \end{array}$$

$$\begin{array}{r} 5 \\ 134\overline{)7065} \\ -670 \end{array}$$

Second step: (Only subtraction part of problem is shown)
1. Borrow from the 7, making
   it a 6. Place "1" to the
   left of 0.
2. Borrow from the "10," making
   it a "9." Place "1" to the
   left of 6.

1. Subtract 0 from 6. Put
   down 6.
2. Borrow from the 7,
   making it a 6. Place
   "1" to the left of 0.
   Student should have
   subtracted 0 from 6
   without borrowing.

$$\begin{array}{r} 6 \quad 9 \\ 7\,10\,16 \\ -6\ 7\ 0 \end{array}$$

$$\begin{array}{r} 6 \\ 7\,10\ 6 \\ -6\ 7\ 0 \\ \hline 6 \end{array}$$

Third step:
1. 16 − 0 = 16. Put down
   6 and carry "1" (10), which
   makes "9" a "19."
2. 19 − 7 = 12. Put down
   "2" and carry "1," which
   makes "6" into "16."
3. 16 − 6 = 10. Put down "10."

1. 10 − 7 = 3. Put down
   "3."
2. 6 − 6 = 0.

$$\begin{array}{r} 16 \quad 19 \\ 7\,10\,16 \\ -6\ 7\ 0 \\ \hline 10\ 2\ 6 \end{array}$$

$$\begin{array}{r} 6 \\ 7\,10\ 6 \\ -6\ 7\ 0 \\ \hline 3\ 6 \end{array}$$

A third approach includes an emphasis on the interactions between task analysis factors and other important variables (Dickinson, 1980). Dickinson suggests a "direct assessment" approach that begins by pinpointing the student's problem in a clear and precise way. For example, the specific vowel sounds a student does not know are listed. The next step is to determine whether the student has ever made the desired response. If he or she has, the conditions under which errors and correct responses are made are examined and environmental adjustments are made to increase the correct response rate. If the correct response has not been made, a task analysis of the learning task would be completed and teaching would focus on sequential task components that the student needs to learn. Dickinson recognizes a close relationship between task analysis and the environmental conditions in which the task is carried out. He presents several helpful suggestions and examples of how to precisely pinpoint the component of the task that may be difficult for a student.

Academic-behavioral approaches such as these are likely to be helpful with some problems. By themselves, however, they lack two important things. First, they say nothing about *how* to teach. In the example we used above, a problem with subtraction was found. But how is the teacher to present the new information to the student? Should the student be told? Should a concrete example be given? Should rote drill be used? Do the language or thinking abilities of the student affect how a particular skill is taught? None of these questions are answered by task analysis and criterion referencing.

Second, these approaches fail to explain why a problem occurred in the first place, although some regard such explanations as superfluous in cases where teaching is successful without them. Lidz (1979) has suggested that criterion-referenced testing should be carefully used because objectives are not agreed upon and because evidence for the effectiveness of teaching and efficiency of learning based on lengthy objective lists is lacking. In many cases, the sequence of skills so important to an accurate task analysis has been determined by logic, not by definitive data. Is knowledge of the subtraction process essential before one studies multiplication? If a child knows letter names, is the learning of sound-symbol correspondences more efficient? What kind of and how much short-term memory is necessary for learning to spell?

Although reasonable answers to these questions have been suggested, we have little firm evidence of which hierarchy of skills is best. Academic-behavioral approaches often account for only those aspects of individual characteristics that are related to specific academic or skill deficits. The content that needs to be taught is identified, but how the learner learns is not always examined (Lidz, 1979). The result can be that the most efficient teaching techniques are sometimes not used, as illustrated by the following example.

In a film titled *Behavior Modification: Teaching Language to Autistic Children* (Appleton-Century-Crofts, 1972) a teacher attempts to teach Pamela, an echolalic autistic child of about 10 years. Pamela is asked to answer the question, "What is this?" when shown a picture of a cookie. In the beginning of the teaching sequence, the teacher says the question and answer. Pamela, who has been rewarded in the past for echoing what the teacher says, repeats the question and answer. She discovers, however, that she is not rewarded. Let us assume the teacher has correctly identified *what* to teach—the response of giving an answer to questions without repeating the question. The teacher repeats the stimulus several times. Each time, Pamela's response is louder and more emphatic, but still echolalic. After an interruption by the narrator, the teacher changes techniques, and Pamela begins to respond as required. The narrator's comment about the teaching reveals that academic-behavioral approaches sometimes place too much emphasis on what to teach and not enough on how to teach. Specifically, the comment is made that "We tried techniques like these for several hours."

It is important to note that Pamela did eventually respond as desired. In this sense, the teacher did arrive at appropriate techniques. At the same time, it is apparent that the teacher may have changed her techniques sooner had she asked, "What is Pamela thinking?" or "Why is she responding this way?" The apparent answer is that Pamela thought the task was to repeat everything the teacher said. Several hours of teaching time may have been saved had this been considered.

Finally, it appears that the teacher, perhaps without realizing it, did actually consider how Pamela was thinking, since the techniques were changed. Thus the teaching technique began to be based on Pamela's peculiar way of thinking (or of behaving, a behaviorist would say), not just on curriculum sequence. In this sense, individual characteristics that relate to more than external evidence of skill deficits may be used in academic-behavioral approaches. If so, the distinction between these approaches and the next type of analysis we discuss is not absolute. The point of the above example, however, is that a teacher who considers mental structures and thinking strategies in addition to observable behaviors will be more likely to choose appropriate teaching methods.

Reliance on academic-behavioral approaches to assessment will probably result in teaching that incorporates the misconceptions about learning presented in Chapter 1. Some professionals may assert that task analysis and the study of specific skill deficits provide a reasonable starting place in the assessment of learning disabilities. They may suggest that, if a student learns rapidly with analysis of this type and teaching based on it, digging deeper is wasteful of professional time. We caution that teaching based on the assumptions of academic-behavioral approaches may not result in true learning as we define it. Even if effective teaching results from this type of analysis, we suggest that some students need additional types of analysis, especially if the student has complicated and severe learning difficulties. In fact, individuals who respond easily and quickly to academic-behavioral approaches may not be learning disabled by our definition. Our definition includes the idea of severe information processing deficits. Learning disabled persons fail to learn under ordinary conditions. Why would they learn more efficiently after a task analysis reveals performance deficits? Teaching methods must also change. The individual characteristics of the person with processing deficits need to be considered in more detail. The next approach we discuss attempts to do this through the study of behaviors that may indicate processing deficits.

Information Processing Approaches

Information processing approaches to assessment assume the necessity for going beyond straightforward descriptions of academic behavior. Learning disabilities are regarded as a set of unique processes, processes that must be examined to determine what the individual does to gain information from stimuli, how the information is stored and made available for expressive responses, how problems are solved, and how the individual thinks. Farnham-Diggory (1978) said that when we give descriptions of behavior such as " 'learning disabled children have trouble drawing' we are not explaining what is wrong. To analyze what is wrong, we must find ways of monitoring the steps in the program" (p. 91). A more complete description of the drawings of a learning disabled person still does not provide much information about what is happening in the information processing system of the individual. In some way, the behaviors need to be interpreted in terms of the information processing system being used. How can this level of analysis be carried out?

Careful study of the behavior of the individual is the place to start in the evaluation of learning processes. In some cases, the way a person processes information is reasonably apparent from such a study. A learning disability specialist who has extensive knowledge about information processing is able to form reasonable hypotheses about the nature of the internal mental structures of the subject. We have given previous examples of how this can be done (see Chapter 1 and the example of Pamela in this chapter). Note, however, that specific behaviors and the end products they produce are not direct evidence of what is happening in the brain. A very practical approach to understanding the relationships between mental structures and behavior is required. Interpretations of behavior must be stated in hypothetical terms, and then these hypotheses must be tested through teaching if this type of analysis is to be meaningful. General statements about global processing problems have little value. Stating that an individual has a short-term memory problem or a perception problem based on a test score, even in those rare cases where a reliable and valid test can be found, yields no direct information about what and how to teach. Interpretation of information processing differences must be related to specific tasks. Two approaches that study processes in this way are protocol analysis and cognitive-functional analysis. Each is described below.

Farnham-Diggory (1978) suggests the use of "protocol analysis" (p. 114), which she contrasts with task analysis: "Protocol analysis is based on behavior—on a sample of what the individual has actually been doing in the course of solving a problem, or writing a word, or 'thinking out loud.' Task analysis is a theory or model of what he might have done—of what the task is all about" (p. 114). Farnham-Diggory believes protocol analysis keeps the professional focused on what the child is doing rather than on other aspects of interpretation and that it generates remedial ideas. Her approach has parallels with Dickinson's (1980) "direct assessment" described earlier in this chapter. In both, actual child behavior is carefully compared with a model of the specific task. Correct responses and errors in response are analyzed in an attempt to isolate the precise problem. The child is assumed to be governed, at least in part, by internal mental events, and analysis of these mediational processes is regarded as important. Task analysis and information processing approaches appear to be moving closer together. We have incorporated major aspects of both of these approaches in our mental structures approach.

Meichenbaum (1977) describes a "cognitive-functional" approach to assessment and teaching that is much like that of Farnham-Diggory and Dickinson. He recommends "focusing on the intellective activity, the nature of our client's cognitive strategies, and the content of his internal dialogue rather than merely the intellectual product or test score" (p. 245).

Assessment is conducted by careful manipulation of the environment in three ways: (1) modifying the task (e.g., require faster performance, present stimuli through a different modality, or increase the saliency of stimulus cues); (2) altering nontask environmental variables (e.g., change the noise level, or ask client for descriptions of the strategy used for the task); and (3) providing the client with supports (e.g., give direct task aids, memory prompts, or task descriptions, or suggest attention focusing, or self-evaluating strategies).

Information processing approaches to assessment add an important dimension to the analysis of learning disabilities. Study of the direct relationships of specific behaviors and probable mental events leads to remedial activities that include both what and how to teach. If the teacher can determine how the student is thinking, methods of teaching that relate to that thinking can be used. Is such an approach likely to be reliable and valid? Technological and theoretical problems arise when information processing approaches are used in assessment. Farnham-Diggory (1978) stated that the speed with which these processes take place presents one area of difficulty. Related issues involve how these rapid internal processes should be subdivided and studied as well as how they are related to brain function.

Although much has been learned in relation to these problems, even more remains to be done (Gaddes, 1980; John et al., 1977; Luria, 1980; Powers, 1973; Rose & Fernandes, 1977; Sommerhoff, 1974; Sternberg, 1979). The work of the above authors indicates some possible ways to study internal mental processes.

Their work is encouraging because it indicates that meaningful measurement is possible. On the other hand, the technology for accurate measurement in the ways they suggest is not generally available in educational settings. Teachers and diagnosticians in learning disability will need to use other alternatives for the time being. Meichenbaum (1977) noted that "we can develop instruments to tap our client's cognitions that meet the psychometric requirement of reliability and validity" (p. 257), and he cites considerable evidence to support this contention.

We suggest that internal mental processes can be meaningfully evaluated as long as the professional regards the interpretations as tentative and hypothetical and demands that the hypotheses about processes be checked out through teaching. In some cases, formal test results may provide data about information processing. However, reliability and validity questions make it apparent that test results must also be regarded with caution (Salvia & Ysseldyke, 1981). Basically, interpretations about how a person processes information rely on clinical expertise, not on the direct interpretation of test scores. Are expert diagnosticians more reliable and their interpretations more valid than test results? We believe that because of the complexity of human learning, the human mind is more likely to approach reliability and validity than are test results. In spite of the obvious variations in the way learning disability specialists interpret learning processes, we are convinced that efforts in this area are not wasted. A study of learning processes should be completed in assessment. Teachers should form hypotheses about processing and design teaching methods that take information processing abilities into account.

Having said all this about the necessity for meaningful interpretation of mental processes, we need to say one more thing about their measurement. Detecting processing deficiencies is not the major goal of assessment. Information processing problems may be hypothesized about and apparent deficits may be taken as supportive evidence of a learning disability. In our definition of learning disability (Chapter 1) we said that apparent deficits in essential learning processes lead to learning that is at an inappropriate level. But the goal of identifying all of the mental structures of the student takes precedence over the goal of identifying processing deficiencies. Whether processing deficiencies directly cause learning disability in a specific case is less critical than identifying how and what to teach the individual.

We are not interested in determining causes although we recognize that the identification of causes of a disability is important if treatment changes as a result of the identification. In medicine, the treatment of disease is typically directly dependent on the cause of the problem. Someone who cannot walk because of a tack in his or her foot is treated differently than someone who cannot walk because of a sprained ankle.

Cause-effect study of a problem is important in other areas too. If a car does not start after several attempts, it is necessary to find out why. Repairs are made dependent on the type of problem.

With problems in human learning, the situation becomes complex. Frequently, direct cause-effect links are hard to find. Apparent logical connections do not always hold true. Persons with mixed dominance (i.e., the right eye is dominant, the left hand is dominant) sometimes learn to read; sometimes they do not. Measurement of problems is not precise. Causes behind the *causes* are not clear, and the evaluator often does not know how far to pursue the search. If the major symptom is school failure, for example, is the "cause" a lack of reading ability? Or is lack of reading ability a symptom of an auditory discrimination problem? Perhaps auditory discrimination problems were caused by minimal brain damage, which was caused by a head injury at birth, which was caused by the relative sizes of the bone structure of the mother and the baby's head, which are, of course, related to genetics, nutrition, prenatal care, etc.

The educator needs to decide where to stop the search for causes. We suggest that the study of structures provides the most economical solution. Other professions may need to look for causes of a different sort, and the educator needs to know when to seek help from other professionals. But the responsibility of the educational professional is to study structures. Incomplete, inadequate, undeveloped structures may be regarded as the cause of learning problems. Modification of structures becomes the most basic goal of treatment. Learning may be defined as the modification of internal mental structures.

When we speak of identifying causes of a disability, therefore, we seek to communicate a specific view about causes. We go beyond observable behavior to inferences about the mental structures indicated by behavior. Inadequacies, inaccuracies, and idiosyncrasies in structures provide an adequate account of the causes of a learning disability in most cases.

In a very important sense, however, identification of causes is just a subgoal. The question in assessment is "What are this person's structures?" not "What are the causes of the disability?" Identification of causes, as such, may be important when placement or funding decisions are made. Then the professional may need to decide if the structures of the individual are typical of a learning disabled person.

The study of processes provides only one set of information that is helpful in determining how, what, and when to present content to the individual. Knowing the cause of a problem does not, by itself, tell the teacher how to correct it. Rather, we must evaluate the total situation of the individual and attempt to identify all of the important aspects of the person's thinking and learning. Learning problems are unlikely to result from unitary causes. Descriptions of learning disabilities must consider a variety of dimensions, not just deficiencies in learning processes.

A Mental Structures Approach

The final type of analysis we will present is the one that is the focus of this book—a mental structures approach based on the model presented in Chapter 4.

Details about use of the model for assessment purposes are described in Chapter 6. We will introduce the approach here by discussing how it is similar to and different from the two approaches just presented and by specifying the major components of the approach.

Academic-behavioral and information processing analyses can be used together. Torgesen (1979b), for example, has suggested that task analysis and process analysis should be combined, with assessment efforts concentrated on understanding the processes only in relation to specific important tasks. Our approach attempts to accomplish this integration. The structures approach has some similarities to academic-behavioral approaches. We also study the component parts of tasks and may evaluate which of these parts a student can do. Our approach is similar to the information processing approach in its emphasis on how a student thinks while working on a task.

How is the mental structures approach different? The major difference, we believe, is the emphasis we place on identifying the student's *level* of response. Our assessment procedures are based on a specific theory of the psychology of learning disability that is designed to point directly to the kind of instruction a learning disabled person needs. Teaching principles are attached to each level of response, and each level involves qualitatively different mental structures.

Assessment involves deciding about the level of response of the individual. This decision depends on the thorough analysis of all the mental structures used by the individual, which, in turn, requires analysis of the task, the information processing abilities, and the specific strategies the person applies. Note, however, that identifying the specific immediate structures of the student is only a part of the process. We are not interested only in how the student approaches problems in mathematics or in the structures that are evident in reading comprehension tasks. We want to know how all structures of the student are interrelated—how the entire performance of the student holds together and what this means for teaching that individual. The concept of levels of response provides a perspective for interpreting structures in an integrated way. At the same time, teaching goals (or response goals for the student) can be set based on the idea of levels. If a 10-year-old demonstrates some evidence of appropriate Level IV responding but also clearly shows inadequate performance on many tasks at that level, teaching and response goals will focus there.

In assessment, the individual is regarded as an active learner who comes to the situation with an enormous set of mental structures that can be evaluated. The result of assessment is not some kind of final, unchanging product that will answer all questions about the nature of the students and the instructional techniques essential to teach them. Processing problems are not "discovered" or "diagnosed." Rather, the examiner seeks to ask the major questions that are important and determines a way to *begin* to teach the individual.

Is a Processing Problem Present?

Some rather strange twists appear when assessment is looked at in this way. For one thing, processing problems are said to be present on the basis of what might be termed circumstantial evidence. Each level of response is directly associated with one of the five learning processes from the model. If the student is able to perform some tasks at a higher level than others, a processing problem is presumed to be present related to the tasks that are performed at the lower level. If reading is performed at Level III, but spelling is not, a processing problem with memory is assumed because memory is the process associated with Level III. We are, of course, speaking of dramatic and significant differences in level of performance here.

This is how analysis might proceed. A student is able to read sight words in a way that is typical of his age group but is unable to spell any of these words if they have more than three letters (in spite of normally adequate instruction in spelling). This student shows Level III ability in reading but not in spelling. Such performance would be taken as evidence that the person is not using memory processes adequately in the spelling task. It appears from the information gained so far that a strategy for learning how to learn spelling words may be needed for this student.

Two rather subtle but very important points must be made, however, lest we leave the wrong impression about how teaching should proceed. First, the teacher should not attempt to remediate the memory problem per se. That is, if the learner apparently uses only three "slots" in memory during spelling tasks (only three-letter words were spelled correctly), stretching memory capacity to four or five slots is not the major goal. Instead, the teacher aims at enabling the student to use memory processes efficiently so that the learning task is accomplished. An efficient way of "chunking" or grouping information (e.g., by approaching spelling at the syllable level instead of letter by letter) may enable the student to learn how to spell in spite of a limited memory capacity. The second point is that teaching probably will not focus *only* on a strategy for teaching new spelling words. More analysis of the student's structures would be essential before the decision about how and what to teach is made. An integrated perspective about the student's levels of response is essential for effective teaching. Given that additional analysis shows a need for more adequate Level III responding, teaching would focus on developing and selecting strategies at this level. Obviously, these strategies would aim at efficient spelling, but adequate performance in all tasks at Level III is the more important goal. The emphasis is on adequate Level III responding, not directly on teaching a particular academic skill.

One could argue that identifying a memory difficulty in this way shows circular reasoning and does not establish that the child has a memory deficit. However, information processing deficits are *never* directly measured. They cannot be because they are hypothetical constructs, not objects with physical dimensions. We must rely on interpretations of behavior if we are to understand how information is processed in the human brain.

Formal and informal tests provide some information that helps us make reasonable inferences about information processing, and we would use these when needed to gain information about the structures of a student. But the results from a test do not answer the question about whether an apparent deficit has a direct effect on learning. Test results frequently indicate perception problems. Can we infer from poor performance on a short-term memory test that the student will be unable to spell? Of course not! Performance in spelling can be examined by asking the student to spell, which is exactly what we would do. Our reasoning is the opposite of going from a test result (showing poor processing) to an inference about spelling. We infer inadequate use of memory processes on the basis of poor spelling performance. But note that we make inferences about memory processes *only* in relation to spelling unless we also find specific evidence of similar performance in other tasks. We are actually saying, in this case, that the student shows apparent inability to use memory processes appropriately to learn spelling words, in spite of adequate instruction. We have made the assumption that spelling is a Level III task; we have found that the child is unable to perform in this area at Level III; and we attribute the inability to perform to inappropriate or inadequate use of memory processes. More importantly, we have gained information about the learning needs of the student. We have evidence of the need for strategies that allow for efficient temporary storage and rehearsal, the major kind of processing required at Level III.

Is Teaching Modified?

Another dramatic consequence of identifying the level of response in assessment is that the usual teaching sequence and the usual "developmental" principles of teaching are sometimes turned upside down. The sequence that is regarded as extremely critical in academic-behavioral approaches may be tossed out. Again, let us illustrate how this might occur.

We will continue with a description of the hypothetical student from the previous example—the person who was unable to spell but able to read sight words. Suppose that this child is 11 years old and that additional evaluation shows the child is capable of Level IV performance in tasks such as reading comprehension or solving story problems in mathematics. An academic-behavioral approach would still recommend teaching direct spelling skills at the level of breakdown. An information processing approach might come closer to our approach because it involves examining how the child thinks about the spelling task. Still, the information processing approach does not deliberately take account of qualitatively higher thinking abilities and attempt to use these in teaching spelling.

The structures approach attempts to enable the student to approach the spelling task (and other tasks) in a new way—a way that is consistent with the highest level of thinking available to the child. All the structures the child brings to the task are regarded as significant and potentially important for learning how to spell. Once these structures are analyzed and evaluated, the teacher is better able to design the learning environment so that the student can take advantage of those structures most closely related to the task. The teacher no longer attempts to "fix" a spelling problem by replacing broken or missing parts. The student constructs a system for learning how to spell. The teacher makes the components of the system available to the student so learning is more likely to take place.

With an 11-year-old, specific attempts might be made to use the logical thinking and language abilities of the child. Instead of teaching spelling in the usual developmental sequence where rote drill plays the major role, the teacher might help the student develop a learning strategy based on spelling rules. The emphasis is on *using* the strategy the student develops as a system for learning new spelling words and as a system for spelling words correctly any time the words are needed.

Mental Structures and Types of Analysis

Four types of analysis and levels of description are included in our structures model (order is not critical here):

1. The *specific knowledge structures* or plans (see Figure 4-1) are examined to determine the particular skills the individual has acquired. Incomplete or inaccurate plans, especially in relation to traditional academic areas, are described.
2. *Intellectual capacity* and *motivation* are evaluated. The effects these control structures will have on learning and performance, given their makeup in the individual, are described.
3. Mental structures in the *intent to respond* and *strategy selection* areas are carefully assessed. The specific structures the individual appears to use for making decisions related to responding and strategy selection are identified.
4. For each important task and academic area, the control structures that involve the use of *specific strategies* and *processes* are described.

This analysis enables the evaluator to isolate the level at which the individual is performing with each task. The type of problem the individual has with any task is described in terms of the level of response shown, the processes engaged in, and the strategies used. Note, however, that identification of significant *disabilities* does not complete the assessment process. Examiners must also identify the other structures of the learner. In addition, they must decide which problems are most important.

In nearly every case, more than one major area of difficulty is found. Should all problems be regarded as equally significant? Should they all be addressed simultaneously? We do not think so. Simultaneous treatment of several problems often seriously dilutes the effectiveness of teaching. The professional needs some basis for deciding which of several problems is most in need of attention. The structures model provides that basis. It may be used as the theoretical justification for deciding to work on one problem and to ignore others. For example, an examiner may decide that a problem with short-term memory is less significant than a problem with verbal comprehension because of the age of the student and because of environmental expectations. The levels-processes approach shows that short-term memory problems may become less significant as age increases because new types of thinking emerge and environmental demands change. Thus, even though an individual appears equally deficient in the two areas mentioned, the structures model indicates that verbal comprehension may be a more important disability for an older student.

By engaging in the four types of analysis presented above, the study of mental structures is made reasonably complete. At the least it is comprehensive enough for the specialist to identify specific teaching strategies.

To summarize this section, we regard assessment as a matter of arriving at appropriate teaching strategies through evaluation of the total mental structures of the student. Effort is directed toward describing these mental structures in each important dimension of thinking and learning. The description is based on the behavior of the individual as a variety of tasks is completed. The extent and type of difficulties the individual has are described, and the need for special teaching strategies is determined. Specific teaching strategies are designed and implemented. It should be noted, however, that assessment does not end when teaching begins. Teaching and testing are closely allied. The way an individual responds to teaching, by itself, provides excellent information about mental structures. In addition, any time a person learns, structures change. Reevaluation of the person's structures thus becomes a continuous process. Each time something is learned, content, goals, and strategies may change. Teaching and testing are continuous and cyclical. We regard them as so closely allied, in fact, that including separate chapters about assessment and teaching in this book was a difficult decision. We may leave the undesirable impression that the two processes should be separated.

The structures model (Figure 4-1) provides one meaningful way to look at behavior and make decisions about teaching. It does not provide a model for the description of all aspects of normal thinking, but it does guide in the analysis of structures. This type of analysis makes possible the specification of how and what to teach.

Finally, note that historical, ecological, and medical factors must be carefully considered as a part of any type of assessment. Although these factors will not be explained here, we recommend careful study and analysis of them. Many excellent texts on assessment present information related to one or more of these areas (See, for example, Anastasi, 1976; Salvia & Ysseldyke, 1981; Sattler, 1974; Wallace & Larsen, 1978).

Chapter 6

Evaluating Mental Structures

INTRODUCTION

In this chapter we develop in more detail the specific considerations that are critical to the evaluation of mental structures in learning disabled persons. The ideas are developed from the perspective of the assumptions and purposes explained in the previous chapter. The first section presents three major components of assessment: (1) the selection of tasks; (2) the observation of responses; and (3) making inferences about internal mental structures. The last section applies the concepts developed to actual procedures for evaluating mental structures in relation to the structures model.

THREE MAJOR COMPONENTS OF ASSESSMENT

Simply put, the evaluation of mental structures involves determining what a person does and does not know. We use the term *know* to refer to more than the facts the person has stored in long-term memory or the academic skills the person can perform. The ways in which experiences or tasks are approached, thought about, and carried out are part of internal mental structures.

Since every aspect of structures cannot be evaluated, the professional needs to choose which components to assess. The choice depends on the theoretical orientation of the practitioner and the task demands of the student's environment. If short-term memory is regarded as important for learning, the examiner will select short-term memory tasks. Mental structures related to solving story problems in arithmetic need not be evaluated unless this task is required in the person's environment.

How is the task of evaluating structures accomplished? At least a three-step process is required. First, a task is selected and presented to the individual. Then, the evaluator makes careful observations as the subject works. In the third step, the professional forms inferences about the meaning of the performance. That is, the structures that underlie the performance are analyzed, and hypotheses about them are proposed.

Task Selection

Each step in the evaluation of structures demands considerable expertise. The first step, selection of tasks appropriate for evaluation, requires general knowledge of internal structures and human learning, as well as specific knowledge about assessment tasks and the environmental demands surrounding the individual. We regard task selection as a matter of asking the right questions. Based on general or specific knowledge about the subject, knowledge about the learning process, and knowledge about the individual's environment, the examiner decides which areas need investigation. Questions about the internal structures of the subject are formulated. These questions may take the form of working hypotheses—tentative explanations of the person's behavior—that are systematically explored. Tasks are selected to provide information about the hypotheses. Sometimes formal tests provide the needed tasks. Frequently, the examiner needs to devise informal tasks that both teach and test.

Note the importance of choosing relevant tasks that allow for the analysis of structures. Tasks are not selected because they are found in someone's test. They are selected because the individual's environment demands the kind of thinking required in the task. In assessment, we must be aware of the age-related demands placed on our subjects. In addition, we must determine the type of thinking that is required in any particular task.

The structures model can be directly applied here. It shows how the level or type of thinking changes with age, thus providing a guide for the selection of tasks that fit with age-related expectations. The general rule we follow is to concentrate on tasks that match with the mental age of the student. That is, if the student is seven years old, we would select tasks that can be accomplished through Level III processing. If the student is 10 years old, we would want tasks that can be related to Level IV. The environment, both in and out of school, is likely to require that individuals of particular ages show responses at a level corresponding to that age. Obviously, the most relevant tasks are those closely related to environmental demands.

When this approach to assessment is taken, tasks will often not be sequenced in easier to more difficult fashion. The examiner is more likely to begin with tasks that can be approached from several different levels or higher level tasks that demand the kind of thinking typical of the student's age. The level of thinking a student actually uses can be determined from tasks that are readily approached from more than one level. If a student is incapable of performing a higher level task, lower level tasks may be administered, in addition to other relevant tasks that fit the highest probable level of functioning of the individual.

An important distinction between *relevant* and *academic* tasks must be made here. The tasks used in assessment need not be identical to other tasks in the environment in order to be relevant. The tasks must enable the analysis of structures that are significant for the student. Sometimes, the best analysis can be accomplished if a task is identical to one demanded in school (or outside of school). In other cases, the individual's structures can be analyzed better by choosing tasks that are never specifically required in other contexts. For example, word attack strategies may sometimes be more obvious if nonsense words are used. Interference from previous learning is less likely if a student has never seen the words before. The key concept is that the task must require a type of responding and thinking that is relevant to the student's situation. Frequently, learning disabled students react more positively to tasks that appear to be dissimilar from school tasks.

Appropriate task selection requires a "clinical method of enquiry" (Bovet, 1981, p. 2). Our efforts in assessment should be directed at understanding the thought processes of the student. We want to know how and what the individual thinks and whether concepts are stable, accurate, and complete. Bovet (1981) suggests that the same task may be given to children at different ages. Adolescents may be asked to explain simple concepts, not because we do not expect them to be able to accomplish the task (nor because we want them to have a "success" experience), but because the task enables the examiner to determine the level of thinking. Young children may be asked to explain something we are certain they will explain inaccurately for the same reason.

Testing is *not* a matter of obtaining test scores or determining whether a student knows the answer. It is a matter of examining mental structures, and the tasks we select should be aimed at this goal. Note that this clarifies the general rule that tasks should match the mental age of the student. It does *not* always mean that simple tasks are given to younger students and more difficult tasks to older students. Exactly the same question may be asked at both ages. The tasks should allow for a wide variety of responses in order to reflect the thinking of the individual. Herein lies a critical difference between our approach and psychometric or diagnostic/prescriptive models. The testing/teaching process becomes a dialogue (Bovet, 1981) between student and teacher—a dialogue that is focused on the structures of the learner and how to develop those structures. Bovet (1981) suggests the use of "counter suggestions to verify the stability and structure of a concept developed by the child" (p. 2). Tasks are selected that require explanations by the subject. After an explanation has been given, the examiner probes the individual's thinking through additional questions and alternative explanations until the thinking of the student is apparent.

After a student has made a response to a task, the examiner does not simply record the results and select a new, unrelated task. Rather, the next task is selected on the basis of the previous response. The examiner continually adapts the next task depending on the type of thinking the student has demonstrated. Appropriate task selection of this kind requires careful analysis and thought on the part of the examiner. Many teachers find it difficult to interpret the responses of students as soon as those responses are made, and then to select an appropriate subsequent task. Note, however, that informal teaching/testing of the sort we describe does not demand the precision associated with formal testing.

The task demands intensity and concentration but also has an element of playfulness. Students may need an "out" during the process that provides them with the option of not responding. Directly telling them that this is an option often leads to better responding because it removes the need for a power struggle between student and examiner. Mistakes (i.e., poor task selection) can be made by the examiner without devastating effects. False leads are sometimes followed up, wasting a bit of time, but otherwise having no serious consequences. Important aspects of a response may sometimes be misinterpreted or overlooked. Such limitations can be modified and corrected later as the teaching/testing process continues. The important concept is that the process described above should be followed, not that the process should be perfect. Practice in following the process may help an examiner become more efficient. The examiner learns what needs to be done if responses are confusing or difficult to interpret. It may help to ask the question again at a later time, ask a similar question, or set up other means of exploring an area in greater depth.

In many cases, the tasks selected will be in the form of trial learning lessons. A new word, concept, action, or other stimulus is presented to be read, analyzed, imitated, or responded to in some way. The subject responds, and the examiner observes and interprets the response and selects the next task. Always, the attempt is made to select tasks that reveal how the student thinks. As a part of the process, improvements in performance resulting from instruction are carefully evaluated. This information is very helpful in setting up appropriate instructional methods. Both content to be taught and methods by which to teach it are continuously evaluated or reevaluated during the teaching/testing process.

Observation

Step two in the evaluation of mental structures is to carefully observe the responses of the subject and the products of those responses. In this step, the professional must clearly distinguish between *observation* and *inference* to avoid the danger of assuming too much. Problems with attention, perception, memory, and other processes cannot be directly observed. For example, an examiner may infer that inability to copy a circle indicates a problem with perception of the model. Even if this is correct, it is an inference and not an observation.

Careful observations of the performance and product must precede the formation of inferences. In our circle example, the examiner must observe the amount of time the student spends examining the model, the smoothness of the movement, and the force exerted on the pencil. It may be important to observe whether the reproduced circle is closed, shows a continuous curve, or is equivalent to the model in size. Only when observation is thorough and accurate can inferences be drawn that will lead to appropriate teaching.

Observation takes place both while the subject prepares to do the task and during task performance. After the task is completed, additional observations of the product, if any, are needed. Words, facial expressions, or movements of any sort are suitable targets for observation. Products are examined to determine correctness, omitted responses, and error patterns. Observations of errors and error patterns has particular value because errors are seldom made deliberately. Thus errors provide direct clues about which structures need modification.

At first, it may appear that accurate observation does not depend significantly on a theoretical point of view, but this is not the case. Observation does involve some important skills that are not dependent on a particular theory. But more than observation skills are needed. The observer needs to know what to look for and must be able to notice the unexpected. Knowing what to look for probably depends partially on experience, but much of this knowledge comes from awareness of the characteristics of learning disabled persons. The study of characteristics requires theoretical knowledge about the psychology of learning disability. Theory enables the professional to concentrate on some characteristics and ignore others.

At the same time, care must be taken to watch for important behaviors that may deviate from what is expected, given a particular theory. The examiner's task is not to fit a subject to theory but to fit theory to the subject when appropriate. As a goal of assessment, our theory of the psychology of learning disability seeks to identify the major *level* of individuals' performance. The theory also guides the examiner in identifying which learning processes are deficient.

A broader goal, however, is to identify *all* of the important internal mental structures of the subject. Some individuals who are referred for evaluation will not have processing deficiencies, and their learning difficulties will not clearly fit the theory we present. The need to remain open, to allow for alternative explanations, and to abandon an interpretation of learning problems, when necessary, is obvious. The evaluation of the subject's internal mental structures is always important in assessment, but the appraisal process demands more than this. In some cases, interpretation of the individual's total life situation leads to the conclusion that no learning disability is present. The point is that the examiner must be capable of observing carefully enough to notice the characteristics of the individual that do not match a particular theory, even though that theory is being used as a guide for assessment.

In the observation step, then, the examiner concentrates on careful, thorough recording of the responses of the individual. For learning disabilities, it is particularly important to look for evidence of the level of performance for each task. Does the subject approach and respond to Level III tasks in a Level III manner? Does the student act as if a comprehension task requires a mechanical strategy or is a logical strategy appropriately applied? Careful observations, carried out in the framework of levels and strategies, provide a basis for the next step, inferences.

Inferences

A third major step in assessment requires the formation of *inferences* about what a person knows or does not know. The purpose for making inferences about internal mental structures is to enable the teacher to decide how and what to teach. If these inferences are drawn in relation to an accurate model of the teaching/learning process, effective teaching should follow.

Inferences must be clearly distinguished from observations. An hypothesis about internal mental structures is definitely not the same as an observation of a behavior. Of course, inferences are made on the basis of observations. In fact, they usually occur almost simultaneously with the observations on which they are based. The close connections between the three steps in the teaching/testing process become very apparent as we examine this step. The tasks selected form the basis for observations; the observations are the basis for interpretations; and the interpretations take the form of tentative hypotheses, which are evaluated through additional tasks. For each observation, the examiner asks, "What is this student thinking that led to the response?"

Theoretically, an enormous number of hypotheses could be generated in response to this question. Realistically, however, an examiner might select one, two, or three hypotheses to examine further. Teaching/testing tasks are selected to check out each hypothesis the examiner regards as important.

What type of analysis should be carried out? Should the teacher concentrate on interpretations such as "This person appears to have a visual-motor deficit?" We regard this type of inference as relatively unimportant. Such inferences may help, in a vague way, to select the next teaching/testing task, but they are not very helpful for deciding how and what to teach. Incidentally, we find this type of inference made frequently by teachers of the learning disabled. The "identifying problems" approach it reflects seems to be very ingrained. When effective teaching is the goal, this type of analysis is not sufficient. We urge teachers to replace it with a "This student thinks . . ." statement, which forms the basis for additional appraisal or teaching.

The major goal of drawing inferences in any stage of the teaching/testing process is to determine the current thinking of the student in relation to important tasks and to decide the nature and direction of necessary changes in that thinking. With this concept of learning, inferences that specify how a student thinks are crucial.

Meichenbaum (1976) suggests that a careful analysis of cognitive strategies and the circumstances under which they are used needs to be conducted. This analysis depends on careful selection of tasks and introspection about what kind of thinking is needed to accomplish those tasks. Meichenbaum finds that asking the subject to verbalize about the processes they use as they do the tasks may be helpful in the analysis. We recommend the use of this technique whenever possible. Ask the students to explain their performance. If this is done in a persistent but nonthreatening way, additional insights about the individual's mental structures are likely. Let us now examine in more detail what needs to be done to evaluate thinking from the perspective of the structures model.

ASSESSMENT PROCEDURES AND THE STRUCTURES MODEL

We assume that the structures of learning disabled persons are both qualitatively and quantitatively different from those of the nonlearning disabled. This uniqueness makes assessment especially necessary since the teacher cannot assume that learning will take place in the usual way. In fact, learning has already failed to take place.

The examiner's task is to determine the nature of the individual's thinking and the reasons for failure and then to design an effective plan for teaching. To do this, specific knowledge structures, general capacity and motivation factors, control structures, and strategies and processes must be examined and described. These are the important components described earlier and pictured in Figure 4-1. We will describe important aspects of the teaching/testing process for each of these components. Remember, however, that the process is a holistic one in which simultaneous analysis of the components is typical. The examiner must attempt to determine which factors are important and how these factors relate to the total functioning of the individual. The needs, the preoccupations, the interests, the abilities, and the capacities of the student all need to be considered during the teaching/testing process.

Examiners may wish to begin the teaching/testing process by asking students to explain their problems and give reasons for those problems. Sometimes this question leads to the denial of problems. More often, however, the student's answer identifies many variables important to that individual. Most learning disabled persons are aware of their problems and have built up stable concepts about them. Students who have faced years of failure in school, for example, are likely to have "I can't do school work" structures that have an important impact on their performance and on the way the teaching/learning process should be approached. As one method of obtaining significant data, we advocate asking the individual to explain.

Evaluating Specific Knowledge Structures

The specific knowledge structures or plans that an individual has available comprise an important component of performance. As educators, our major concern about knowledge structures is the academic skills that the student may or may not have. A student who is achieving adequately in school is usually not a candidate for help through a learning disabilities service. Analysis of this component is obviously important if valuable and expensive professional time and expertise are to be used responsibly.

Appropriate analysis of knowledge structures depends on the evaluator's knowledge of environmental demands, curriculum, and academic testing procedures. The examiner must be aware of the expectations that are placed on the student, especially in relation to classroom situations. When these demands are known, a direct guide exists for deciding which knowledge structures to evaluate.

Extensive knowledge about curriculum is also required at this point. Knowing the response expectations in the classroom is not enough. The examiner must understand the thinking required to meet those response demands. If the task is to complete a page of subtraction problems, many previous concepts are also required. In a sense, every school task is a problem-solving task, and the student must have a set of structures for solving the problem. Thus, even during the evaluation of knowledge structures, the examiner needs to concentrate on more than responses. The student's understanding of the task and ways of approaching the task must also be considered.

Tests of academic skills and textbooks about academic assessment are numerous. Our intent is not to review these tests nor to present another text on academic assessment. We do regard a thorough knowledge of academic test instruments and of academic testing procedures as essential parts of the repertoire of teachers of the learning disabled. Wallace and Larsen (1978), Salvia and Ysseldyke (1981), and Mann and Suiter (1974), among others, provide information about how to evaluate knowledge structures in academic areas. The information in these sources is helpful for the teaching/testing process even though we regard analysis of how and why a student performs in a certain way as more important than skill performance in a narrow sense.

One task of the learning disability specialist, then, is to decide whether the individual is significantly below norms in relation to type and extent of knowledge structures. This decision is not always easy since school environments and teacher expectations vary. Many important questions arise. Should national or local comparisons provide the norm? Should gifted underachievers be considered? How far behind should a student be before intervention becomes critical? Will a program that allows students to receive assistance from a learning disability specialist when they are one standard deviation low on a standardized achievement test be cost effective?

Our purpose is not to answer these questions. Definitive criteria for answering them are not available. For each, state or local level decisions will need to be made, based on needs and resources. Our concern is that the learning disability specialist recognize the need to evaluate the knowledge structures of students. Even though we regard regular education as primarily responsible for teaching this component, learning disability specialists must determine whether the student has the necessary knowledge structures in reading, mathematics, spelling, writing, and other academic and nonacademic areas. Only in the presence of significant difficulties in this component would we advocate providing learning disabilities services.

Evaluating Capacity and Motivation

In Chapter 4, we described the intellectual capacity and motivation components and indicated why they are important. Our descriptions also indicated some ways in which these factors can be evaluated, so our comments here will be brief. Although standardized tests may be helpful in evaluating intellectual capacity, our interest is in true capacity to learn and process information, not in a score on a test. We also do not believe an individual must obtain a particular score on a test to be identified as learning disabled. We suggest that the learning disabilities specialist should evaluate the learning and processing capacity of the individual so that teaching content, rate, and methods can be designed to match. For the most part, analysis of this component can be integrated with analysis of other control structures. We present capacity as a separate component primarily because broad limits and capacities that are not apparent in other parts of the model do have a significant impact on individual performance and learning.

Similar comments are appropriate about motivation. This component is included in the model because a student's "affective structures" obviously have an impact on content and methods. Teachers need to be sensitive to the emotional reactions students display, not just apparent skill performance and intellectual functioning. This component is evaluated, in most cases, through careful observation and interpretation of the emotional status of the student during the entire teaching/testing process. Extreme behaviors and reactions may require the assistance of other professionals who specialize in affective areas.

Evaluating Intent to Respond and Strategy Selection

Two "metastructures" are especially important in the teaching/testing process. These components are identified as *intent to respond* and *strategy selection*.

Evaluation here may be regarded as having both global and specific levels. That is, a set of important questions needs to be asked in general and specific terms as these components are evaluated. The examiner needs to ask each question for each task separately and for tasks collectively.

Intent to Respond

In Chapter 4, we explained why the intent to respond component is significant in learning disabilities. Learning disabled individuals may either fail to inhibit responses or may fail to actively engage the task appropriately. Two basic types of responses are made as a part of this component—bypass or strategy selection responses. Learning disabled persons may use the bypass but select the wrong plan, or they may bypass when no plan is actually available. The latter we referred to as impulsive guessing.

Strategy Selection

Similar concerns were delineated in Chapter 4 regarding the strategy selection component. Failure to actively engage the task could be rephrased as a failure to select a strategy when one is needed. An individual may also select a strategy that is ineffective because it is from the wrong level or because it does not match the nature of the task even though the level of the strategy is appropriate. Finally, learning disabled individuals may have difficulty shifting flexibly to different strategies when required by the task.

These concerns give rise to a set of questions that should be asked as a part of the teaching/testing process. The questions can all be stated in the same format: In doing this task (or set of tasks) does this individual:

- respond when no response is needed

- fail to respond when a response is needed

- respond incorrectly when strong evidence exists that the correct response is known

- respond rapidly but incorrectly when strong evidence exists that the correct response is not known

- respond with a strategy that is from a level other than that demanded by the task

- respond with a strategy that shows an appropriate level of response but does not fit the specific task

- fail to respond with a different strategy when the previous strategy is not effective

Each of these questions attempts to evaluate one of the areas of difficulty we addressed in explaining the intent to respond and strategy selection components. If the individual appears to respond in one or more of the ways referred to, the examiner may form hypotheses about instructional needs relative to the metacomponents under discussion.

Evaluating Strategies and Processes

The strategies and processes components of the model are the primary focus of the teaching/testing approach we advocate. Careful study of the levels of response and the strategies and processes used at each level provides the information a specialist needs to teach effectively. The task of the learning disabilities specialist, we suggest, is to emphasize the teaching of specific strategies and ways to choose appropriate strategies.

Principles to Follow

Analysis of how the student thinks is of primary importance here. The evaluator must present tasks that enable the strategies the individual uses to be studied in considerable detail. Several other "rules of thumb" set the stage for appropriate assessment. First, the examiner must provide tasks that relate to *teaching*. That is, the tasks must require the type of thinking needed in the student's environment. When the student does not exhibit the type of thinking needed, the examiner explores how the student thinks and attempts to teach the student as a part of the evaluation procedure. Direct attempts at trial teaching are an integral part of the process.

A second rule is that students' explanations must be sought and evaluated. As with previous components, students' explanations of the strategies they use provide very meaningful data. If an individual cannot or will not explain, the examiner can form a tentative hypothesis about how the student may be thinking and then present a task that evaluates this hypothesis. For example, if a student appears unable to read a word in a reading selection but cannot explain the approaches he or she is attempting to use, the examiner might hypothesize that the student thinks context cannot or should not be used to decode the word. One way to test this would be to present a sentence with a word left out. If the student is asked to fill in an obvious missing word and does so, the examiner can ask how he or she knew that was the missing word. Usually the student will explain, at this point, that he or she knew from the meaning or context of the sentence. The examiner can then ask if the same strategy can be used in the reading passage. If the student says it *is* possible and proceeds to do so, the examiner probably formed an incorrect hypothesis, or the student just learned something new. Alternatively, if the student says the strategy *cannot* be used, the examiner has identified one aspect of the student's thinking that may need to be modified. In either case, the student's problem-solving structures are made more apparent.

Notice how the student's lead is followed in this process. Tentative hypotheses and tasks are chosen not only on the basis of a testing model, but also on the basis of the thinking of the student. A model provides a guide to tell the examiner what is usually important. It provides a way to interpret the structures and strategies of the subject. Many tasks are selected to explore the explanations of the student or the examiner's hypotheses about the thinking behind the responses. If we are to understand the strategies the individual uses, we must follow and explore them until their nature becomes reasonably apparent.

A third rule of thumb is to always study both the *product* of the student and the *procedure* used to produce it. The product, the final result of the attempt to do the task, is important not only because it reveals whether the student is right or wrong. In fact, as indicated earlier, this is often not a highly significant question. Rather, the product indicates something about the mental structures that lie behind it. A response of "Leif Ericson" to the question "Who discovered America?" reveals something different about the structures of the individual than a response of "Christopher Columbus," whether we agree that the response is correct or incorrect. The procedure used to produce a response is often even more revealing than the product. Procedure may be apparent from verbalizations or other responses made by the student. The order in which responses are given, the speed at which they are produced, the control demonstrated, and the motions and partial responses made all can be interpreted in relation to the structures they reflect.

A final rule is to always consider age-related and environmental expectations during the analysis of strategies and processes. Age-related and environmental expectations tell us what to examine and what to expect. The structures model tells us that, if a child is seven years old, we may wish to begin with tasks that require Level III thinking. Environmental expectations help us identify many specific tasks that are required at this age. Both the model and the environmental expectations show that children at this age are likely to be able to read several sight words, solve simple addition problems, name and define common objects in the environment, and use other mechanical strategies to solve problems and learn new things. The point is that our first concern should be those expectations that are typical of the age and environment of the student. "Does this student exhibit the thinking and responding required and expected of seven-year-olds?" should be our first question, not "What is this child's problem?" In this way, realistic and relevant tasks are likely to be selected.

Procedures for Levels, Strategies, and Processes

Some suggestions about what the examiner may wish to identify during the early stages of the teaching/testing process may be helpful. We find the concept of levels of response to be especially useful here. We assume that the way in which people respond indicates the level at which they are interacting with the task. Through careful task presentation, observation, and interpretation, a learning disabilities specialist is able to make the necessary decisions about teaching. Three aspects of performance related to levels need to be identified. They need not be regarded as a sequence. The examiner must identify: 1) the level(s) where difficulties appear to be present; 2) how the student uses strategies and processes at age-related levels and levels where difficulties are identified; and 3) the actual levels of performance shown. Let us examine each of these in more detail.

Identifying the level or levels at which the student has difficulty is one important aspect of evaluation. Start this process by presenting the subject with an age-related task. Nearly any task will do as long as it has some components that require the kind of thinking expected at the mental age of the student. Usually, we select typical school problems since these are most relevant to educational needs. For example, a seven-year-old might simply be asked to read a passage from a book to determine the child's approach to the basic skills of reading. A 12-year-old might be asked to solve a complex story problem that requires Level IV logic in mathematics. As soon as a response is given, the examiner initiates the observation/interpretation process. A tentative hypothesis about the level of response demonstrated by the student is formed.

But which response level is actually indicated? First, since the examiner cannot know for sure, tentative hypotheses, not statements of absolute truth, are made. Second, the tentative hypotheses can be further evaluated. As more data are gathered, the level of response becomes more apparent. Third, the structures model is a guide for thinking and decision making. It should not be regarded as absolute truth either. Rather, it provides a set of constructs that are helpful for guiding instruction. Finally, the examiner must thoroughly understand a theoretical framework to interpret behavior adequately. If the model we present is to be used, knowledge of the structures model is essential, and there is no substitute for careful study of it. Only if the reader studies and understands earlier chapters in this book will decisions about level of performance be made appropriately.

The analysis of which level of response is indicated by any particular task may not be as difficult as it first appears. For the most part, the decision is a matter of understanding the model and making a logical decision. Does the task require only a response showing that the stimulus was noticed or received? Is the type of response required usually learned between birth and 18 months? If so, the task is probably at Level I. Few formal tests attempt to measure this level, but we might test young children informally by moving a colorful object in front of them to see whether they follow it with their eyes. With older children, it is usually possible to determine if they have persisting difficulty with Level I. Such children approach tasks in an extremely impulsive way, ignore many of the important stimuli, or do not respond at all, apparently because they have not received the stimuli. Such responses make it clear that processing at Level I should be examined more closely.

Does the task require the student to identify likenesses and differences in stimuli on the basis of sensory characteristics? Is the type of response required usually learned between one and four years? If so, the task is probably at Level II. Level I responses are also required, of course, but, if the task appears to require a higher level of response, we regard it as being a higher level task. Many tests attempt to measure Level II responding, and many informal and school tasks require it. We might test this level by asking a student to tell us whether two similar words look or sound the same. Again, determining whether the student is approaching the task from an appropriate level is usually possible. If the student appears to look carefully at the word and to recognize the component parts (the examiner may ask for the names of the letters in the word), the task is probably being approached through a Level II strategy. If the student seems to simply guess at the word without relying on perceptual analysis, a Level II strategy is not indicated. Note that the precise type of processing the student may be doing is not the issue here. At this point, we are only attempting to decide whether the subject has difficulty with certain important levels of responses. If the product is incorrect or the procedure is inappropriate, the examiner may hypothesize that difficulty with the level of response demanded by that task is indicated. Further evaluation of the level is probably needed.

Similar analysis is needed for the remaining levels. Two types of questions provide the necessary guidance for a decision about whether a particular task fits at a certain level. One question asks whether the task fits the basic components of the level as we describe it. The other asks when the type of responding required in the task is typically learned. Because the levels are age-related, the time when a response is typically learned often identifies the level with which the task corresponds.

Identification of which level the task matches does not tell how the student responds, however. In fact, when we wish to evaluate how a student thinks, we usually present tasks that can be approached from more than one level. Again, reasonable hypotheses can be formed on the basis of careful observation and interpretation. Consider the following example. Three students are asked which row of blocks has more, a row with six red blocks that are spread out or a row with six green blocks that are close together. One student says the row with red blocks has more because "I like red blocks." Another student says the row with red blocks has more because it is bigger. The third student counts the blocks in each row and says they are the same.

Which level of response did each student use to approach the problem? The first child reacted on the basis of a perceptual characteristic (color) and an affective response to that characteristic. This response might be regarded as Level II because the decision was made in relation to a perceptual attribute. However, this attribute is insignificant in relation to the task, and all of the potentially more important attributes are ignored. Therefore, we might decide that the response is indicative of the lowest level of responding, the awareness level.

The second child's response appears to be more typical of Level II. The perceptual characteristic used to make the response is apparently the length of the row. This is an attribute that is typically attended to by young children, and it is sometimes related to the concept of *more*.

The second child is approaching the task in an appropriate way for a Level II strategy. In this case, however, a Level III response is required. Only the third child approaches the task from this level. This child attends to the important stimuli and recognizes the salient perceptual characteristics. In addition, the need to label the parts of the stimuli and compare their number is recognized, and this Level III strategy is applied to solve the problem.

Careful analysis of this sort enables the examiner to decide which level the student is using and whether difficulties with a particular level of response are indicated. An individual who approaches a task in a mechanical way that depends on relatively simple, overlearned labeling strategies is working at Level III. Someone who attempts to understand the major concepts involved in a problem-solving task, relates these concepts to one another, and comes to a logical answer is working at Level IV. The expression of highly meaningful concepts in a fluent manner indicates Level V functioning. An understanding of the structures model and the logical, creative thinking (at Level IV) of the teacher are the essential components for this aspect of evaluation.

A second major aspect of the evaluation process is the identification of how the student uses strategies and processes at age-related levels or levels where difficulties are identified. Analysis of the age-related strategies and processes is usually more important than analysis of levels where difficulties are apparent. Frequently, of course, the age-related level and the level of difficulty are the same. Obviously, if a child is not old enough to be expected to function at Level V, we would not be concerned if difficulties are apparent at that level. But what about the student who seems to have difficulty functioning at levels that should have been surpassed?

The decision about how much to explore the individual's thinking at earlier levels depends on two considerations. First, if the student appears to function at a later level with many tasks, in spite of the difficulty with the earlier level, it may not be necessary to evaluate the earlier level extensively. In these cases, teaching will typically focus on the highest level of functioning, making full understanding of how the student uses strategies at the previous level less essential.

The second consideration is the severity of the problem in the earlier level. Typically, the more severe the problem, the more it interferes with later functioning. Thus, we may have a child who is generally capable of Level III functioning but who is unable to read (at the beginning Level III stage) because of extreme difficulty with Level II strategies and processes. The more an earlier level problem appears to interfere with later level functioning, the more necessary it is to evaluate the earlier level.

Suppose a decision has been made to evaluate the processes and strategies of a student at a particular level. The next step might be to attempt to enable the student to function appropriately with problems that match this level. The evaluator attempts to teach the student to use a strategy. Although teaching may take the form of simply telling the student how to use a strategy, more information will be gained about how to teach the student if teaching takes the form of helping the student discover a workable strategy for the task.

In trial teaching the examiner first selects the level, chooses an appropriate task, and then examines the strategies and processes the student uses. Suppose, for example, that you decide to evaluate processes and strategies at Level III. From the structures model, you know that temporarily storing an impression of stimuli and rehearsing by repeating stimuli internally are important aspects of processing at this level.

You assume that the student has difficulty with the area of reading, so you decide to select a task from this academic area that demands Level III thinking. You select four words—cat, mat, rat, and bat—that you want the child to learn to recognize. The child does not know these words by looking at them. After reading the words to the student, you ask him or her to learn these words. You ask the student to think of the fastest way to learn the words.

Several alternate ways of temporarily holding and rehearsing the stimuli should be explored at this point. If the student does not spontaneously generate several strategies, some can be suggested. In this example, strategies that might be discussed include writing each word 10 times, putting each word on a flash card and practicing with the cards, recording the words on a tape recorder and listening to the words while looking at them, or remembering that they are all "at" words which can be recognized by sounding out the first letter and attaching this ending.

Next, one of these strategies is selected to actually learn the words, and, again, the student may be able to help in the selection. The strategy is tried out and the evaluator carefully observes and interprets the responses in relation to the corresponding level. Does the student appear to use the strategy appropriately? Does the student appear able to store a temporary impression of the words? Does the student rehearse the information? Does the strategy result in learning? These questions cannot always be answered immediately or with a single trial. But remember that testing is not a single, one-shot affair. It is a process, integrated with teaching, and the process takes time and effort. In this case, the examiner may need to check whether the words are remembered the next day or the next week. Also, it is unrealistic to expect to discover the ideal strategy on the first try. Several additional strategies, with new sets of words, may be tried.

Isn't this just a complicated way of saying that, when you find an academic problem, you should teach trial lessons and select the method that seems to work best? Why is it necessary to put in all the information about strategies and processes? We stress that the answer to the first question is *no!* Teaching academic content is the regular teacher's job. The learning disabilities specialist needs to teach strategies—strategies that can be applied in a variety of situations. Thus, even though the task in our example involved learning to recognize certain words, the examiner is actually attempting to determine how the student functions at Level III. The responses of the student must be looked at in a broader, more integrated way.

For each level that is significant for a particular student, then, a variety of tasks are presented and evaluated so that strategies and processes can be examined. Attempts to teach the student at the level of concern are integrated with testing tasks. The examiner assesses how the student thinks in relation to specific tasks, and especially in relation to the total level. The strategies and processes—the internal mental structures—the student uses are delineated.

A third aspect of the evaluation process is to identify the actual level of performance of the student. The levels of performance are identified by analyzing a relatively large number of tasks and deciding at which level the student approaches them. Usually, if a student is near average in intellectual capacity, some tasks will be approached from a level that matches with chronological age. That is, if the student is 10, some tasks will be approached from Level IV, the typical level of performance for 10-year-olds. If the child is six, some tasks will be approached from Level III, the typical level of performance for six-year-olds, and so on.

The decision the examiner makes at this point is a rather general one, but it has important implications. In essence, the decision helps to determine whether the student needs assistance from the learning disabilities specialist. In addition, the decision identifies the level of performance that will be the goal for instruction. By our definition, a person may be said to be learning disabled when some behaviors are age-appropriate and others are not. The services that a learning disability specialist can and should provide may be appropriate for such a student.

Even more important, the decision enables the teacher to select goals and methods. The goals for the student are to learn and use strategies that are at the highest level of performance demonstrated. If the highest level of performance is Level IV, teaching should aim for performance at this level in all areas. If performance is, at best, at Level III, teaching focuses there. When functioning in an important area reaches this level and the student demonstrates readiness to progress to a higher level, the emphasis in teaching shifts upward. The methods used are guided by the principles for the level at which the goals are set. These principles and methods are explained later.

As with other aspects of the teaching/testing process, the requirements for making a decision about the actual levels of performance of the individual are a thorough knowledge of the structures model and an ability to analyze tasks and performance. The following example illustrates the process.

An adolescent girl is asked to explain the spoken sentence "John and Mary are playing the flute." She replies, "They are kissing" (Wiig, 1978). This task, since it requires logical analysis of syntax and verbal explanation, probably is a simple Level IV task. Which level of response is indicated by the response? Perhaps the student did not attend, heard only the "John and Mary" part, has acquaintance with a John and Mary who often kiss, and impulsively made this response. If so, a Level I approach may be indicated.

But this response may be at Level II. The student does not discriminate the phonemes in *flute,* perceives the word *field* instead, and interprets "playing the field" as kissing.

Or, perhaps, at Level III, the student does not know the meaning of the word *flute,* so she either ignores the word or guesses at the meaning. From the reference to playing, she decides they might be kissing. This is, after all, a rather typical form of play among adolescents. Note that each of these hypotheses is possible, but are they highly probable? Each time, we find that some amount of meaningful understanding of concepts was still needed for the girl to make her response. In a general way, then, we may have simply identified some possible difficulties with processing at earlier levels, rather than the actual level at which this student approaches the task.

The procedure we prefer to follow is to look first at the level where the student would be expected to perform. An adolescent is expected to respond from Levels IV and V. What is the thinking of the student that leads to the observed response? At Level IV, the concept in the sentence needs to be examined. The sentence means that two people are playing two flutes, but the word *flute* appears to be singular. Perhaps the student thinks that only one flute is indicated, so she visualizes John and Mary standing face to face, lips pursed and nearly touching, as they try to play the flute together. How can we state the problem in "This student thinks . . ." terms? Stated in reference to this specific example, "This student thinks that because *flute* has an *s* at the end whenever it is plural and because it has no *s* in this sentence, it must be singular even though the subject of the sentence is plural."

Perhaps the student is a bit confused by this, but for her the only logical solution is to regard John and Mary as playing the same flute. If additional evaluation indicates that the student thinks in a similar way about other sentences of this type, we might conclude that "This student thinks that when a plural *s* is ordinarily used to show that a particular word is plural, the absence of the *s* must mean the word is singular in every case." If our hypothesis is correct, an inability to identify the specific meaning results from inadequate knowledge about sentence structure. Sometimes a word that appears to be singular has a plural meaning. Strategies for understanding sentence structures of this type may be needed. We must decide whether the concept is needed and exactly how to teach it.

The above "This student thinks . . ." hypothesis might be the most probable because it matches the age-related expectations and the level of the task. A Level V interpretation is also possible. Perhaps the student intended to say, "They are having fun." The difficulty may be with recalling the correct words for the expression of the idea. As with the hypotheses about the first three levels, this idea seems less acceptable than the Level IV hypothesis.

Forming an Integrated Hypothesis

When the levels of difficulty have been identified, the structures of the student have been analyzed, and the actual levels of thinking and performance determined, an integrated hypothesis about how and what to teach can be made. The teacher must decide what is most important, given all the available data. Deciding to remediate all of the problems is not satisfactory since time is limited. More seriously, attempting to solve all the problems encourages a piecemeal approach and takes away some of the responsibilities of the regular classroom teacher. The learning disability teacher should focus on learning strategies that the student can use in any learning situation.

How can an appropriate decision about how and what to teach be made? Typically, some type of difficulty can be specified for nearly every level with most learning disabled individuals. The teacher's task is to decide which level of response to emphasize at a particular point in time. The structures that the student needs most must be identified. The highest level of responding shown by the student is determined as we described earlier, and performance at this level becomes the goal.

To determine which specific strategies to emphasize, the teacher examines the nature of strategies and processes at this level. Thus, if the goal is Level IV responding, the student must recognize, identify, associate, and infer meanings (the components of the cognition process) in all important areas of performance. In school tasks, the student will need strategies for comprehending what is read, for solving complex mathematical problems, for organizing and understanding concepts in social studies and language arts, for taking meaningful notes from lectures, and so on. In most cases, the thinking of the student needs to be modified in similar ways for all these diverse areas, and this provides the basis for an integrated teaching approach. Often, the specific content area doesn't matter because the strategy the teacher works on is applicable to many areas.

The crux of the matter is to identify how the student currently thinks in relation to the level for which goals are set. We suggest that hypotheses about teaching be stated in the form of "This student thinks. . . ." and "This student needs to think. . . ." These statements do *not* attempt to identify only the immediate structures relevant for a specific academic task but the broader question of how the person approaches tasks at the age-appropriate level. Thus we might have hypotheses that say "This student thinks that pattern and organization are not found in language. This student needs to think that pattern and organization are present in language and that these can be used to perform tasks in spoken, read, and written language." Specific strategies that teach the pattern and organization of language are selected. These strategies are aimed at teaching the student to perform in an age-appropriate fashion, in spite of the processing differences that are present.

Using Formal Tests

Formal tests can be interpreted and used in much the same way as any other task. However, when used according to formal testing rules, they have less value than informal teaching/testing tasks because additional exploration of responses is so limited. In the context of the structures model, formal tests are seldom used in formal ways. Since test *scores* are not very useful in analyzing mental structures, the value of formal instruments lies in the analysis and exploration of the responses made. Formal tests do provide a ready source of tasks that may be appropriate for the teaching/testing process. Relating tasks from formal evaluation tools to students' structures and ways of thinking is no more difficult than doing so with any other task. The learning disability specialist must understand the levels, processes, and strategies that are important in the model. The demands made in any formal test can then be analyzed in reference to the level of responding, the type of processing, and the strategies required.

Chapter 7

Teaching the Learning Disabled: Goals, Strategies, and Principles

INTRODUCTION

Teaching is vitally important. Although most teachers love their work most of the time, the task is difficult and exhausting. How can professionals translate knowledge about teaching into direct practice? How can teachers help students change and develop their mental structures, especially when they have been struggling with learning for several years? Obviously, we don't have all the answers. We expect that much will be learned about effective teaching in the learning disability field as it matures. We do have some suggestions about how to apply what is known about the teaching and learning process, and we present these ideas in the next two chapters. Part one of this chapter is about the goals and strategies of teaching. The second section presents principles or guidelines for teaching that are based on learning processes. The last section explains principles related to the levels of the structures model.

TEACHING GOALS AND STRATEGIES

Teaching is special in learning disability and is not the same as teaching in the regular classroom. Learning disabled persons have not learned as expected in typical settings. They also process information in unique ways, which results in unique mental structures. Specialized techniques and approaches are required for effective teaching in learning disability. Of course, the learning of learning disabled persons is not totally different from that of others. Many similarities exist between the processing and structures of the learning disabled and those who are not disabled, and many aspects of teaching and learning are identical. Major "laws" of learning hold across all ages and types of learners. Even persons with obvious sensory disabilities such as deafness and blindness do not learn in totally unique ways. But, as with deafness and blindness, we suggest that the learning disabled can benefit from a specialized approach to teaching. They are unique enough to require special teaching. Let us examine how the goals and strategies of teaching are affected by this idea.

Goals of Teaching

The most basic goals of teaching in learning disability are identical to those of teaching in general. The goals are to educate, to enable the student to learn, and to encourage the development of mental structures. This may sound too general to be helpful, but setting these goals assumes several significant concepts about what teaching is *not*.

Frequently, we hear teachers say that their task is to teach academics to the learning disabled. Others, especially at the high school level, say that the most essential task of the learning disability professional is to enable the students to receive vocational training. Still others say that the major goal should be to return the students to the regular classroom.

These goals may sometimes be desirable side benefits, but we believe that an emphasis on any of them is misplaced. If learning disability professionals stress academic training, they are taking over the task of regular education. Why assume that the special educator can do it better? If vocational training is the goal, professionals are again available in that specific area. Additionally, preparing an individual for one specific job is far too limiting. It avoids important areas of life such as social interactions, preparations for change in a changing world, recreation and leisure time activities, and preparation for future learning in and out of school. Returning students to the regular classroom (assuming they were removed in the first place) seems like an admirable goal, but it has a major weakness. It places the emphasis on helping a student conform to a system that may or may not lead to an education, and it tends to make the teacher of the learning disabled function as a remedial tutor.

Our goal is to educate, but what does it mean to be educated? We can make some general suggestions, but the specifics must be determined by individual teachers. Students must be prepared for all phases and aspects of life, for the changes they will face, and for the environmental demands that will be placed on them. Obviously, teachers cannot teach students *everything*. But as much as possible, teachers should assist students in the development of mental structures that are both broad enough and specific enough to promote continuing contributions to society and to personal development and satisfaction. This goal translates into the learning of strategies and metastrategies for selecting among them. The task of the teacher of the learning disabled is focused on the strategy selection and specific strategies (by level) components that are a part of the control structures in Figure 4-1.

The goal of teaching in learning disability is to enable the students to function effectively at an age-appropriate level. Remediating deficient learning processes or academic deficits is *not* the primary aim. When the emphasis is placed on age-appropriate functioning, two consequences follow: 1) some curriculum components are not taught; and 2) some apparently deficient processes are ignored. Brief explanations of these consequences follow.

Deciding which curriculum components are critical is an important task of the professional. In some academic areas, later learning is very dependent on earlier learning. But many parts of a typical school curriculum are not essential for thinking and learning at later levels. These components can be eliminated when teaching emphasizes an appropriate level of responding, based on the individual's age.

The teacher may decide to teach the use of a calculator as a substitute for memorization of multiplication tables for a ninth grader who is studying algebra. Multiplication tables are usually memorized before ninth grade algebra is taught. If the student has the conceptual ability to study algebra, however, the convenience of a calculator may be substituted for the convenience of memorized facts. Knowledge of the facts is not essential. Learning to think about algebra in an age-appropriate (ninth-grade) way may be more important. Noncritical content is eliminated, and learning to respond in a way that matches the actual age and developmental level is emphasized.

The same concept applies to deficiencies in learning processes. Tests or observations may show significant deficiencies in attention, perception, memory, or other processes. These problems may need to be carefully evaluated to determine how they affect the individual's learning. Teaching methods may need some modification because of the problems. But if the student is able to perform at an appropriate level, remediation of apparent processing problems is unnecessary. If a learning disabled seventh grader can adequately comprehend what he or she reads, it matters little (in reading, at least) that this student has only four "slots" in short-term memory or a deficient score on the Digit Span subtest of the *Wechsler Intelligence Scale for Children.*

One additional aspect of the suggested emphasis on age-appropriate functioning is worthy of mention. This approach enables the educator to move away from a "disease treatment" or medical model of learning disability. The professional in learning disabilities concentrates on the development of appropriate internal mental structures, not on the treatment of internal disabilities. Teaching remains unique because the structures of the learning disabled are exceptional, but the emphasis is placed on reaching age-appropriate response goals.

Teaching goals, then, are based on response levels. The methods and materials used are determined by the level of response that is sought, not by the processing problems the student may show. Specific methods are decided upon in relation to the mental structures the particular student brings to the task (the processing and strategies the student currently uses) and the level of response set as a goal. As age increases, the goals of teaching shift to higher levels, and methods and materials also change.

Strategies of Teaching

"Ditto sheet teaching" is not enough. Many approaches to teaching, both in learning disability and other areas, emphasize a *testing* approach in which a small amount of information is presented to the student and then the student is handed a ditto sheet to "practice." In reality, the practice is a test, which the student is expected to complete. Frequently, the strategies the student uses when doing the test are not analyzed by the teacher.

In contrast to this, we find an increasing emphasis on the teaching of strategies in the learning disabilities field. What are these strategies, and how are they taught?

What Are Strategies?

Are strategies something a teacher uses or something a student uses? Our answer is both. However, important distinctions should be made between teacher strategies and student strategies. Carefully examine the strategies in books such as Alley and Deshler's *Teaching the Learning Disabled Adolescent* (1979). In some cases, the strategy under discussion appears to be a method that the teacher can use to enable students to complete a task. In others, a way for the student to think about the task is explained. Both the way in which the teacher should teach and the strategy the student should use are not always presented.

In our view, teachers should think in terms of strategies to use to teach effectively *and* in terms of strategies for students to use. Teachers should not limit themselves to presenting a curriculum sequence and then testing (through "practice" exercises) whether the students can perform. Strategies that can be used to acquire new information, to solve problems, and to transfer learning to related situations are needed. Teachers also need strategies for teaching students to use them.

Appropriate strategies take many forms because they are needed for unique individuals, each with different structures. We have found, however, that effective strategies for teachers and students have the following six characteristics in common:

1. The strategy takes account of how the student is currently thinking about the task.
2. The strategy provides for both the action of the teacher and the action of the student.
3. The strategy encourages generalization and transfer.

4. The strategy matches the highest level of thinking of which the student is capable.
5. The strategy corresponds to important environmental demands.
6. The strategy is generated through teacher-student interaction.

Implied in these six characteristics is an entire approach to teaching. An understanding of these concepts is critical for effective teaching. A discussion of each characteristic follows in the next section.

How Are Strategies Taught?

Unless the teacher knows how the student is currently thinking, instruction is certain to be significantly misdirected. To prevent this from occurring, teachers must carefully develop the evaluation skills explained in earlier chapters. The first characteristic of good strategies emphasizes the importance of understanding students' mental structures, which is possible only through evaluation of those structures during the testing/teaching process.

The second characteristic listed above implies that a strategy is more than a statement about behavioral objectives and materials to be used. Strategies should specify action, process, and method. A strategy involves the precise steps a teacher goes through and the specific components of thinking and behaving expected of the student during the learning process. Behavioral objectives only say what the student will do at the end of the lesson. In most cases, they do not state how the student is to arrive at the final product, and they do not present the intermediate steps in the thinking process.

It is possible to teach a strategy that helps a student accomplish one specific task in one setting. Strategies that can be generalized to many different tasks and transferred to many settings are more useful, however. Teachers should direct their efforts at enabling students to develop thinking and learning abilities that can be applied in many ways and places. Knowing how to approach and solve mathematical problems that frequently arise in daily life is more important than developing a specific strategy for the completion of a single story problem in a mathematics book. Knowing how to take notes from a teacher's verbal presentation is probably more important than learning a specific set of facts about the American Civil War. We urge teachers to repeatedly ask themselves, "How can I incorporate strategies that can be generalized as I teach this lesson?"

Strategies should match the highest level of a student's thinking. Some tasks may not require high level responses, of course, but, for tasks that do, the teacher should encourage their use. Students who are capable of approaching reading comprehension tasks in a highly meaningful, logical (Level IV) way should be helped to do so. The alternative, to drop back to an earlier, more mechanical strategy, ignores the cognitive ability of the student and probably slows the learning process. "Readiness" approaches, in which learning of specific skills in sequence is assumed to be necessary, frequently ignore this concept.

Unless a strategy is applicable to important environmental tasks, teachers should deemphasize it. Pressures from parents and other teachers sometimes make it easy to concentrate on tasks or strategies that are of only temporary and limited value. In our view, teachers of learning disabled persons must set the priorities and select the strategies for their students. When conflicts with parents or other professionals arise, we must tactfully negotiate, firmly insist on the essentials, and compromise on the details if necessary. A teacher who permits students to spend significant amounts of time on trivial or unnecessary tasks is not meeting professional responsibilities.

Strategies will probably be more effective if they are generated through a process of interaction between a student and a teacher (Guthrie & Seifert, 1978). If students help design a strategy, they are likely to have more invested in it and may tend to recall and use it when it is needed. As Torgesen (1977) suggests, "a child's use of active and efficient strategies . . . depends not only on the level of his general cognitive awareness, but also on his purposes and goals in the situation" (p. 29).

The interaction between teacher and student should focus on strategies that are useful for that particular student, given the nature of his or her mental structures. This characteristic of strategy teaching is especially critical because it incorporates the assumption that students actively construct new mental structures. The entire nature of the teaching/learning process is involved. If all the teacher does is "teach" by imposing a strategy on a student, we are back to regarding the student as a passive learner.

Strategies imposed on the learner may appear to force some accommodation, but forced accommodation is not real learning. Teaching does not create learning. As teachers, we can guide students toward thinking about things and solving problems in particular ways, but we do not have direct control over what happens inside their brains. The roles of teacher and student are intimately related but not identical. The student must learn to use a strategy, and the teacher must decide how to facilitate the learning process.

In many cases, the teacher knows several possible important strategies and knows that the student probably can learn and use these strategies. At first glance, simply imposing these strategies on the student appears to be very efficient. The process of developing a strategy through interaction between a student and a teacher takes much more time.

Why should the limited time available be used in this way? The answer, of course, is that students may not use the strategy if it is imposed on them. If this happens, time is also wasted, and, more importantly, the student does not learn. When a new problem is presented and the imposed strategy is needed, the student comes back to the teacher still unable to perform. The teacher may present the strategy again, but again it probably will not transfer. This may be especially true with learning disabled persons, who appear likely to fail to activate strategies even when they are capable of using them (Torgesen, 1977).

We have found in a study with learning disabled adolescents that imposed strategies for solving difficult tasks are usually not applied to the task even though the subjects appear to understand the strategy (DeRuiter & Wansart, 1981). We suggest that unless students are aware of the need to restructure their concept of reality, unless they know that a strategy is available and useful for them, and unless they understand that they need to select a strategy to solve a problem, they will continue to respond as if they are inactive learners. They will not learn to become independent problem solvers who can respond in new, more appropriate ways.

At a general level, then, a teacher needs to be aware of the necessity for using transferable strategies that enable the student to meet important environmental demands at the highest level of response. In a specific situation, a teacher may have several alternative strategies in mind and may arrange the teaching/learning situation so that the student discovers one or more of these strategies. Often, students develop alternatives of their own. The components or steps in a strategy are not necessarily elicited from the student without teacher assistance.

The teaching/learning process involves *interaction* between teacher and student. Direct instruction and modeling (Hallahan, Tarver, Kauffman, & Graybeal, 1978) should be used when necessary, as long as the student is ready to learn in this way. Sometimes leading questions are used to help the student discover a strategy, and sometimes alternatives are directly suggested by the teacher. In some cases, a strategy is put into practice as it is discussed, but at other times the strategy is evolved first and then applied. Sometimes the strategy is applied in role-playing or simulated situations before it is used in real life settings. Teachers should not be confined to a unidimensional approach to strategy teaching. Rather, strategies need to be developed through interaction between the teacher and the student. Teaching becomes a creative, problem-solving process, a dialogue between student and teacher.

PRINCIPLES OF TEACHING RELATED TO PROCESSES

We divide principles of teaching into two categories—those related to learning *processes* and those related to *levels* of response. This section develops a number of ideas about how differences in essential learning processes may affect teaching.

The work of the learning disabilities teacher is directed at teaching students how to select and use learning strategies. The task is not to remediate deficient learning processes. This does not mean, however, that difficulties with efficient processing are unimportant in teaching. In fact, because learning disabled persons have extreme difficulty with information processing, special teaching is particularly necessary. We regard three considerations as especially important in selecting and using methods for persons who have significant processing deficiencies. We will state these considerations in the form of principles related to learning processes and discuss each principle in the following sections. The three principles are: (1) select methods before materials; (2) avoid overload; and (3) activate the essential processes.

Select Methods before Materials

In many teaching situations, teachers first decide *what* to teach, and then *how* they will teach it. We believe the sequence should be reversed when teaching persons with severe processing problems. Methods that match the unique thinking of the learning disabled person are needed. Since traditional methods did not work, we must now select special methods that both enable the person to accomplish the necessary information processing and result in reaching an age-appropriate level of response.

Once a particular method has been selected, the materials may be chosen based on two major considerations: (1) whether they work effectively with the method; and (2) whether they fit age-related expectations. These two items reflect a rejection of a common approach to materials selection. If materials are chosen to fit the method, they may not fit grade scores from tests. In the area of reading, for example, designation of independent, instructional, and frustration levels is frequently suggested (Kirk, Kliebhan, & Lerner, 1978). These levels are determined from an informal reading inventory. Materials are selected to match the independent reading level if the student is expected to read without assistance and from the instructional level if new learning is expected.

This approach is very different from the one we suggest. For one thing, it provides no information about which method to use. It also assumes that the age of the student is unimportant because materials are likely to be the same for a person who is 7 years old and one who is 14 if they receive the same test score. Obviously, this shows acceptance of the misconceptions about testing and teaching we have discussed.

Professionals do not have full agreement on what constitutes a grade level of reading. No one knows how many errors a reader should be permitted before an instructional or frustration level is specified. There is wide debate about which skills should be taught in which sequence. How can teachers designate a precise instructional level in the face of these uncertainties?

Even more serious, we believe, is that age differences are ignored. A method that enables the student to think and learn at an age-appropriate level should be selected first; then materials that fit the mental age and interests of the student, as well as the particular method used, should be selected.

Consider, for example, a high school student who is capable of Level IV functioning and who needs to understand syllabication and word structure rules in order to apply these rules in spelling, writing, and reading. Assume that this student has a fourth-grade instructional reading level. Does this mean that the words chosen for study are from a fourth-grade level? Definitely not! Words are chosen that are appropriate for the method applied and the particular rule studied. If the student is studying how to divide a word into syllables when it has two identical consonants in series, the teacher obviously would not choose the word *will* simply because it matched the student's reading level. Words like *bookkeeper* or *fissure* or *illness* might be chosen because they illustrate a rule, are interesting to the student, and are age-appropriate.

Words from supposed earlier grade levels are not necessarily easier for students. Consider words such as *the, then, there,* and *three.* Such words are usually considered to be at early reading levels, but they often cause difficulty long after the learning of many words from "higher" reading levels. Why is this so? The reason may be the visual similarities between the words, the low content value, or lack of concreteness. The students may have worked on these words for five years and may have a stable "I can't read that word" structure about each. Whatever the reason, we see no support for the notion that materials should be selected before the teaching method or that they should be selected based on a grade level score on a test.

We are not intimating that students should be asked to read (without assistance) a book that has many words they do not recognize and cannot decode. The method must allow for a suitable level of successful responses. Methods that simply test what a student already knows in the hope that more will be learned during the process are not really methods at all. Appropriate methods require teacher and student interaction.

Notice also that we are not suggesting a "teach to the strengths" approach as this concept is often applied. Methods should match the age-appropriate abilities of the student. They should use the cognitive and language skills the student has, and they should lead students to function at the highest level of responding of which they are capable. This concept is very different from teaching students to read through "visual methods" because they are "visual learners."

Avoid Overload

Overloading causes frustration, and frustration may inhibit performance. Not all frustration is necessarily detrimental. Sapir and Wilson (1978) note that many learning theorists believe learning is enhanced by an appropriate amount of frustration although they caution that handicapped children may typically have huge amounts of frustration in their lives. We explained earlier that learning does not occur unless the learner feels a certain amount of disequilibrium. How are the ideas of overloading, frustration, and disequilibrium related?

Disequilibrium is not the same as frustration. Disequilibrium refers to an intuitive or conscious awareness that a mismatch exists between outside stimuli and internal structures, or between old ways of thinking and new information. When we attempt to create disequilibrium in a student, we do not seek to create frustration. Frustration may sometimes be a side effect if the student is unable to bring reality and mental structures into balance. Most of the time, however, frustration is a consequence of inability to perform at levels that individuals expect themselves to perform.

Frustration of this sort is usually avoidable. One way to prevent it is to enable students to maintain a very high success rate, but this poses a problem. If students are only giving correct responses, they may not be learning anything new. Instead, they may be repeating something they already know. Being successful, by itself, does not assure learning.

As we see it, two shifts in emphasis are needed if learning is to occur without undue frustration. One shift is to present information just different enough to cause the student to feel disequilibrium. A second shift is to an emphasis on the processes of learning instead of the products of performance. Most of the time, students are praised for their products, but the processes they go through are ignored. We suggest praise for appropriate thinking and processing, even if the final product is not particularly praiseworthy. This approach helps students feel successful at the same time that they recognize a need for more learning.

If a student appears frustrated and is not successful with either the learning process or the product, overloading may be the problem. Cohen and Netley (1978), for example, conclude that learning disabled persons may overload because of an inflexible memory system. They suggest that a central feature in reading and spelling problems is an inability to cope with overload.

What does this mean for teachers of the learning disabled? If the learning processes of this group are easily overloaded, we must be especially conscious of this possibility. Perhaps it will mean teaching three new spelling words or reading words on Monday and adding three additional words each day rather than presenting all 15 words the first day. The number of new concepts taught in a lesson may have to be reduced, and the number of sensory stimuli presented to the student may have to be kept to a minimum instead of bombarding the learner with multisensory input. It almost certainly means that the teacher will not move to new information before the old is learned. A new page in the workbook may not be completed every day. The student may finish 2 experiments in science class instead of 15. But the concepts and skills studied are maintained by the student.

The approach we advocate here takes time. A student may spend several weeks learning one integrated concept. Careful selection of skills and concepts to teach is essential. It seems obvious to us, however, that the time is well spent if the student eventually learns, retains, and uses the concept. Certainly, this is better than ''teaching'' every concept in the student's mathematics book with the result that none of them are remembered or used. Interestingly, we find that learning may accelerate very rapidly when this approach is taken, once the first few concepts are acquired.

Students probably have very different overload capacities. Also, capacities probably differ within an individual based on the nature of the task. Therefore, we cannot specifically state how many skills or concepts should be taught in a particular lesson. We suspect many teachers have a tendency toward presenting too much too fast, with an emphasis on changing activities frequently so the student does not become bored. We prefer highly integrated methods, with built-in variety, but a concentration on maintaining efforts toward a goal until that goal is attained. Whether a student needs to learn that $2 + 2 = 4$ or needs to understand how to use the scientific method, a teacher can present the concepts in sufficient variety to keep the student interested and involved. We urge teachers to change goals only when reasonable assurance exists that learning has occurred. The number of concepts, that rate at which they are presented, the level of abstraction, and the kind and variety of stimuli used—all must be considered and selected on the basis of individual learning structures. Teachers should attempt to find the balance that works best for the particular student, a balance which aims at avoiding overload and achieving maximal learning.

Activate the Essential Processes

The principle that heads this section has two terms that require explanation— *active* and *essential*. Activation of processes requires intense concentration and hard work on the part of the teacher. A certain subtle pressure is placed on the student so that thought processes are activated. The student is not left to daydream or play games except when these are essential parts of the educational plan. We are not arguing against providing students with considerable "integration time" in which to consolidate and stabilize what they have learned, but we are suggesting that too much valuable time is wasted in learning disability classrooms.

Students with learning disabilities often have normal intelligence. Teachers should hope for and expect normal achievement. Our students will not reach this level, however, unless our instruction has a high level of intensity. *Intensity* implies concentrated effort, a sense of direction, and interaction between the student and the environment. It implies the opposite of saying "What would you like to do today, John?" when a student walks into the resource room. Intensity does not eliminate time for play. It does not suggest that the teacher present many concepts rapidly so the student has no time to think, to reflect, or to discover. Nor does it refer primarily to external actions on the part of the student. It *does* mean that the teacher is constantly aware of the need to activate the internal mental processes of the student.

The term *essential* is important because it shows that activation is not enough. The teacher must have a clear idea of the goals of instruction and must emphasize the processing that is essential for doing the tasks appropriately. If the goal is to activate processes, such as rehearsal at Level III, the student is guided toward the use of this process rather than being permitted to accomplish the task by some other means. Haring and Bateman (1977) state that "Circling a thousand worksheet pictures of things that start with /m/ provides exactly zero practice in looking at *m* and responding "/m/" (p. 151).

We have observed a teacher who asked a student to respond rapidly by giving the answer to problems such as 5 + 3 = ___ which were presented on flash cards. Her goal, she reported, was to have the child rehearse the problem several times so that the facts under study would become automatic. The process the student activated was to count on his fingers under the table. If the teacher wanted to activate the rehearsal process, a better approach would have been to present the student with the entire problem, including the answer, and then to ask the student to repeat the problem several times in varied ways.

Frequently, we find teachers asking students to try to come up with an answer without assuring that they know how to do so. One notable example is from an observation taken during the teaching of a reading lesson. The teacher gave the student a book and asked him to read it. When he came to a word that was not in his automatic sight word vocabulary, the teacher provided varied suggestions about how he might decode the word. The goal of the teacher appeared appropriate—she wanted to activate the process of accurate reading with adequate speed. Try to identify the specific processes she attempted to activate as we present the suggestions she made to the student. On one occasion, when the student hesitated, she told him the word. On another occasion, she told the student to "sound it out." Later, she said, "You know that word. We learned it yesterday." Twice she said, "What do you think might fit here?" Once she said, "It means the same as 'finished'." On another occasion she said, "It means *this*," as she moved her hand rapidly forward. The gesture was intended to demonstrate the word *push*.

You may have identified: (1) a "rely on the teacher to give you the answer" strategy; (2) a "use phonics and word attack" strategy; (3) a "use your sight word vocabulary" strategy; (4) a "use the context" strategy; (5) a "match to the definition" strategy; and (6) a "match to concrete gestures" strategy. Whether each of these strategies activates important learning processes is not the only important question. Observation of the student clearly showed that he was not able to correctly read the words no matter which strategy the teacher suggested. Instead, he consistently activated guessing processes and waited for the teacher to monitor and correct him. When we asked the teacher whether she had taught the student how and when to use the strategies she asked him to use in reading, she reported some scattered and partial attempts to do so. It was obvious, however, that the emphasis in previous teaching had not been on building a repertoire of alternative strategies and metastrategies for choosing among them. By using the "testing" method described above, the teacher was virtually assuring the activation of inappropriate processes.

The task of the teacher, then, is to activate the processes essential for performance at the appropriate response level. At each level in the structures model, a corresponding learning process has been identified. If the student is working on tasks that demand responses at Level I, attention processes are activated. At Level II, perception processes are activated, and so on. The efforts of the teacher are not directed at curing or fixing deficient processes. Rather, the goal is to teach "learning how to learn" strategies that enable the student to respond at the age-appropriate level. These strategies demand a certain amount of processing of the type designated at the corresponding level. Teaching sessions are organized around strategies chosen on the basis of the capacity and mental structures of the student.

PRINCIPLES OF TEACHING RELATED TO LEVELS

Let us explain the most basic principles that guide our teaching. We suggest that teaching in learning disability should follow two important guidelines:

1. Learning disabled students should be taught a repertoire of specific "learning how to learn" strategies that enable performance at an age-appropriate level.
2. Learning disabled students should be taught to select appropriate strategies from their repertoire as demanded by the task.

Implied in these concepts is a particular view of the learning process. Students are regarded as active learners who build internal mental structures through experiences. When students come to the teacher, they come with internal mental structures that form the basis for additional learning. At the same time, these very structures must be modified for learning to occur. Structures will not develop or change unless disequilibrium is created in the learner. The task of the teacher is to create this disequilibrium so that the student acquires "learning how to learn" strategies. These strategies are applied, transferred, and maintained as long as necessary. The goal of instruction is to move the student to an age-appropriate level of response. Both general principles for teaching related to the levels and specific principles for each level are described below.

General Principles Related to Levels

We derive three general principles for teaching from the concept of five distinguishable, age-related levels of response. We assume that responses at each level are qualitatively different and that learning disabled persons have particular difficulty at each of these levels. The three principles are:

1. Use age-related abilities even for earlier level learning.
2. Incorporate teaching principles from earlier levels at later levels as needed.
3. Apply "upside down" concepts to teaching.

Use Age-Related Abilities

We assume that age makes a difference in the structures of the student. As development and learning proceed, new mental structures are created in the learning disabled person, even though the structures may be incomplete or inaccurate. The result is that the learning disabled individual develops many age-appropriate abilities. Language and cognitive abilities that are present in the learner can and should be used to encourage learning at the appropriate level. For example, teachers should deliberately choose logical cognitive strategies, not mechanical memorizing strategies if the student is capable of performance at Level IV.

We regard this principle as particularly important in very severe cases of learning disability. In such cases, progress at an age-appropriate level may not be possible although we urge teachers to move to the age-appropriate level as soon as possible. For example, a student may have severe perceptual deficiencies that interfere with the acquisition of basic reading skills or severe memory difficulties that interfere with the use of language labels. In such cases, the student may be unable to comprehend reading passages or solve certain problems (i.e., respond at Level IV) even if cognitive abilities in other areas are age-appropriate and the student is 15 years old. Does this necessitate teaching the student exactly as a younger student would be taught?

This principle suggests an alternative. Age-related abilities that are present may be used to teach at earlier levels. For example, language mediation processes may be used to guide perception (Miller & Rohr, 1980) and discrimination (Reese, 1976). Labeling of conceptual categories may occur more readily when a highly structured, categorically ordered context is provided (Robson, 1977).

Students do not come to the tasks, no matter how simple they are, with a mental vacuum. The structures they bring are significant and should be used to enable more effective learning. Adults would feel insulted if they were taught as though they were inactive, mechanical learners who could memorize content only through rote repetition. Even if adults are novices in a particular field, they approach new learning as adults with logical thinking abilities, not as children. This concept is especially important in learning disability because this population is out of developmental phase. By definition, some of their abilities are age-appropriate and some are not.

Incorporate Earlier Principles at Later Levels

The second principle directs us to incorporate teaching principles from earlier levels at later levels. In the next section, we state several teaching principles for each of the five levels. It is those specific principles to which this general principle refers. Sometimes a student is working on a Level III task, such as developing a strategy for learning spelling words, but shows continuing problems with focusing on the critical stimuli. The latter problem indicates that the student may still have difficulty with the awareness level. In such cases, instruction continues to focus on Level III but principles such as reduce stimuli to essentials and increase size and intensity of stimuli are incorporated into the teaching methods. These principles are presented and explained later as particularly applicable to Level I, the awareness level. Whenever continuing problems with an earlier level are present, the teacher may wish to incorporate applications of principles from those levels.

Apply "Upside Down" Concepts

The third principle suggests that we apply "upside down" concepts to teaching in learning disability. Kass (1970) has suggested that many basic developmental concepts widely accepted in psychology and education need to be turned upside down in learning disability. The rationale for this idea has already been expressed—learning disabled persons have a unique mix of age-appropriate and nonage-appropriate structures, which result in atypical developmental patterns.

Basic differences between a typical developmental approach and the approach we suggest are presented in Exhibit 7-1. In the left column we list several interpretations from a developmental point of view. In the right are alternative interpretations that may be applied based on the structural model we propose.

In fairness to those who urge a developmental approach, we note that the developmental interpretations presented in Exhibit 7-1 are limited or inappropriate applications of developmental concepts. That is, good developmentalists would probably not accept the interpretations (in the left column) without reservations or explanations. We find, however, that teachers often put these developmental concepts into practice in a way that reflects these limited interpretations.

We have discussed most aspects of the first concept (start where the student is) previously. Note that the structural model interpretation does not regard knowledge about scope and sequence as unimportant. Teachers must know this information if they are to set appropriate goals within a level and if they are to teach in ways relevant to school demands. However, typical developmental sequences may not work effectively with older learning disabled students. Schevill (1978) reports, for example, that tactile training with five- to seven-year-old poor readers had positive results. The same VAKT (visual, auditory, kinesthetic, tactile) training for learning letters did not lead to increased learning in students aged seven to nine.

Exhibit 7-1 Comparison of Developmental and Structural Model
Interpretations

Concept I: Start where the student is.

Developmental Interpretation	Structural Model Interpretation
1. Refers to academic, pre-academic, or language skills.	1. Refers to the *level* at which a person is, can, or ought to be functioning.
2. Fit student into a pre-determined "developmental" sequence of skills.	2. Enter at the age-related level and teach sequentially. Skip the sequence of skills when possible. Move to levels above a deficient one if appropriate based on age. Use higher level functions to develop lower level functions.
3. Use materials at the student's instructional or independent level.	3. Use materials at the student's mental age level.
4. If student cannot do the task, move to easier tasks.	4. If the student cannot do the task, teach an age-appropriate strategy so it can be accomplished.

Concept II: Provide for success.

Developmental Interpretation	Structural Model Interpretation
1. Refers to success when the student is being tested and is alone with the task.	1. Refers to success under teaching conditions. Success means the student is using appropriate processes and is operating at an appropriate level.
2. Refers to making the correct responses all the time.	2. Success means the student is thinking on the correct level and has a pattern of success even though errors, by adult standards, are frequent.

Exhibit 7-1 continued

Concept III: Teach to the whole child.

Developmental Interpretation	*Structural Model Interpretation*
1. Use as many input channels or modalities as possible.	1. May decide to teach using one modality.
2. Teach concepts and facts or skills and comprehension at the same time.	2. May teach specific facts or skills in isolation from concepts and comprehension.
3. All significant factors should be dealt with simultaneously.	3. All related factors are considered, but the significance of the factors changes, and some aspects of learning are emphasized more than others in particular contexts.

Rees (1973) concludes that research shows no real basis for saying that the discrimination aspect of auditory processing has a direct causative relationship to later development of articulation difficulties, aphasia, or reading problems. Bovet (1981) points out that "at different levels of competence, identical learning situations lead to cognitively divergent reactions" (p. 7). Each of these authors lends support to the idea that going back to earlier levels of performance may not be necessary.

The second concept (provide for success) sometimes falls short of its intent because teachers do not adequately distinguish between teaching and testing. Teaching is regarded as telling students how to perform and waiting for them to perform correctly. In our view, such an approach is a testing approach. Testing is carried out any time the student is asked to perform from long-term memory. As explained in Chapter 5, teaching and testing should be regarded as inextricably linked. Success does refer to appropriate performance during the teaching/testing process, but the emphasis is on the process, not on the product alone.

The third concept (teach to the whole child) is included to show that teaching in learning disability is not simply a matter of using the methods that work best in the regular classroom. Certainly, teaching is frequently effective in learning disability when a variety of input channels is used. Holistic teaching, in which all important aspects of a task are taught in an integrated fashion (e.g., using a language experience approach in reading), appears to be highly effective with learning disabled persons in many cases. In fact, we find most teachers in the field have a tendency to be too oriented toward specific isolated skill sequences. We must recognize that we face unique learners, and special interpretations of what it means to teach to the whole child sometimes become necessary.

Specific Principles for Each Level

Teachers of the learning disabled must understand that the method of teaching makes an important difference. They must continuously be aware of the exact method they are using, the reason for using this method and not some other, and the relationship of the method to the characteristics of the students. When a student says "1 + 1 is 3" and the teacher says, "Is it?," the method is different than if the teacher says, "No, it isn't. It's 2," or "Yes, because 3 − 1 is 1," or "Let me show you what you just told me with this set of blocks."

This is how methods *really* differ based on student attributes. The entire *level* of teaching changes depending on student characteristics. Methods do not match student characteristics as determined by test results that show weak and strong channels or processes. Characteristics are matched based on the level of performance expected from the student. Once a level of performance is selected, methods that encourage that level of response can be chosen. However, knowing the goal (the level at which you want the student to perform) is not the same as knowing the method. That is, even if the individual's mental structures and the strategies the person needs to know have been identified, the teacher still needs to decide how to teach those strategies. The teacher needs to decide exactly how to create the necessary disequilibrium.

Our observations of teachers indicate that selecting an appropriate strategy is apparently much easier than teaching that strategy efficiently. Assume, for example, that the strategy to be taught involves the use of a basic phonics skill (specifically, knowledge of vowel sounds and how to decode them) in combination with learning a basic sight word vocabulary. One teacher strategy to use would be to present the students with words appropriate for the strategy, ask them to read the words, say "stop" each time they make an error, and ask them to try again. Possibly, this strategy would teach them to look more carefully before guessing, because the saying of "stop" might cause some disequilibrium. More likely, however, the students will continue to make many errors because they do not have a good model to imitate, they practice errors frequently, and they learn that the teacher will monitor their performance so they do not need to think for themselves.

A second approach might be to directly teach all of the words (tell the students what they are), require numerous repetitions immediately after a word is read, ask the students to read the words independently, and anticipate errors by providing "corrections" even before the errors are made. This method is usually fast, and it frequently works well at Level III. It demonstrates good modeling. If the students participate in developing an active "rehearsal strategy" and are encouraged to transfer it to similar situations, the method will probably be appropriate for some students.

A third approach would be to use what we call the "Columbo Method," which is described in detail later. In essence, the method requires the teacher to ask probing questions that force students to examine their erroneous thinking about a task. Disequilibrium occurs for the students as they recognize a mismatch between the way they think and the way they must think to accomplish the task. Strategies for efficient learning of the task are devised by the students with teacher assistance. The strategies are then used to learn new information and are transferred to other situations. Often, this method is the most efficient over time because it focuses on active learning.

Selecting strategies and deciding how to teach them is a highly creative, problem-solving process that evolves out of direct interaction between teacher and student. We cannot tell you exactly how to select and teach strategies; however, we have developed some principles that can serve as guidelines for the selection and teaching of strategies at each level. These principles are presented and explained in the remainder of this section.

Level I Principles

The five principles at Level I, the awareness level, are:

1. Reduce stimuli to essentials.
2. Increase the size or intensity of stimuli.
3. Use attention-getting and high motivation materials.
4. Use successive approximation techniques.
5. Enable the student to respond repeatedly and rapidly.

Level I responding does not involve being right or wrong so much as making a response that shows awareness of the presence of important stimuli. Before the attributes of stimuli (Level II) can be noted and labels can be attached to them (Level III), one must be aware that important stimuli exist in the immediate situation. But what should a teacher do if someone does not pay attention to significant stimuli? Can a teacher force attention and awareness?

Keogh and Margolis (1976), in their review of attention processes and problems, suggest that remediation should involve careful setting up of the task so the student knows where to start. They say that simply teaching students to slow down is not enough. Tasks need to be restructured; solution techniques need to be developed; and appropriate reinforcement needs to be given. Pick and Pick (1970) indicate that stimuli can be manipulated to increase attention. Sharper contrast, greater complexity, and less redundancy may help. Horner (1977) found that the amount of environmental stimuli experienced by hyperactive children is not crucial to whether these children behave in a hyperactive fashion. Each of these authors indicates that the route to awareness level responses is through stimulus manipulation.

Attention is a process deep inside the individual and is basic to any kind of responding above the reflex level. The process is complex, difficult to measure, and difficult to address in teaching. Learning disabled persons with attention problems may attend too much or too little. Obviously, they attend to some things because they do learn. At the same time, they frequently show a lack of goal-directed behavior and a level of activity that is so high or so low that teachers are distressed.

Because the processes that permit Level I responding are deep within the individual, they are extremely difficult to address in a direct way. The problems that exist are related more to internal mental states than to external stimulus conditions. Although access to internal states is very indirect, stimulus manipulation and direct physical contact with the student comprise the major ways of "getting through" to those who have awareness level difficulties. The teaching principles at this level emphasize this approach.

The hyperactivity of hyperactive children may not decrease when the number of environmental stimuli is reduced (Horner, 1977), but most teachers have students who fail to attend to a task when the fire engine whistles past the window with a blasting siren. Certainly, some relationship exists between the presence of stimuli and the responses of people.

For some students, the number of stimuli may need to be reduced to help them focus on a task. This could include removing extraneous stimuli from the environment. More important, we have found, is the reduction of the number of specific stimuli included in a task. The student is presented with one toy, not three. One or two sounds or words are presented to autistic children in early stages of language imitation programs. When principles from Level I need to be considered during tasks at later levels because of continuing attending difficulties, the student may be given a single page instead of an entire book. A page may contain one problem instead of 100 mathematics facts (to be completed in three minutes).

Another closely allied principle is increasing stimuli in size or intensity. The stimuli to which the student needs to attend might be drawn large on the chalkboard, colored brightly, spoken loudly, and so forth. The teacher attempts to make the important stimuli and the salient features of those stimuli stand out.

The third principle is a rather general one that shows the importance of making a connection with the internal status of the student. The teacher must determine which stimuli seem to be interesting to the student. Stimuli may be made more complex and novel. Direct physical manipulation may also be used. Perhaps the teacher needs to grasp the student's chin and lift the head so eye contact is more likely. The teacher may wish to vary speaking volume from very loud to a whisper if this helps students attend.

Successive approximation techniques may be appropriate at Level I. In using these techniques, a partially correct response is at first rewarded. As more responses are elicited, rewards are given only if the desired response is more closely approximated. Responding is shaped in successive steps until the correct response occurs. Using these techniques probably helps the student move to Level II where clear discriminations are made. At Level I, the emphasis is on noting and rewarding *any* response the student makes that seems to be related to important environmental stimuli and any responses that indicate the beginnings of goal-directed behavior. Combined with these techniques should be direct instruction and "calling to attention" techniques. The young child is told to "Get the *ball,* the ball." Sentences are simplified, and important words are emphasized and repeated. Visual stimuli are enlarged and colored to attract attention.

The goal of this stimulus manipulation is to enable the student to respond at Level I, which is summarized in the last principle. When a student is capable of responding repeatedly to important stimuli and can do so at an appropriate rate, it may be time to move to Level II. Note that we are not referring to correct or incorrect responses so much as responses that show the student has acquired some strategies for staying on task and for noting important stimuli in the environment. The student may have learned to scan the environment visually or to make eye contact. He or she may have learned to listen to words and to explore the environment. The student will play with others when encouraged to do so. Particular desires and needs are beginning to be communicated through gestures and sounds. The young child is beginning to recognize danger and to pull back from it. The child has obviously moved from mostly reflex action to behavior that indicates awareness of significant stimuli in the environment.

Level II Principles

We have identified three major principles at Level II, the differentiation level:

1. Start with large differences and gradually decrease.
2. Call direct attention to distinctive cues and essential features in stimuli.
3. Provide direct practice in discriminating, coordinating, and sequencing.

The student learns attribution strategies at Level II. Essential features of stimuli are noted, and inner language concepts that organize and classify perceptual stimuli are built up.

Chalfant and Scheffelin (1969) suggest beginning with single stimuli and then presenting stimuli that have maximum contrast in discrimination practice. Gibson and Levin (1975) point out that a major aspect of perceptual learning is to form an abstraction in which major features are "pulled out" and conceptualized. They recommend starting with maximum contrast between stimuli and moving to minimum contrast.

Spiker (1959) found that preschoolers did better on a difficult discrimination task if they were first given training on a similar easier task. One group was given 48 trials on the difficult discrimination but no trials on the easier task. They did not do as well as the second group, even though they had more practice. The second group was given 24 "easy" trials and 24 trials with the more difficult task. It appears that, if discrimination tasks contain a high level of contrast initially, individuals learn to identify the most important and relevant features. Therefore, in teaching visual, tactile, auditory, or other forms of discrimination, we suggest beginning with large differences and gradually presenting stimuli that are more and more similar as the student learns to recognize and respond correctly to the important features. Note, however, that we are referring to teaching when the student is at the age specified for Level II (one to four years).

As a child gets older, the opportunities for using language to guide perception increase, and highly contrasted differences in stimuli may be less essential. At later levels, for example, a student may be able to distinguish between fine differences such as whether a sound is voiced or unvoiced by using verbal processes. A teacher may verbally explain the throat vibrations that occur when the sound /b/ is pronounced but not when the sound /p/ is pronounced. Students may be told to place a hand on their throat to feel these vibrations. The verbal guidance may enable a discrimination between these two very similar phonemes without first demanding practice with maximum contrasts.

If, as Gibson and Levin (1975) state, perceptual learning involves abstracting out essential features and relations, students with difficulties in responding at Level II may be unable to identify and conceptualize the important features in stimuli. Difficulty discriminating, coordinating, and recognizing sequence may be apparent. Gibson and Levin (1975) recommend the provision of "uncluttered examples of the invariant property" or "enhancing the feature contrast" (p. 25). They caution, however, that calling direct attention to distinctive cues and essential features is not always as simple as adding color to the stimuli. They report one study in which preschoolers were taught letter names. For one group, visual stimuli were presented in three contrasting colors. For the other group, all of the letters were printed in black. All children were tested on black letters. Both groups did very poorly on the test. The groups did not differ in performance, although the first group did remember the original color in which the letters were presented.

Reese (1976) also notes that cues that appear salient to adults may not be effective cues for children. Hagan and Kail (1975) say that the use of redundant cues (e.g., increased size or added color) speeds discrimination learning for normal students, but that adding more than two redundant cues may not help and may even hinder learning. Zentall, Zentall, and Barack (1978) found that adding color made some tasks more difficult for hyperactive children.

The task of the teacher becomes rather complicated, given these considerations. Teachers must know what the essential features of stimuli are and must aid students in discriminating, coordinating, and sequencing the stimuli. They must carefully evaluate which redundant cues may help and which may hinder learning. Then they must call students' attention to the distinctive cues and essential features. Incidentally, although we know some things about which features are essential at the letter level (Gibson & Levin, 1975) much less is known about the essential features of larger units such as words and concepts. Teachers will need to make reasonable decisions about what to emphasize on the basis of their intuition and the responses of students.

The third principle at Level II encourages the provision of direct practice. We urge teacher observations during this practice to assure that the student is processing in a way that is necessary for learning. If students are left alone to complete discrimination tasks, they may discover ways to complete the tasks without understanding them.

As with the processes at Level I, perception processes are deep within the individual and difficult to address directly. A major way to "teach" discrimination is to provide many opportunities for direct practice of tasks that demand discrimination, coordination, and sequencing. Especially if a student is between the ages of one and four, the use of materials that encourage practice in these areas may be helpful. We are convinced, as are others (Sabatino, 1976; Wiig & Semel, 1976), that a connection exists between perceptual skills and other skills such as reading. We are suggesting the use of discrimination, coordination, and sequencing practice for young children. We are not saying that this perceptual training directly transfers to reading or other tasks, only that students need to learn strategies for discovering and learning the perceptual attributes of important stimuli. As students increase in age, direct practice in perceptual tasks may be unnecessary.

Level III Principles

At Level III, the labeling level, we have identified four principles for the selection and teaching of mechanical strategies:

1. Teach more than test.
2. Provide direct modeling, rehearsal, and drill.
3. Reduce chances for error.
4. Reduce emphasis on logical analysis and comprehension.

Earlier, we expressed the idea that teaching is closely linked to testing. At all levels, input must precede output (Johnson & Myklebust, 1967). However, we find a distinction between teaching and testing especially important at Level III.

Teachers need to be aware of when they are teaching and when they are testing. Confusion on this point is prevalent at this level, probably because of the nature of Level III tasks. Common tasks are learning to count; to name objects and events; to say the alphabet; to respond rapidly with answers to "math facts" in addition, subtraction and multiplication; and to recognize words in reading. The means many children use to learn this information include an emphasis on direct rehearsal. Our first principle suggests that direct rehearsal is most efficient if teaching is emphasized more than testing. The second principle puts this concept into more definite form. The teacher teaches by providing direct modeling and by providing opportunities and encouragement for direct rehearsal and drill.

Note, however, that learning will not occur through rehearsal and drill alone. The student brings active learning processes and previously established structures to the learning situation, and disequilibrium must be present to make learning happen. At Level III, as elsewhere, the learner must recognize the need to learn if rehearsal and drill are to be effective. Therefore, approaches such as the "Columbo Method," described later, may need to be used before the teacher provides direct input. Incidentally, the provision of external reinforcement may improve the use of rehearsal strategies by reading disabled persons, but external rewards alone apparently do not enable them to use rehearsal as effectively as good readers (Haines & Torgesen, 1979). Learning disabled students must understand why rehearsal strategies are necessary, and they must learn how to use them efficiently.

Direct modeling, rehearsal, and drill require a continuous cycle of input from the teacher and output from the student. Little time is spent in requiring the student to produce a response when a stimulus is not presented immediately prior to the response. Many of the tasks at this level have a definite right or wrong answer. When this is true, the most direct route to learning may be best. The teacher may wish to go directly to the essentials and tell the student the correct response (Kohl, 1974). For example, a student may be asked to read a word in context. If the word is not immediately known, the teacher says the word for the student if Level III responding is the goal. Next, the student is asked to rehearse the word numerous times, perhaps by repeating it several ways (e.g., looking at it and saying it, writing it in the air and saying it, etc.). The assumption is that if the student does not know the word, it will be learned most rapidly, at this level, through a rehearsal strategy. If the child *does* know the word but does not produce it rapidly, immediate modeling and repetition may help to stabilize the knowledge and enable more rapid responding.

A similar emphasis is present in learning related to other content areas. The use of rehearsal strategies is encouraged by presenting the student with the entire stimulus *and* the expected response. Addition, subtraction, and multiplication flash cards are presented with the answer showing, and the student repeats the entire fact. Labels for objects and events are provided by the teacher, and the student repeats the label in context.

The first two principles lead directly to the third—reduce chances for error. Prior to the practice of mechanical strategies, students may need to make errors that can be used as a basis for creating disequilibrium. However, once the student recognizes that the response produced does not fit reality, direct teaching begins, and a strategy for learning the new information is developed. As the student applies this strategy, the teacher attempts to anticipate errors and correct them before they occur. Learning disabled persons seem to practice errors long after other students have ceased to do so, perhaps because of perceptual or memory processing difficulties. Whatever the reason, a potential solution appears to be preventing the practice of errors so that confusion is reduced. Students who confuse *b* and *d* or *was* and *saw* are not likely to stop doing so if they continue to use the wrong label 50% of the time when they see these stimuli. Reese (1976) suggests that the practice of errors during associative learning produces proactive interference. That is, practice of the error interferes with the yet to be learned responses.

The last principle (reduce emphasis on logical analysis and comprehension) shows recognition that students who are focusing on Level III have limited logical thinking skills. They do, of course, have a level of understanding of such things as word meanings and basic concepts. They are capable of recognizing patterns and similarities in perceptual stimuli, but they are not capable of the logical problem solving that predominates at Level IV. The strategies they use will be more mechanical and less elaborate at Level III. We should not expect sophisticated written expression, in which sequencing of ideas and logical relationships reach adult levels. Up to the age of eight years, the emphasis should be on learning strategies for acquiring the academic skills that are a basis for later Level IV and V responding. These skills should include the observation and thinking abilities that are available at Level III.

Obviously, we do not want to encourage a move toward the misconceptions we explained in Chapter 1. But especially for the learning disabled youngster who is struggling with the basic skills usually learned in the first three grades of school, care must be taken to concentrate on Level III types of content. Frequently, this translates into an emphasis on what are called basic academic skills.

Level IV Principles

Four principles are particularly important at Level IV, the understanding level, as follows:

1. Reduce or increase thinking time.
2. Present the complex before the simple.
3. Develop the logical steps in the thinking process.
4. Develop a logical structure within which information can be organized.

Thinking begins to be much more complex at Level IV. At this level, the possibility of dramatically varying the presentation and sequence of information becomes more apparent. It may not always be necessary to present all the earlier components of a particular academic sequence the student has not mastered. If the student is directed toward an understanding of the rules and generalizations of age-related content, the earlier skills and content can be quickly mastered.

Some learning disabled persons appear to think too long in problem-solving situations. We worked with one young man of 15 years who nearly put us to sleep during evaluation phases because he responded so slowly. Further probing indicated that he was attempting to use rather elaborate processes to work the problems given him but that these processes were not very effective. For example, when asked to solve the problem $792 \div 8$, he attempted to count on his fingers and toes to arrive at an answer. He was able, eventually, to solve the problem. However, not only did he use a primitive strategy, he failed to use several abilities he was capable of using.

We asked him to respond every time we snapped our fingers (about every two seconds) by giving an estimate of what each part of the answer might be. We found that, at first, he relied on a simple strategy, but soon he made accurate estimates, which he then applied to other problems. Specifically, when first asked to respond rapidly to the first part of the above problem (i.e., how many times can 8 be divided into 79) he estimated "2," then "3," then "4," and so on until he reached 9. After two or three problems, his first estimate was much closer to the correct answer; he no longer proceeded in "one, two, three" sequence; and he began to estimate in a way that "bracketed" the correct answer between an estimate that was slightly too high and one that was slightly too low. This illustrates what we mean by reducing thinking time. When extensive thinking is not needed or in cases where the student is spending far too much time using inefficient strategies, thinking time should be reduced.

In other cases, the student may guess impulsively, hoping that the answer will be correct or that the teacher will monitor (or ignore) the error. In these cases, it becomes necessary to increase the thinking time.

Suppose, for example, that we want a student to learn to use sentence and paragraph structure to identify unknown words in a reading passage. A student who is thinking too *long* may be trying to remember an entire list of words that might fit. We would need to break this mechanical pattern by speeding up the response. The student might be asked to rapidly produce a possibly appropriate word and immediately try it out. In the case of a student who responds too rapidly, we might require the student to wait 15 seconds before a response is permitted, in an attempt to insure an exhaustive search for an appropriate word. Of course, taking more time will not assure appropriate thinking by the student. Logical strategies for exhaustive search may need to be developed, as noted by principles three and four.

The second principle at Level IV suggests the presentation of complex information before simple. Content that matches the highest level of thinking ability may be presented before normally prerequisite content. In the example of reading in the above paragraph, our goal was to teach the student to identify unknown words from context clues. Context clues can be used even if the student does not know word attack skills. The student can be taught to look for and identify the meaning of what is being read and how to use it. In fact, the student should be encouraged *not* to try to recognize the particular unknown word before context clues are examined. This raises word attack to an age-appropriate level and also develops appropriate processing. In this reading example, material from the student's interest level would be selected instead of instructional level material since this presents more complicated sentence and paragraph meaning. Easy, uncomplicated content and examples need not precede more complex content. Depending on the nature of the task and the abilities of the student, the opposite may be necessary.

The essence of teaching at Level IV is reflected in principles three and four. Possibly, the ability to structure thought in an abstract, logical way depends, in part, on formal schooling. Luria (1976) found that adults clung rigidly to very practical or functional classifications of objects until they had been in school for one or two years. Abstract, logical classifications and flexibility became possible even with this limited amount of training but did not occur when no formal training had been given.

Perhaps we can expect the same pattern with learning disabled individuals. Even with nine- and ten-year-old children, Ceci, Lea, and Ringstrom (1980) found that semantic information may be used to recall stimuli if they are told to use it. These children were previously deficient in recall abilities. When given aid in both learning and recalling, the semantic input apparently overcame the deficit. By helping learning disabled persons discover and use logical thinking strategies and helping them develop logical organizations (or internal mental structures) within which information can be placed, we may enable them to function appropriately at Level IV. The students must be actively involved in the generation of these thinking and organizing strategies. These strategies must fit the thinking of the student and must be useful in a variety of contexts.

To show the logical steps in the thinking process, a problem may be presented to a student, and a solution may be requested. To do this appropriately, we should recognize that there are many levels of problem solving. Greene (1975) designates six levels. The first and simplest level is when the problem solver already knows the solution. This corresponds to Level III of the structures model and is characterized by such questions as "Which side won the Battle of Gettysburg?" A second level is reached in problems requiring knowledge of the rules for arriving at a solution. An example might be applying knowledge of the formula for calculating the area of a circle to a given set of figures. Greene's third level involves learning correct responses during the task. An example might be finding a way through a maze. At level four, operations for producing a solution must be selected and evaluated. Greene uses the example of doing a crossword puzzle. Major reformulations or unusual solution methods become important at level five. This level involves tasks such as inventing a better mousetrap. At the sixth and last level, the solver must recognize that a problem exists. Greene (1975) points out, for example, that Newton needed to realize that the falling apple demanded an explanation.

These various types of problem solving may be useful in teaching learning disabled individuals. We may be able to use them as a guide for presenting more complex problems to our students if their problem-solving abilities permit this.

After a student has been asked to solve a problem and has failed to do so, the teacher must analyze how the thought processes of the student are organized related to the problem. The teacher also needs to know the logical steps the student can use to reach a solution. Knowledge of student structures and of an appropriate set of steps for solving the problem are brought together as the teacher attempts to help the student restructure his or her thought through the development and use of logical strategies. Strategies for deriving meaning from sentences may be developed through a study of sentence structure. Strategies for organizing ideas for a test in social studies may center around "mind pattern pictures" (Buzan & Dixon, no date, Buzan, 1976) in which related ideas radiate out from a central concept in an organized but nonlinear way. Strategies for writing original stories, taking lecture notes, answering a series of science questions, developing conversational skills, reading a meaningful paragraph, and hundreds of other tasks may be developed or taken from sources such as Alley and Deshler (1979). Hresko and Reid (1981) review five major theoretical approaches to cognition and point out how each of them may have teaching implications. At least four of these approaches, information processing, metacognition, genetic epistemology, and cognitive behavior modification, seem to be applicable to the development of logical strategies for Level IV.

Keep in mind, however, the essential point that strategies that are simply imposed on students will not produce learning. Disequilibrium must be present, and the student must invest effort in the task. The more direct and explicit the strategy, the greater the chances for its use. It is not enough to simply test the student. If the student is asked to solve a problem and cannot do so, a strategy is required for thinking the problem through and coming to a solution. If a student cannot answer comprehension questions at the end of a reading passage, simply presenting an easier passage will not tell the student *how* to comprehend. The teacher must determine whether the student cannot do the task because of a lack of knowledge about word meanings, sentence structure, paragraph structure, or some other area. Then the teacher must help the student develop a strategy for understanding the meanings of words, for interpreting sentence structure, or for identifying meaning in a paragraph. By doing so, the student begins to function at Level

IV. When students recognize and use a logical, organized structure of information, they are functioning at Level IV.

Level V Principles

We have derived three principles to use for teaching at Level V, the habit level, as follows:

1. Inform the student of the nature of the learning problem and the proposed solution.
2. Change the situation and the sensory feedback system.
3. Help the student unlearn old habits by moving back to earlier levels of response.

Explicit communication between teacher and student about the nature of the problem and the proposed solution is usually as helpful at earlier levels as at Level V, as long as the student is able to understand the explanations. We specify this concept as a principle at Level V because it is particularly important for changing deeply ingrained habits. In addition, student expectations and performance will probably change if the individual is convinced that change is likely. Low performance may also occur if students are convinced that a task is difficult. Errors apparently increase even on simple tasks if the person expects difficulty (Reese, 1976).

At Level V, responses are at a high level of meaning, but meanings are expressed in automatic ways. Individuals with difficulty at this level may have continuing difficulty with expressing personal meanings, with understanding the communications of others, and with monitoring their own output. Frequently, they have incorporated "bad habits" that interfere with efficient processing at this level. Because the responses involve high levels of meaning, but very habitual, overlearned systems, unlearning needs to take place. We are speaking, then, of deeply ingrained ways of responding to meaningful material. When adults read a novel, they may experience a set of meanings at this level. Frequently, when we converse with one another, meaning is grasped on this level. Artists may respond at Level V when viewing the work of others or producing their own. When we express ourselves in verbal, gestural, or written language, many automatic Level V processes are activated.

Changing inefficient or erroneous habits is not a simple matter. The bad habits must be confronted directly and pointed out explicitly. Efforts to change are more effective if the individual consciously recognizes both the error and a means to change it.

Meichenbaum (1977) notes that most behavior is based on habit and that if we are to change behavior we need to think before we act. Powers (1973) says,

"Change demands consciousness from the point of view that needs changing" (p. 201). He goes on to explain that if a response has been learned to an automatic level, consciousness of the details tends to disrupt the behavior and begin reorganization of it. The presence of what we mean by disequilibrium is clearly implied in these ideas. That the need for change should be conscious appears especially important at Level V.

Since the individual is capable of operating at a high level, the nature of the undesirable response, the sources of the difficulty, and the methods and resources for change can be analyzed logically. The first principle reflects the idea that the student begins to consciously say, "I am doing this wrong. I want to change. I know which change I want to make and a way to make the change."

The second principle points out a way teachers can help change habits. Most adults are aware that habits, good or bad, are more likely to be maintained if the conditions under which the habit is usually exercised are present. Someone who drinks six cups of coffee a day at the office may drink none when out of the office for the day. Persons positively addicted to running may find running difficult when away on vacation. If we want to change ingrained behavior, external changes may help.

Changes may be made in the physical surroundings. Perhaps we need to remove students from the classroom situation and teach in an obviously different setting such as outdoors or in the hallway. Changes can be made in the task and the material used for it. Instead of books and paper and pencil, single pages, chalkboard and chalk, or nonwritten "mental" activities may be used.

The second part of principle two suggests changing the sensory feedback system. Such changes enable the individual to use a different monitoring system to determine whether responses are correct or incorrect. Figure-ground aspects of the stimuli may be modified. "Noise" (extraneous or unneeded information) may be added to force the individual to search more carefully for the essential components of the task. A channel of input that is used inappropriately may be masked so that it cannot be used. For example, an individual may be prevented from using the visual channel to check whether letters are formed correctly by writing on a background (e.g., a page from a newspaper) that makes visual checking difficult. Such techniques force the person to attend to the feedback from the senses of touch and movement.

We applied techniques like those described here with a young man of 23 who read in a very halting, word-by-word fashion with many repetitions of words, phrases, and sentences. His comprehension was at a low level, not because he lacked comprehension ability, but apparently because of an extremely slow reading rate. When asked whether he "listened to what he was reading," he appeared confused and uncertain about what the question meant. We suggested that he cup his hand from his mouth to his ear as he read aloud. This technique, we hoped, would change the feedback system. Instead of checking what he was reading by looking again at the printed words, he would listen. We also urged him to read the passage smoothly and fluently as he listened carefully to the words and interpreted meanings. The change in reading habits was immediate and rather dramatic. Oral reading rate nearly tripled and comprehension reached expected adult levels.

Teaching at Level V emphasizes holistic, meaningful patterns of response. If the student demonstrates undesirable habits as a part of these integrated responses, the components that cause difficulty may be "pulled out" and examined. To unlearn these habits, the student may be asked to work on this part of the task at a lower level, as suggested by the third principle.

The first step may be to deliberately practice the error at Level IV. Secretaries, for example, sometimes deliberately type a troublesome word incorrectly (Powers, 1973). That is, if a particular word is nearly always typed incorrectly, this incorrect spelling may be repeated many times. Essential to this process, however, is Level IV analysis of what is happening. The secretary internally repeats "This is my old, incorrect way of typing this word. From now on, I will type it correctly." If the system works, the individual develops a new monitoring system. Each time the word appears, this monitoring system goes into action, preventing the error from occurring again. At Level V, then, the contrast with Level III methods becomes apparent. Errors may be deliberately practiced instead of avoided. Similar systems may be helpful in correcting habitual errors in written or verbal expression.

A more complex example may serve to illustrate the use of the third principle. A young seminary student who was capable of meaningful, appropriately sequenced verbal expression was having extreme difficulty with written expression. Not only were errors in spelling and punctuation numerous, but syntax, paragraph structure, and idea sequencing difficulties made this student's written work nearly incomprehensible. Since verbal expression was age-appropriate, we had evidence that he could perform at Level IV and Level V with language under some conditions. Teaching efforts could be focused on reaching these levels with written language. The first step was to recognize and analyze the errors. Secondly, the teacher helped him develop a Level IV logical sequence of activities to use as a strategy for writing assignments. Dictating ideas into a tape recorder and constructing an outline evolved as essential components of this strategy. After a composition was written, monitoring was encouraged through a variety of editing techniques. Syntax errors were analyzed at Level IV through the study of correct sentence patterns. Spelling and word use were also analyzed at Level IV through the study of spelling rules and of how words are constructed.

Level III "reteaching" was sometimes needed to clarify word definitions or to enable him to spell some words automatically. (We regard automatic, rote spelling as a Level III and not a Level V response.) At times, he was taught and encouraged to use Level II strategies for such tasks as checking the appearance of the paper or the spelling of a word (Does it look right? Are the sounds in correct sequence?). The goal was to unlearn the old way of performing at Level V, to reteach as needed, and to bring the entire process to an automatic level.

Some aspects of meaningful communication remain at Level IV, as is apparent from the ages we attach to the last two levels. Adults function at both of these levels simultaneously, performing some aspects of highly meaningful tasks at Level IV and others at Level V. Perhaps the metacognitive variables that control strategy selection and decisions about when to respond are the most important functions accomplished at Level V.

Chapter 8

Teaching the Learning Disabled: From Principles to Practice

We don't know the children you teach or the mental structures they have. Therefore, we cannot tell you which specific strategies to use or exactly how to use them. Helping students develop, learn, use, and transfer strategies evolves out of creative teaching. In this chapter, we present some strategies for teachers and students that may help in the teaching/learning process. How these are used depends on the individual teacher and the students he or she teaches. In the first section, activating and cueing strategies, which have general applicability to all levels of teaching, are presented. The last section presents specific strategies useful at each level of the structures model.

GENERAL STRATEGIES

Two kinds of general strategies that are useful at all levels of the structures model are explained in this section. The first is called an activating strategy because its use is necessary for activation of basic learning processes. The second type is termed a cueing strategy because metacognitive or external cues are used as a guide for student thinking and responding. Two varieties of cueing strategies are presented. One we call perceptual cueing, the other, language cueing.

An Activating Strategy

The strategy we describe here is intended to activate the essential learning processes of the student. It is, for the most part, a *teacher* rather than a student strategy, although students may be able to use some aspects of it to regulate their own learning and behavior. The main use of the strategy is to provide guidance to the teacher in any teaching/learning situation. The primary goals of the teacher in using the strategy are to create disequilibrium in the student at the exact point of

177

difficulty, to provide new information that is just different enough from the old structures to permit learning, and to help the student stabilize the new learning. Notice as we explain the method how teaching and testing are integrated into the process.

We sometimes call the strategy described here the "Columbo Method" because it has some similarities to the methods used by a detective of the same name. We refer to the 1970's television show *Columbo,* in which the star of the show, Peter Falk, played the role of a police investigator. Columbo's image and style were quite different from the usual portrayal of television detectives. His major efforts were directed toward forcing clever criminals to admit their crimes by providing the guilty parties with "enough rope to hang themselves." The list of techniques in Exhibit 8-1 summarizes much of what Columbo did to accomplish this goal. Examples of typical behavior by Columbo taken from different episodes of the show are presented on the right to illustrate the techniques.

Columbo's technique eventually forces the hand of the criminal, resulting in a full confession and the inevitable question, "How did you know?" We suggest that teachers operate in a way similar to Columbo, although the similarities in the situations may not be immediately obvious.

We are not saying that students are criminals and that the teacher's task is to ferret out their wrongdoings and obtain a confession. Another major difference between being a teacher and being a detective is that students are involved in learning new information while criminals are trying to hide information.

The similarities between the detective Columbo and the teacher Columbo will become apparent as we explain the steps in the method. The seven steps used in the method are:

1. Understand the student's structures.
2. Understand what the student needs to learn.
3. Imagine the steps in between.
4. Generate disequilibrium.
5. Switch roles.
6. Play with the new concept.
7. The student teaches.

Each of these steps is explained below.

Understand the Student's Structures

This step focuses on the evaluation phase of the teaching/testing process. The teacher assesses the mental structures that the student brings to the task. The procedures to be used here are explained in detail in Chapters 5 and 6. The student is encouraged to demonstrate and explain how to do a task. The teacher observes,

Exhibit 8-1 An Example of the Columbo Method

Technique	Examples
1. shared ignorance	*Criminal:* "I don't understand." *Columbo:* "I don't either."
2. seeking help	*Columbo to criminal:* "I'm gonna need a lot of your help."
3. citing irrelevant facts	*Columbo to criminal:* "This painting is by DeGroot. That one is by Rembrandt. Isn't that interesting!" (Often, such remarks were not as irrelevant as they first seemed.)
4. playing humble	*Columbo to criminal:* "I was hoping I could have a couple of minutes of your time."
5. citing the important as unimportant	*Columbo to criminal:* "This isn't important, but it's been bothering me."
6. acting confused or ignorant	*Columbo to criminal:* "I wish you could help me by explaining how the knife could have been put in the kitchen." Or "It seems impossible."
7. playing reasonable	When the criminal explains, Columbo accepts the explanation, often repeating it back to show how reasonable it is. Sometimes, he makes it apparent that the explanation may be *too* reasonable: "In fact, we know exactly what time *you* were there and that *your* car trunk was empty."
8. feigning excitement	Columbo excitedly reaches toward a folder containing paintings, saying, "Do you have a Van Dyck in there?" The move is designed to see if the criminal will stop him.
9. presenting fallacies	Columbo presents a conclusion that is logically incorrect, which leads the criminal to explain. Columbo gains more clues and more information about how the criminal is thinking.

Exhibit 8-1 continued

10. seeking more information	*Columbo to criminal:* "One more thing."
11. going with the resistance	*Columbo to criminal:* "Of course, you're right." This is done even when the criminal is obviously wrong.
12. asking exactly the right question	Columbo gains information primarily by asking the precise question that traps the criminal. The question leads the criminal to explain something that eventually collapses the entire argument due to logical inconsistencies.

questions, and forms hypotheses about the structures that underlie the activity of the subject (Bovet, 1981). The teacher shows respect for the structures of the subject by: (1) praising the student for creative solutions even if they contain errors; (2) regarding structures as providing a basis for all responses, even errors; and (3) regarding them as the basis for new learning. Particularly important, at this step, is to avoid immediate corrections of errors.

Bovet (1981) points out that most teaching aims at economically and simply producing a rapid drop in errors by providing ready-made answers. Generally, the student is not prepared for this kind of teaching. Some of the student's behavior may change, but thinking and learning may stop, and the new learning may be temporary.

The teacher aims at pinpointing the structures of the student in relation to the task. Both appropriate and inappropriate structures are noted. Hypotheses about those structures are stated in "This student thinks . . ." terms.

Understand What the Student Needs to Learn

Specific, detailed knowledge about content and skills related to school and other aspects of the student's environment is essential for this step. The teacher must understand curriculum, the prerequisites for successful performance, and the specific skills the individual needs. Since the student's structures are understood from step one, the teacher compares this information with immediate and future environmental demands and decides what the student needs to learn. Specific learning goals are set.

Imagine the Steps in Between

The learning that is of interest to the teacher of learning disabled persons usually does not involve a single simple concept or skill. Most things worth learning take time to learn, and several steps may be involved. The teacher imagines, as specifically as possible, the steps that may be necessary to change the student's structures.

Although this process may sound difficult, we regard it as natural and creative. The process evolves out of the teacher's knowledge of curriculum and the nature of learning. The teacher should expect that learning will progress slowly since important learning takes time. The learning may proceed stage by stage, as new structures are developed and are then modified or even destroyed when other structures take their place. As these stages are imagined, the teacher must be aware that the student actively participates in the entire process. Opportunities for discovery and exploration must be presented.

Generate Disequilibrium

This step is perhaps the most complicated. It includes most of the techniques used by the detective Columbo. Notice, first, that a teacher cannot directly create disequilibrium since this is an internal process. Disequilibrium depends on the learner's recognition that a mismatch exists between internal ideas and external stimuli. A teacher may be able to encourage the generation of disequilibrium, however, if appropriate techniques are used. As we noted before, simply giving the student the necessary information will not result in stable learning unless the student is already in a state of disequilibrium relative to that information. Bovet (1981) states the goal of the teacher at this stage clearly when she says that "the learning procedures must be designed in such a way that they create a positive disequilibrium between the child's schemes" (p. 6).

The assumptions and anticipations of the student must be challenged at this step. The challenge is directed at those specific structures that are in need of change. Although different authors express this idea in varying terms (e.g., Alley & Deshler, 1979; Bovet, 1981; DeBono, 1968; Moses, 1981; Powers, 1973), the concept is very similar. The student must experience internal disequilibrium, which the teacher should help to develop through the creation of conflict and challenge. How can this process be encouraged?

The current inaccurate or inadequate structures of a student can be interrupted, first of all, by permitting the student to present that structure and *going with the resistance*. This technique is used to avoid the creation of greater resistance in the student. As in swimming across a river, it is better to swim downstream, allowing the current to help you across, than to strike out against the current. With either approach, you usually end up downstream. The student explains, and the teacher recognizes and encourages that response. Let us use an example of a problem we

presented in Chapter 1. The student is asked to solve the problem $33 - 17 =$ _____
(written vertically). She writes the answer "24." The following dialogue ensues:

Teacher: I see. You have 33 minus 17 is 24. So, 3 minus 7 is 4. Hmm. I don't
understand how you get 4. Let's see . . . 3 minus 7 . . . If I have 3
can I take 7 away? How did you get 4?
Student: Seven minus 3 is 4.
Teacher: Oh! Seven minus 3 is 4. That's right!

The conversation continues as the teacher begins to ask exactly the right
questions.

Teacher: Let's look at these blocks. We have 33 blocks, so how many are we
taking away?
Student: Seventeen.
Teacher: Alright. Take 17. (Child does so.) How many do we have left?
Student: Sixteen.
Teacher: Is that right? (Student counts again.)
Student: Yep.
Teacher: Hmm! Let's look at this problem. When we had 33 and we took
away 17, how did we get 24?

This exchange was carried out to establish the concept that the quantity in the
student's original answer was not correct. This is particularly important because
the student must recognize the mismatch between reality and the way she operates.
She now knows and has made a commitment to the idea that 33 minus 17 is not 24.
In the child's mind, it is not just numbers, but real quantity, that is involved.
Disequilibrium is created. The teacher continues to ask questions and go with the
resistance, at the same time beginning to introduce countersuggestions and playing
reasonable.

Teacher: Let's try another problem. If I have 25 blocks and you take 14
away, how many are left? (Child takes 14 away.)
Student: Eleven.
Teacher: How do we write this problem? (Child writes problem vertically.)
Can you work the problem? (Child does so and writes the answer,
11.) Did you do that the same way you did the last one?
Student: Yeah.
Teacher: Well, in this problem, you took the 3 away from the 7, which is the
top number away from the bottom. In this problem you took 4 away
from 5, which is the bottom number from the top. Can you subtract

either way with any problem? How do you know which way to do it? Why did you take the top number from the bottom with this (the first) problem?

Student:	Because there wasn't enough.
Teacher:	Because there wasn't enough. What do you mean?
Student:	Because 7 is more than 3.
Teacher:	Oh! I see! You always take the small number from the large number when you're subtracting.
Student:	Yeah!
Teacher:	You can't take away something you don't have, right?
Student:	Right!
Teacher:	That's correct!

Now the teacher moves to create disequilibrium in direct relation to the structures that need to be modified. This child apparently thinks she should always take the smaller number from the larger. She thinks there is no relationship between written number problems and the quantities they represent in reality. Even though she knows about real quantity, she does not apply this information to "ditto sheet" problems. Now the teacher acts ignorant and carries the logic to the absurd in an attempt to create internal conflict.

Teacher:	Now I understand why you did it that way. We didn't have enough on top. But when we solved the problem with the blocks, we got a different answer. How did that happen?
Student:	I don't know.
Teacher:	Can you just go in any direction? I must be confused. I thought you always took the bottom number from the top. But if there isn't enough on top, I guess we can't do that. Maybe we should try another problem. How about 10 minus 1? (Teacher writes problem vertically and student writes the answer, 9.) Wait a minute! One minus 0 isn't 9. Where did you get that answer?
Student:	One minus 0? The problem says *10* minus *1,* which is *9.*
Teacher:	That's right! But . . . I don't understand what you did here. One is bigger than 0, and I thought you said we always took the smaller number from the larger. Isn't that what you did before? I guess you'll have to explain this to me again.
Student:	I guess you don't *always* take the smaller number from the larger one.
Teacher:	I see. Maybe if you already know the answer, as you did in 10 − 1, you can forget about that rule, right?
Student:	I guess so.

Note in the above dialogue that the teacher deliberately presents problems that will make the student likely to violate her own rule. This begins to create conflict because the student recognizes a contrast between reality and the way she is currently thinking about the task. Exaggeration of the concept until it becomes absurd creates disequilibrium.

The teacher has not reached the point, as yet, where the student is ready to learn new information. The next steps probably should involve presenting additional problems to the student. We recommend the continued use of concrete materials at this point. Two types of problems, those that fit the student's current structures and those that do not, should be presented.

Each time, the problem should be written down, and the child's attention should be called to the written form to assure that she knows when the top number in the one's column is larger and when it is smaller. The teacher should continue to ask the student to explain and should be careful to ask questions directly relevant to the precise misunderstanding of the student. The student is enabled to actively explore the alternative ways of correcting the problem. She generates new hypotheses about an accurate way to explain what needs to be done to solve problems of this sort. If the student does not generate these hypotheses, the teacher presents suggestions and helps the student try them out.

Sometimes, a student is capable of the inductive reasoning necessary for reaching a correct conclusion. If so, the teacher can proceed directly to step six of the method. Frequently, however, the concluding dialogue at step four goes like this:

Student: I guess it isn't right to take the smallest number from the largest with those problems because then the answer is wrong. But sometimes the bottom number is bigger, so there's no way to do those problems.

Teacher: I guess you're right. Maybe you'll have to just skip those problems if your teacher gives them to you. I sure can't figure this out, can you?

Student: Nope! I'm all confused.

Teacher: The problem is, it seems like the other kids answer *all* the problems. Do you think your teacher will say it's OK for you to skip some?

Student: I'll probably get an "F".

Switch Roles

Assuming that the student now clearly recognizes the mismatch between her mental structures and the arithmetic problems she needs to solve, sufficient disequilibrium has been created to move to a new step in the teaching process. The teacher switches roles. This usually works best if it is done just as the student shows signs of understanding the procedure. The teacher may then present a new problem to make it apparent that the student can "borrow" from the 10's place. Again, the use of concrete materials will probably be helpful. As the student begins to "discover" that borrowing is possible, the dialogue continues:

Teacher: Guess what! You just took a bundle of 10 popsicle sticks from the 10's pile. Now I'm going to tell you a secret. That's *exactly* what you need to do! It's called "regrouping."

The dialogue proceeds with the teacher providing new opportunities for discovery and, simultaneously, providing verbal information about the process. The teacher has switched from the role of being ignorant and confused to the role of "teacher."

Play with the New Concept

Playing with the new concept enables the student to stabilize the structure and makes transfer likely. The teacher helps the student exercise the new structure. First, several examples that are not confusing or difficult may be presented, and the student solves the problems. The teacher praises the use of appropriate processes. Next, more difficult problems (in this case, problems that require regrouping) are presented. The teacher again switches roles and may again pretend to be confused and in need of the student's assistance. There are some important differences from step four, however. First, the teacher presents problems and works out the answers herself, sometimes incorrectly. Secondly, when she solves problems incorrectly, she does so from the point of view of the student's old, erroneous structures. That is, the teacher demonstrates and verbally expresses *exactly* what the student previously did, a means of presenting fallacies in true Columbo style. This provides a check of whether the new structure has stabilized and provides the student an opportunity to see what was wrong with her old structures. It enables the student to practice and further stabilize the new structure by explaining it again. If the student does not object to the erroneous demonstrations of the teacher, it often works for the teacher to say, "I tricked you." At this point, a brief explanation (rather than going back to step four) may be all that is needed. We sometimes mark down "I tricked you" and "You caught me" points during this process. The points may be tallied at the end but are then thrown away. Few students need any additional reward or feedback. The learning itself is usually reward enough.

A third difference between this step and step four is an increased emphasis on anticipating the student's thinking. Phrases such as "I'll bet this one is different" or "This problem doesn't follow the rule," followed by an example that might confuse the child if the structure has not stabilized are frequently presented. In a sense, the teacher deliberately tries to make the student respond incorrectly because an error tells her that more teaching is needed. Of course, the teacher actually is hoping no errors will appear.

In this step, the teacher is forcing the child to think for herself. Student questions are answered with teacher questions. The student's task is not to find out what the teacher is thinking or to wait for the teacher to provide an answer. In fact, the student does not know whether the teacher is giving correct or incorrect information. The goal throughout steps four, five, and six is to enable the student to construct a version of reality. Teaching becomes a dialogue, an active interaction between child and teacher (Bovet, 1981).

The Student Teaches

The final step in the Columbo method is begun in step six, but it is so important that we have listed it separately. The student explains the new concept to the teacher or to other students. The emphasis is on transferring the new learning to other situations and to similar problems.

Other Uses of the Columbo Method

We have applied the Columbo method to a wide variety of tasks and are convinced that it can be used with nearly any content. It appears to be an excellent means of creating the disequilibrium that is essential to learning. We find, however, that the dynamic, flexible, playful nature of the technique is sometimes difficult to communicate. The interchange between student and teacher demands much from the teacher, but also provides a much more interesting way to teach than simply telling students what to do and how to do it.

We urge teachers to try this method in a variety of settings and with different kinds of problems. The method can be used with students at all levels of the structures model. The following dialogue is a partial example of how the method might work with a student who confuses the words *when* and *then*. Although this student is expected to perform at Level III with this task, some difficulties with accurate perception of letter shapes may also be involved in the problem. We take the dialogue only to the point where disequilibrium is created. The next steps would probably include helping the child evolve a Level III rehearsal strategy for learning these two words as well as others.

Teacher:	What is this word? (shows *when*)
Student:	When.
Teacher:	Right! What is this word? (shows *then*)
Student:	When.
Teacher:	Right! This one says "when" (points to then) and this one says "when" (points to when).

Student:	Yep.
Teacher:	These two words are exactly the same, right?
Student:	Right!
Teacher:	Right, because they are spelled the same way. This one is spelled *t-h-e-n* and *this* one is spelled *w-h-e-n*. (The letters in each word are said with similar emphasis as if the teacher said exactly the same letters, even though this was not the case.)
Student:	Um. You said *t* and *w*.
Teacher:	Oh! Does that make a difference if the words are exactly the same?

Sometimes, the student will not notice the "mistake" the teacher made and it may be necessary to carry the fallacy further. The teacher may have the student trace the letters (in giant size on the chalkboard, if necessary) and may state that the letters are obviously the same because they are made the same way, so the words must be the same too.

The method tends to work even better with older students and more complex tasks. Older students are better able to understand the logic and the fallacies upon which the method, in part, depends. Also, higher level tasks tend to have more logic and more complex components to analyze. For example, suppose a junior high student writes disorganized paragraphs. An analysis of the student's structures indicates that he thinks paragraphs are simply a collection of sentences grouped together with the first line indented. The teacher decides on the goal of teaching him that paragraphs are a set of related sentences with a topic sentence, several sentences that support or explain the topic sentence, and a summarizing sentence at the end. The teacher imagines the steps that the student will need to go through to reach the final goal. Then the teacher analyzes several alternative strategies that may be useful to the student. The teacher also thinks of alternative ways of carrying out the steps in the Columbo method. Again, we will present only part of the dialogue from step four. We assume the student has just written a paragraph at the request of the teacher.

Teacher:	I see you wrote five sentences in your paragraph. That's good. Can you tell me what the paragraph is about?
Student:	Well, it's about riding motorcycles and playing baseball and learning to roller-skate and other stuff.
Teacher:	Sounds interesting. You must like sports. But tell me, what's the main idea of the paragraph?
Student:	Main idea?
Teacher:	Yes.
Student:	It doesn't really have one.
Teacher:	Hmm. Oh, I get it. It's just a bunch of ideas put together in a paragraph, right? Hmm. How can you tell it's a paragraph then?

Student:	Well, you told me to write a paragraph, so I did.
Teacher:	Oh, I see. It's a paragraph because that's what I said it was supposed to be. Is there any way to tell whether a bunch of words in a group is a paragraph or not?
Student:	The words have to be in sentences, and the first line is set in like this. (Points to his paragraph.)
Teacher:	OK, so you must have written a paragraph because you have words in sentences and you indented. But how many *sentences* must there be before they make up a paragraph?
Student:	I don't know. Two, I guess.
Teacher:	Hmm. I don't get it. A paragraph has only two sentences. You have five sentences here. I guess this is *not* a paragraph.
Student:	No. This is a paragraph too. Some paragraphs have more than two sentences.
Teacher:	I see. Some paragraphs might have lots of sentences. Could they have just one sentence? Never mind. Let's forget that. (The teacher realizes this is the wrong question.) Anyway, it doesn't matter what the sentences say, as long as they are sentences and the first line is indented, right?
Student:	Yeah.
Teacher:	So I could be writing this story about hunting elephants and right in the middle of the paragraph I could say something about tiddledy-winks, is that it?
Student:	I don't know. I guess so. But it would have to make sense in the story.
Teacher:	Oh, now I've got it! If it makes sense in the story, it doesn't matter if it makes sense in the paragraph. Have I got it right now?
Student:	I don't know. It doesn't seem like you could write a story about hunting elephants with tiddledywinks.
Teacher:	You're probably right, but I wonder if we can put anything we want to in a paragraph. It seems that if we have to be careful about what we put in a story, we may need to be careful about what we put in a paragraph too. What do you think?
Student:	I don't know. Maybe so.
Teacher:	How about if we look at some of the paragraphs in this book and find out how they do it?

From here, the teacher would read a paragraph with the student and then suggest that obviously the sentences in the paragraph have no relationship to one another. The student is likely to object and is well on the way to recognizing that his paragraph structure does not match the example. The lesson continues with the remaining steps of the method until a strategy for constructing good paragraphs is developed, explained by the student, and used.

Objections to the Columbo Method

When we teach prospective teachers about the Columbo method, three common objections are frequently raised. They suggest that the method takes a lot of time, that they will not be able to do it effectively because it takes a special type of personality to teach that way, and that the method will upset the students.

The method does take time. The teacher needs to monitor the process, of course, to be sure that time is not wasted and that the method is not used to excess. But if the choice is between effective teaching and simply presenting a large amount of content which students fail to learn, the time is obviously worth taking. If appropriate disequilibrium is generated and the students really learn a concept, it is not necessary to "teach" it again. If the students do not really learn, it will become necessary to provide additional assistance every time the concept needs to be applied. The end result may be that more time is used, and the students still may not have learned the concept.

We find that the method does not depend on a certain personality type, although it does demand a high degree of awareness and fairly intense effort on the part of the teacher. The effort should not be a problem since teachers are accustomed to hard work. The necessary awareness for efficient use of the method comes from practice with it. We suggest trying the method with an eye toward refining your skills as you go along. Sometimes it helps to deliberately practice key phrases like those we included in the dialogues (e.g., "Right!" "Oh, I see!" "I get it now!" "Sounds interesting."). The strategies in this method do not require an aggressive or outgoing personality, just an understanding of the essential components of learning and a sensitivity to the structures of students.

For the most part, the method does not bother students. In fact, they often enjoy it immensely, perhaps because it has gamelike aspects. Many students, especially at the secondary level, become so absorbed in their own thinking and learning that they enjoy it for that reason alone. Humans seem to like to think, once they get used to the idea. Occasionally, students do appear to become frustrated or to object that the teacher is playing dumb. As we explained before, creating disequilibrium is not the same as creating frustration. Disequilibrium is an internal mismatch. If the method is causing extreme frustration, it is either being used improperly or is being carried too far. The teacher needs to be aware of when it is time to switch roles.

At the same time, the students must be urged to think for themselves. Phrases such as "I'm sorry, I could do it for you, but I already know how to do it so neither of us would gain very much" sometimes help. Incidentally, going with the resistance and praising creative solutions, techniques that are built into the method, often help too. When accused of playing games by the student, we usually admit to doing so, and we may explain why. Another technique is to say, in a pleasant but facetious way, ''Would I do that?'' If the method is used consistently in the classroom, it soon becomes an unspoken game. The students expect you to play it, and they also begin to expect to think for themselves.

One final note about this activating strategy is necessary. The emphasis is always on reconstructing knowledge in a strategy-oriented way. Perhaps the major strategy students learn is to think for themselves. This goal is obviously implied in the Columbo method, and it can be explicitly stated by the teacher to the students. The examples we used in this section show an emphasis on academic skills, which is obviously the general arena in which teachers of the learning disabled work. As we explained earlier, however, the teacher in this area should focus on the learning, use, and transfer of strategies and not on academic content for its own sake. The examples used were kept somewhat simpler than most actual uses of the method in order to avoid excessive length and complicated explanations.

Cueing Strategies

We have identified two types of cueing strategies that are often helpful as guides for learning disabled persons. One type is designated perceptual cueing, the other, language cueing. Both are designed to enable students to use learning strategies effectively at all five response levels. The basic features of these general strategies are described and examples presented in the following sections.

Perceptual Cueing Strategies

For the most part, perceptual cueing systems involve presenting visual cues to help remind students to use a strategy or the steps in a strategy. This approach is based on the notion that for some learning disabled individuals visual cues may help to call attention to or sustain attention on important stimuli. Sykes, Douglas, and Morgenstern (1973) found that hyperactive children attended more efficiently to visual than auditory stimuli. However, this effect may be present only with younger children (Swanson, 1980). These authors were concerned with sustaining attention rather than cueing students to use strategies. It may be possible, however, to identify the kind of stimuli that students attend to best and then develop cueing systems that use these stimuli. For example, Meichenbaum (1977) reports that cue cards can be used as a means of providing students a signal to ask questions.

Cueing systems can be used as a way to teach students to regulate their own functioning instead of depending on the teacher. Many forms of cueing strategies are commonly used by teachers. For example, teachers frequently ask students to chart their performance. If the chart is placed in view of students, it may serve as a cue to begin work or even to approach the work in a particular way such as by not getting out of their desk seats. Simple perceptual cueing systems such as a red dot in the upper left corner to show on which side of the paper writing should begin are also common. We have found that more elaborate visual cues may help some students follow the steps in a strategy. The same cues may remind them to use a strategy rather than a random approach. Specifically, if students have learned to use a four-step strategy to enable them to comprehend what they read, the steps can be designated by visual symbols (e.g., a star for the first step, a square for the second, etc.). These symbols can be placed in sequence at the top of a page or on a desk. At first, the steps may need to be written next to them. Later, the symbols may be used alone. Eventually, students may internalize them so that self-regulation no longer requires an external cue. At this point, the cues are dropped, although students may continue to need occasional reminders to use the system.

If, as Torgesen (1977) suggests, some learning disabled students are inactive learners, perceptual cueing strategies may help to activate strategy selection. Especially for younger children who may not be able to use the language cueing strategies described in the next section, teachers may wish to provide perceptual cues. The obvious goal is to enable the students to internalize the process so that strategies are selected when needed.

Flexible use of strategies (that is, using first one strategy, then another, and so on) presents a problem for some individuals. Again, perceptual cues may provide a guide. In reading, for example, a set of visual symbols may be placed at the top of a page to cue the student to use different systems (such as determining the word from context, sounding it out, associating it with other words with similar spelling, etc.) for reading an unknown word. The student would need to have learned how to use these strategies previously, of course.

Perceptual cues other than visual cues may be helpful for some students. A sound or a touch may also serve to remind students to use appropriate strategies.

Language Cueing Strategies

Once language has been learned, it appears to play an important part in controlling internal mental events. Luria (1969) suggests that language may be regarded as a "second signal system" (the first signal system consists of perceptual signals). Language begins to be used to mediate incoming stimuli and the responses of the individual. It "establishes rules for generalizing any new bit of information" (Miller & Rohr, 1980, p. 319).

Professionals in learning disabilities have recently begun to place increasing emphasis on the active internal processes that organize and regulate behavior. Hresko and Reid (1981) review these "cognitive approaches," as they call them, and suggest that they "promise to lead to instructional strategies that are inherently child-centered and at the same time carefully structured" (p. 241). The four approaches Hresko and Reid suggest may be useful are termed information processing, metacognition, genetic epistemology, and cognitive behavior modification. Each of these approaches, to a greater or lesser degree, emphasizes the active involvement of the learner in controlling cognition and the use of language as one means of controlling or activating learning strategies. Although research on the effectiveness of these approaches is in early stages, we suggest that teachers should attempt to use language to guide perception (Miller & Rohr, 1980; Sabatino, 1976), to guide behavior (Bornstein and Quevillon, 1979; Meichenbaum, 1977) and to guide other aspects of cognition (Abikoff, 1979; Meichenbaum, 1977; Weithorn & Kagen, 1979).

In our view, the use of language as a cueing strategy should be consciously applied to teaching learning disabled persons. As with perceptual cueing strategies, the goal is to activate the selection, flexible use, and transfer of learning and problem-solving strategies. Internal, self-regulated cognition and behavior is an even more basic goal.

The techniques teachers use to teach these strategies should be based on the concept that learners actively construct knowledge. Therefore, direct participation of students in the process of developing and using language cueing strategies is important. Approaches in which language cueing strategies are imposed on the learner, as cognitive behavior modification tends to do, are likely to result in less stable and transferable learning. Other approaches that involve the learner in generating strategies that are useful specifically for them are more desirable. Of course the student is not left alone to devise a strategy. The teacher must be there to create disequilibrium and to guide the student.

Language cueing strategies actually provide more than cues. They can encompass the entire thinking and problem-solving process. That is, they not only tell the student what to do next, they tell how to do it. This is especially true with tasks that require problem solving at Level IV, although younger children are also capable of using them in some cases. More guidance may be needed with younger children, and perceptual cueing strategies may need to be used concurrently.

Both the perceptual and the language cueing strategies that students develop may not transfer to other situations unless special efforts in this direction are made by the teacher. The student may learn a strategy for using spelling rules to spell numerous words correctly, develop a language cueing strategy for activating the strategy, and still fail to use it on the next spelling test. Sometimes teachers encourage this by urging students to perform more rapidly than the strategy permits. Sometimes teachers themselves abandon the strategy by switching the student back to rote rehearsal and automatic spelling for a final test or by praising a student more for appropriate products than for using the strategy. Teachers should emphasize the use of the strategy at every appropriate opportunity. Students can be directly told that they are expected to use the strategy and that the teacher will check frequently to see that this is happening. We may even go so far as to follow students to other settings, where we observe whether the strategies are being used. Teachers can present a variety of problems that require use of the strategies. The Columbo method can be used to test whether the new strategy is stable and functional and whether the student can explain and teach the strategy. Each of these techniques may help the student transfer and use the strategy more appropriately.

The essence of language cueing strategies, then, is to enable students to think, to solve problems, and to control their behavior through self-regulated internal language. Language is used to guide perception, behavior, and cognition. Although these three areas are closely related, we will present an example of a language cueing strategy that emphasizes guiding perception, then one for controlling behavior, and, finally, a strategy that focuses on higher level cognition. Notice that these are only examples and not necessarily techniques that we recommend. Actual cueing strategies would evolve out of active dialogue between a teacher and a student.

Language may be used to guide perception by simple means such as labeling the movements that need to be made to write a particular letter of the alphabet. In the following example, however, we make somewhat more complicated uses of the language system to accurately identify visual similarities in words. The goal of the teacher is to enable the student to accurately recognize, read, and spell words that fit a particular pattern. Note that the goal indicates that the student will be expected to learn to respond at Level III, even though we are illustrating a technique for guiding perception (the Level II process) through language.

Two more general goals are also involved—using the language cueing strategy with other word patterns and learning to use a self-regulated, language-mediated strategy whenever it is needed. The latter two goals are extremely important but are not readily apparent as we explain the example.

The specific content the teacher uses for the lesson is a "word family" made up of the following words: mat, cat, bat, rat, fat, and sat. The steps in the strategy are carried out on a large piece of paper which covers a table. We present the steps in the method beginning at the point where appropriate disequilibrium has been created. We also assume that the student has been involved in the creation of the strategy. The steps in the teaching/learning process might be:

1. The teacher writes the six words from the "at" family on the paper, reads the words, and states that these are the words the student will learn in the lesson. The teacher asks the student to repeat each word after her as she reads them again.
2. The teacher says that the words are all similar in an important way and asks the student to examine them carefully, listen as she reads them again, and state all the possible ways that the words are alike.
3. The student responds that the words rhyme and that the last two letters of the words are the same. If the student is not able to identify these similarities, the teacher asks questions that guide the student to do so or directly states that these are the similarities.

4. The teacher tells the student that these words are all members of the "at" family because they all end with the letters *a* and *t*. She then goes on to a variety of "tests" of the concept (see steps six and seven of the Columbo method) to be sure that the student understands and can use it. She particularly encourages the recognition of the words as members of the "at" family each time they are seen or need to be spelled. The concept that many other word families exist and will be learned later should probably be presented during this part of the lesson.

The anticipated outcome of this teaching/learning process is that the student will now perceive this set of words in a new way—as members of a family—and that this will increase word recognition and spelling ability. This simple example of using language to guide perception uses techniques that are already familiar to most teachers. By using a familiar example, we want to show teachers that such techniques have a direct effect on perception and on internal mental processes. We also want to emphasize that such techniques should be used more consciously and deliberately by teachers.

In our second example, we illustrate how language can be used to directly guide behavior. We describe a complex situation although much simpler uses are possible. We all use language to guide behavior when we count to 10 before we respond, tell ourselves to relax, or "talk to ourselves" about which way to turn a bolt when we cannot see it. In the example we use here, a teacher is responsible for a small group of adolescents who are frequently in trouble. When conflicts arise, these students tend to use their fists, to run away, to burst into tears, or to respond physically in some other way. The steps the teacher follows to help the students learn better ways of responding are:

1. The teacher writes a short vignette of a typical conflict situation between a student and a teacher. The students participate as actors in a video tape of the scene.
2. The students view the tape with the teacher.
3. The teacher guides a discussion about the scene. Alternative ways of responding *verbally* instead of physically to the conflict are solicited from the students. The teacher helps the students develop these alternatives, and the discussion centers around using them in similar situations. Probable consequences of the verbal responses are compared to those likely to result from physical responses.
4. Students participate in writing, taping, and discussing additional scenes.

A typical scene written by the teacher might involve a conflict between a student and a teacher in which the student is accused of not completing an assignment correctly. The student responds by tearing up the assignment and running from the room. Notice that the emphasis in using this technique is not on talking about problems, but on using language to guide the responses of the students. Language is used, in fact, in two ways: (1) to guide the students toward using language mediation to monitor and control their behavior; and (2) as a response system that replaces physical responses.

In step three, the students learn to think through the problem situation in words and to internalize a set of verbal statements (e.g., "How can I respond in words?," or "Is there a way I can answer that will help work this problem out?" or even "Careful, now. Don't get angry and lose control.") that they should say to themselves in similar situations. Such statements can provide direct control over behavior through language. The students also learn about some of the specific verbal responses they can make in problem situations, thus replacing physical responses with verbal responses.

The fourth step in the above technique also provides an opportunity for the teacher to integrate this task with many other kinds of learning. Strategies for writing stories, for reading scripts, for operating video equipment, and for participating in discussion groups can all be a part of the system. As before, the teacher encourages use of these strategies in all situations to which they can be transferred.

Language can also be used to guide cognition in the sense of solving the problems a student may encounter with academic subjects or other situations. This use is very similar to that of cognitive behavior modification (Meichenbaum, 1977) except that we urge much more direct interaction with students in developing the strategies instead of imposing strategies designed by the teacher.

To illustrate how language can be used to guide cognition in solving problems, we use an example of solving arithmetic story problems. Our hypothetical student is in junior high school and has a Level III approach to solving story problems. Specifically, he very mechanically selects what he presumes are the important numbers and words in a story problem and performs the arithmetical operations that he believes are appropriate. For illustration purposes, let us examine how he solves the following story problem.

Mrs. Jones planned a three-day trip to visit her cousin in Chicago, which was 1,340 miles from her home. The first day she travelled 372 miles. The second day she travelled 481 miles. How many miles did she travel on the third day if she reached Chicago?

The student adds the numbers 1,340, 372, and 481 and writes the correct sum, 2,193. When asked what that number means, he replies, "It means miles." Further inquiries indicate that he thinks this is the total number of miles that the woman travelled on her trip. The teacher probes even more and discovers that this student thinks he can solve story problems by identifying key words specifying the operation needed (in this case, *"How many* miles did she travel . . . ?''") and then selecting the numbers that are used in the operation. In the story problem, all three numbers the student added were followed by the term *miles*. Therefore, all were used in the addition. The student's strategy is not totally inappropriate but is used in a mechanical way instead of in the context of the total problem. Let us assume that the student approaches most story problems with this strategy.

The steps the teacher might use to help this student use language as a guide for a problem-solving strategy are presented below. The steps begin at the point where the teacher has determined the strategies the student currently uses and has decided upon what the student should learn—a language-guided, logical strategy for solving story problems.

1. The teacher creates disequilibrium by using a set of probing questions that enable the student to realize his or her solution and strategy are inadequate. (E.g., How many miles was Chicago from her home? How could she travel more miles than the total distance? Why did you add 1,340 to the other mileages?)
2. The teacher helps the student design a four- or five-step problem-solving strategy that works with this problem. The technique involves components of telling the student some steps (e.g., Maybe our first step should be deciding what the problem is really asking.) and eliciting others from him or her (e.g., What are the operations this problem is asking for? Should I always decide which operations are needed in story problems? Should this decision be one of the steps in our strategy? How would you write the rule for the decision about operations so we can use it in our strategy?).
3. The problem-solving strategy is tried out in varying contexts with many problems, modified as necessary, and internalized for transfer to other situations.

We have illustrated only three of many possible applications of language cueing strategies. The emphasis in every case is on the deliberate, conscious use of language to guide perception, behavior, and cognition. Teachers are limited in employing similar strategies only by their own creativity and the language abilities of the students they teach.

SPECIFIC STRATEGIES FOR EACH LEVEL

Most strategies for learning include important components related to more than one level even though they may be focused primarily on a particular level. As the response goals are set on higher and higher levels, the processing necessary at earlier levels must either already be present or be incorporated into the instruction given. That these concepts are assumed may not be clear in the examples we present in this section because our emphasis is on strategies as they are used at each level.

For each level of the structures model, a description of some strategies that may be important is presented, followed by a detailed example. In the examples, we use the principles from Chapter 7 to guide in the selection of teacher and student strategies. Exhaustive lists of strategies at each level are not presented since the number of possibilities is too great. Each example includes both the teaching strategy for presentation and the student strategy that is learned.

Three notes of caution about the specific examples for each level are important. First, they are not more significant than other strategies at that level. Rather, they are typical strategies that may be useful for most students whether they are individuals learning the strategies at an age-appropriate time or persons with severe learning disabilities learning them at a later age. Second, the specifics we present will need some changes when used with particular students. The use of strategies always depends on the mental structures the students bring to the teaching/learning situation. Third, we have not included some preliminary steps in the teaching process. For example, the important steps that are needed to create disequilibrium are not always described.

Level I Strategies

At Level I, students learn sustained, goal-directed exploratory strategies. Students increase their awareness of significant stimuli through the attention process. To function appropriately at this level, the individual must learn to scan, focus upon, sustain in focus, and shift from focus (when the stimuli are no longer needed) the stimuli that are significant. Strategies at this level are very simple and do not involve logical analysis or highly conscious internal monitoring and control. Rather, they emphasize ways of exploring the environment, attending to important stimuli, and disregarding the unimportant. Perhaps the most comprehensive strategies an infant learns at Level I are that "it pays (in terms of new learning) to explore and it pays to attend" in relation to significant objects, events, and people in the environment. The infant learns to make eye contact with others, to respond to others' voices, to react differently to various noises and tones, to move about the environment (getting into everything), to seek information through the senses by touching, tasting, smelling, looking, and listening, to respond differently to some shapes than to others, to pursue moving objects with the eyes, and so on. From the hundreds of strategies for learning and responding that are built up over the first 18 months of life, we have chosen a strategy for learning to pursue moving objects with the eyes. The specific steps for teaching such a strategy are:

1. The teacher selects several attractive objects of varied colors, sizes, and shapes. Objects may include a ball, a block, a piece of paper, toys, food items, etc. Objects are selected based on their probable or known interest to the students.
2. Objects are picked up one at a time and held close to the students' eyes. When the eyes appear to fixate on the object, it is slowly moved from side to side, up and down, or in other patterns.
3. When the first object is fixated upon and followed, the object, verbal praise, a hug, or some other reward may be given to the students. Then the other objects are used one at a time in the same way. Students learn the strategy of following objects with their eyes. In other terms, the students learn to think that information and desirable consequences may be gained from pursuing objects with their eyes.
4. The objects are placed, one at a time, in students' hands. The teacher grasps the hand and moves it slowly as the student follows it with his or her eyes. Again, appropriate rewards are presented. The students learn to think that information and desirable consequences may be gained by following a moving object with their eyes when the object is in their hands.

The simple nature of the strategy learned through these techniques is apparent. Level I strategies are not complex although they may be difficult to measure. In the example, whether the student learned the strategy would be determined by observing to see if the student used the visual pursuit strategy frequently in varied situations. If the teacher was working with a severely disabled student, for example an autistic child, hundreds of repetitions might be necessary before the strategy is efficiently used.

Some important teacher actions that may be necessary are not specified in the above steps. For example, what should the teacher do if the student is not making the initial response, fixating on the object? The teacher may need to hold and move the student's head or may need to reward the student for responses that approximate the desired one. At each step, the teacher must provide the assistance the student needs so that an appropriate level of response results. No one can force a student to fixate on and follow a moving target. The desire to do so must come from inside the individual, and the strategy is learned through active interaction between student and teacher. At the same time, the teacher can set up the teaching/learning situation to foster and encourage the learning of strategies.

Level II Strategies

At Level II, students learn attribution strategies that enable them to form inner language concepts. The major process at the differentiation level is the process of perception, through which students learn to discriminate stimuli, coordinate stimuli from more than one sensory system, and sequence stimuli correctly. The basic components of this kind of processing are learned between one and four years of age.

Strategies at this level are still relatively simple, indicating a beginning level of concept formation, which does not depend on a language system. Of course, children are usually learning language during this age, and most teaching includes the presentation of language labels and simple language explanations. We designate Level II as a separate level because learning disabled persons sometimes have particular difficulties learning the strategies needed at this level. These strategies appear logically to be separate from the labeling strategies at Level III.

At Level II students learn strategies for perceiving the differences between sounds (e.g., "slowing down" the rate at which a word is spoken), for locating the position and direction of sounds, for recognizing and producing fine and gross motor movements, and for distinguishing the essential features of visual objects, events, drawings, pictures, and symbols. Strategies for classifying and categorizing objects and events are acquired and used. Generalizations about perceptual similarities and differences are formed and become the basis for strategies and structures that enable the student to respond efficiently at Level II. The "logic" of this level is very simple and perceptually based. Events that occur may be interpreted in terms of what appears to happen, not on the basis of adult logic.

The strategy we describe to illustrate a typical structure a student may acquire at this level involves discriminating and producing correct phonemes. The strategy is intended to enable the students to develop an approach to learning new sounds and pronouncing those sounds correctly. Potential steps in the teaching/learning process are:

1. The teacher selects sounds with which the students have difficulty. The students are unable to distinguish between these sounds or are unable to pronounce them correctly, or both. One sound is selected because it has distinctive features. This sound is pronounced by the teacher, and the students are encouraged to imitate it. If the sound is not reproduced, the teacher moves to step two.
2. Distinctive features of the sound are emphasized by the teacher. This may involve one or more of the following substeps:

   - The students discover the distinctive features through the teacher's suggestions or questions. For part of a sound, for example, the teacher may ask, "Where is your tongue when you make that part of the sound?" To help the students notice that a sound is voiced, the teacher may have the students touch their throats and feel the vibrations.

- The teacher directly tells about or demonstrates a distinctive feature. For example, the teacher may say, "Put your lips like this," as the lip position is demonstrated.

- The teacher may physically assist the students. For example, the teacher may press their lips together with two fingers for the sound /m/.

In this step, the students learn that each sound has distinctive features that can be used to distinguish the sound from others. They begin to think that new sounds can be acquired by noting how the articulators are placed and how the air moved in the oral and nasal cavities. After the distinctive features of the sound are known and practiced, the teacher encourages use of the sound as part of a word. The production at this point is usually imitative, and many opportunities to practice are given.

3. Additional sounds are presented following steps one and two. The student is not asked to distinguish the sounds from one another, but to produce each sound in words. Sounds that are very similar are not presented close together.

4. The teacher presents tasks in which the students are required to distinguish between sounds, beginning with sounds that are dissimilar and gradually presenting more similar sounds. The students learn that similar sounds can be distinguished from one another through analysis of the distinctive features that make them slightly different from one another. The substeps from step two may be used again to help in the development of strategies for noting and using distinctive features.

5. The teacher helps the students develop a classification strategy for similar sounds on the basis of their distinctive features. Classification may rely on voicing and the place and type of articulation. Labels for these classifications are used if possible, thus providing for simple Level III responding. The students begin to understand that the sounds of language have similarities and differences that can be learned and used in production.

This process might be called a "distinctive features strategy" for learning and producing sounds. The strategy should always emphasize using the sounds in the context of larger language units. Learning to discriminate sounds at Level II is a matter of learning the basic strategies needed to acquire and produce language. Pronouncing isolated phonemes is not important in itself.

With many students, the strategy may not be carried through all of the steps. In addition, strategies such as this would not be used with students who are not at an age level where the production of accurate sounds is expected. This strategy is more applicable to older students who are beyond the age where the sounds they have trouble with are usually learned.

Level III Strategies

Level III, the labeling level, is especially important between the ages of two and eight. Students learn mechanical strategies involving the efficient use of the memory process. To function appropriately at this level, students need strategies for temporarily storing and rehearsing information. Strategies such as rote repetition are frequently used, making it obvious that the students are deliberately using strategies to acquire information. As the students learn more language, it is used to regulate both behavior and the components of the learning process.

Some of the major strategies students learn at this level include strategies for acquiring labels for objects and events, for learning to count, for reading words, for remembering arithmetic combinations, for learning the alphabet, poems, stories, and other sequences, and for studying and learning word meanings. Perhaps the most basic strategy learned at this level is that repetition of stimuli results in retention.

At the same time, however, students are learning to use their own classification systems to reorganize the information they wish to learn. Incoming stimuli may be changed before they are rehearsed. In fact, as the stimuli are modified, they become more meaningful, and associations are built up. As a person develops more associations rote rehearsal is less necessary. Students learn that words have many similarities in spelling, for example, and they may classify certain words in a group rather than rehearsing each word separately. The system becomes more and more efficient as it expands and develops. The students no longer need to rehearse a set of stimuli hundreds of times the way they may have in learning the alphabet. A few repetitions and a network of meanings serve the same purpose. The thinking of individuals at this level is still not the logical thinking of Level IV, however. Meanings are still more concrete and not as advanced as at the later level.

To illustrate a typical learning strategy at Level III, an example is taken from the area of spelling. The teaching/learning process might go as follows:

1. The teacher selects several sets of words with varying characteristics, such as a "word family" set, a nonphonetic set, a phonetic set, or a set that fits easily with mnemonic devices (e.g., words like *geography*, which can be remembered by using the first letters of each word in the sentence "*G*eorge *E*dward's *o*ld *g*randfather *r*ode *a* *p*ig *h*ome *y*esterday"). The sets are presented separately, and the teacher asks questions or makes suggestions regarding: (1) similarities and differences between the words in the set; and (2) strategies that might be used to learn the set. The students learn that words follow different spelling patterns and that different strategies can be used to learn how to spell.
2. The sets of words are compared with one another, with an emphasis on how the strategies developed in step one might fit with one set compared to how

they fit with the others, based on the spelling patterns in each set. The teacher leads this discussion, again using questions and suggesting alternatives. The students learn that different strategies may fit better with some spelling patterns than others.

3. With the teacher's assistance, students match rehearsal techniques with word sets and apply the strategies to learning those sets. For example, word families may be remembered by rote memorization of the identical part of the words (e.g., -ight) and phonetic analysis of the parts that are different. The phonetic set may be learned by repeating the words syllable by syllable, analyzing the sounds, and writing down the letter for each sound. The nonphonetic set may be learned through rote repetition—writing the words 20 times as the letter names or sounds are repeated. The students are tested for retention of the words. They learn which strategies work effectively with different spelling patterns.

4. The teacher leads a discussion of the effectiveness of the rehearsal techniques. Techniques are modified, tried out, and reevaluated, as necessary. Students learn more about which strategies work for them, how the strategies can be evaluated, and how to carry out the evaluation.

5. The teacher leads a discussion about how and when to transfer the strategies that students have found effective and sets up a system for moving from teacher monitoring (of whether students are using the strategies) to student self-monitoring.

The approach outlined here emphasizes the use of active student involvement in selecting rehearsal strategies. The techniques use the students' current structures at as high a level as possible, but mechanical rehearsal strategies are used instead of rule-based strategies because the teaching is at Level III. Implied in the above steps is the concept that the teacher has already carried out a thorough analysis of English spelling patterns and rehearsal techniques for learning them. This knowledge is essential for the questioning technique (and the direct suggestions made by the teacher) that is used at every step.

Level IV Strategies

At the understanding level students concentrate on learning logical strategies that permit the application of concepts and rules. From the age of nine through adulthood these strategies become increasingly important. The cognition process used at this level involves recognizing the presence of meanings, identifying specific meanings, associating those meanings with others, and forming inferences related to meanings. Students learn to function in a logical fashion through the use of strategies for comprehending material that is read; for analyzing word parts, whole words, sentence structure, and paragraph structure; for understanding the spoken communication of others; for solving complex mathematical problems; for interacting with others socially; for producing meaningful verbal and written language; for critically evaluating varying interpretations and concepts; and so on.

Learning disabled persons should not be expected to know and use the strategies at this level unassisted. Simply providing them with easy to difficult tasks with the hope that they will somehow begin to use logical strategies is often ineffective. Specific strategies must be developed and applied through interaction with the teacher. Students must learn that strategies are available for recognizing, identifying, associating, and inferring meanings. Once developed, these strategies require deliberate application and transfer. Too frequently, teachers expect learning disabled students to know how to take lecture notes, to understand multiple meanings for words, to know how to conduct a science experiment, or to use strategies for answering a set of questions related to a social studies reading assignment. Students at this level have the logical thinking abilities to do these tasks, but this does not mean they will be used. When students fail to complete such tasks, the tendency to simplify the task must be avoided. Instead, strategies that match the logical thinking abilities must be developed.

Teachers must recognize that problems with reading comprehension, for example, are not really problems with reading. The problem is with *language* comprehension. Understanding language requires knowledge of words, syntax, paragraphs, and larger language units. Each of these language components has structure and organization. Strategies for understanding that structure can and should be developed and used at Level IV.

Our illustrative strategy at Level IV involves taking meaningful notes from a lecture. The teacher and students follow these steps:

1. The teacher tells the students the goals of the lessons and the steps that will be used to enable them to take better notes.
2. The teacher presents a 15-minute lecture on a suitably complex topic as the students take notes.
3. The teacher uses the Columbo method to analyze the students' structures, create disequilibrium, help them evaluate their note-taking abilities, and develop a strategy for taking notes effectively. The following questions may be useful in evolving a strategy:
   a. Do teachers organize their lectures? What kinds of organization do they use?
   b. Is everything a teacher says during a lecture equally important? How can you tell if something is important or unimportant?
   c. Should everything the teacher writes on the chalkboard be copied? Should what is said be written down word for word?
   d. How can spoken information be reorganized so it can be written down in a way that is meaningful and contains the essential information?

    e. What are some specific strategies we can use to take good notes?

    f. What can we do if we are not good spellers or if we write very slowly?

During the questioning process, the teacher suggests alternatives as necessary. The students learn about the difficulties they now have with taking notes. More importantly, they begin to think that alternative strategies for note taking are available. They think that these strategies can provide a meaningful organization for taking notes.

4. Students are guided to the selection and use of one or more note-taking strategies. Strategies that the students developed in step three are used. They may include tape recording of lectures for later review, comparing notes with other students after class, representing the major ideas in the lecture through drawings instead of words, identifying and writing down only the key words or ideas and filling in the rest later, asking the teacher to specifically identify what should be in their notes by writing these ideas on the chalkboard or placing an asterisk next to them, and so on. The teacher presents another 15-minute lecture with which students try out the strategy each has selected.

5. The teacher helps the students evaluate the effectiveness of the strategy. Earlier steps of the process are repeated as necessary to modify the strategy and try out the modifications. The students develop structures that enable them to understand and use specific note-taking strategies that work for them individually. Some students may learn in this step that they are unable to use certain strategies. For example, a student may not be able to pick out what is important in a lecture. In some cases, the teacher may need to switch strategies to an emphasis on a strategy for understanding language structures so important ideas can be identified.

6. The teacher helps the students develop specific strategies for activating the note-taking strategies when they are needed. Perceptual or language cueing strategies may be developed, again through interaction between the teacher and the students. The emphasis is explicitly on the direct use and transfer of the learned strategies in a self-regulating fashion. The students learn to think that they can control and regulate the thought processes necessary for note taking and they learn specific strategies for doing so.

Notice how each of the above steps attempts to actively involve the students. At the same time, students are not expected to accomplish the task without understanding how to organize their thinking related to the task.

Level V Strategies

Integration strategies are learned at Level V, the habit level. Beginning at age 11 and throughout adulthood, individuals learn to respond appropriately and relatively effortlessly with many highly meaningful tasks. The internal mental process most closely associated with this level is encoding, which involves recalling, organizing, and monitoring meaningful responses for the purposes of communication and thinking. Integration strategies include ways of automatically comprehending the meaningful communications of others; speaking fluently; writing meaningful thoughts at appropriate speeds; performing complex motor acts such as driving a car, operating a computer, and playing a piano; and interacting with ease and grace in social situations.

Many of the acts we carry out at Level V are closely related to Level IV responses. For example, in writing a short story, an author may automatically sequence the events appropriately, use correct syntax effortlessly, write words without needing to carefully analyze their meanings, and so on, all of which indicate Level V responding. At the same time, many aspects of plot and characters, sequence and timing, and even word meanings and usage may be thought about at Level IV.

Teaching at Level V is aimed at enabling students to "put it all together." To illustrate the teaching/learning process at this level, we use an example of interviewing for a job. The steps begin after the students have completed a Level IV analysis of the components of job interviews. Specific strategies for interviewing effectively have been learned. The task at Level V is to enable students to use these strategies effortlessly. The steps in this task are:

1. The students are informed about the goals of the learning process and the steps that will be used to make job interviewing an integrated skill.
2. The students and teacher design a setting similar to a job interview situation. The physical surroundings may be made to resemble an office, for example. Specific components of the situation, such as the type of job, the personality characteristics of the prospective employer and employee, the nature of the working conditions, the previous training of the prospective employee, and so on are determined through discussion and planning by the teacher and students. A script for the employer and employee may be written if desired. Students recognize that preparation for interviews is possible and necessary, and they begin to think that specific strategies for making an interview go smoothly are available.
3. The students role-play the actual interview developed in step two. Other students observe and record any difficulties that occur during the interview and note the aspects of the interview that appear to be appropriate and helpful.
4. The teacher guides the students in a discussion of the interview. The positive aspects of the interview are analyzed to determine why they were successful. The ineffective responses of the prospective employee are discussed in detail, and strategies for improving them are proposed. The emphasis in this

step is on appropriate self-monitoring and developing new strategies as needed. Much of the teaching moves to Level IV as these strategies are designed. In some cases, teaching may even move briefly to earlier levels. For example, if a student uses an incorrect word, word meanings (Level III) may be explored. If a student mispronounces a word, correct pronunciation (Level II) may be developed. The students are learning to monitor their responses at the same time they are learning precisely how to correct errors.

5. Additional interviews are role-played and analyzed using steps two through four. Emphasis is placed on monitoring as responses are formulated, as they are executed, and after they have been produced (Deshler, Ferrell, & Kass, 1978). The students develop strategies for responding automatically in job interview situations. They learn to monitor their own responses and to use the strategies in appropriate ways.

6. The teacher sets up simulated interviews with actual prospective employers. The students prepare for the interviews by discussing what to expect and how to accomplish their goals in the interviews by using the strategies they have developed. Students participate in the mock interview, performance is analyzed, and the previous steps are repeated as needed. The students develop job interview strategies to the habit level.

CONCLUSION

The strategies we have described are not necessarily useful only for learning disabled persons. In fact, much of what we suggest is appropriate for all learners. Learning is always an active process of constructing internal mental structures. Learning depends on the creation of disequilibrium for every learner. The mental structures of the learner are always important related to the teaching/learning process. But teaching the learning disabled individual is also special. Learning disabled persons have unique mental structures and unique ways of processing information that make it necessary to analyze how they think and learn. They especially need to learn how to deliberately and efficiently use learning strategies. Each strategy a teacher uses must be consciously aimed toward a particular level of response. Teaching must incorporate basic theoretical principles to be effective. Teaching strategies must be frequently modified each time learning has occurred. Teaching should become a dialogue between teacher and student. Teaching must be deliberately and clearly based on a theory of the psychology of the learning disabled.

In our view, the psychology of learning disabilities requires the study of the unique mental structures of this group of learners. The model of structures we propose is presented in Figure 4-1. The important levels and processes of the model are summarized in the Appendix. Specific teaching principles for each level are also included. In addition to these specific components, teachers need to understand the more general components and principles we have explained.

Application of the structures model of learning disabilities in a thoughtful, creative way should aid in effective teaching of the learning disabled. The learning disabled will learn to select and use strategies that match their true abilities.

Levels of Response, Corresponding Learning Processes, and Principles of Teaching

Level I: *Awareness.* The awareness level refers to the physiological arousal of the system that occurs as the organism attends to stimuli. This level is a focus of learning from birth through 18 months.

   1. Major learning process:
   Attention: The process by which stimuli in the environment are scanned, focused upon, and sustained in focus or shifted from focus. It involves:
      a. scanning the available stimuli in the environment
      b. focusing on the distinctive cues of relevant stimuli
      c. sustaining focus for as long as stimuli are relevant
      d. shifting focus to new relevant stimuli
   2. Principles of teaching:
      a. Reduce stimuli to essentials.
      b. Increase the size or intensity of stimuli.
      c. Use attention getting and high motivation materials.
      d. Use successive approximation techniques.
      e. Enable the student to respond repeatedly and rapidly.

Level II: *Differentiation.* The differentiation level refers to a basic understanding related to the use of inner language and the ability to discriminate likenesses and differences and perceptual detail. This level is a focus of learning from one year through four years.

   1. Major learning process:
   Perception: The process by which the stimuli attended to are discriminated, coordinated and their sequence is recognized. It involves:

        a. discriminating distinctive differences between stimuli within any one sensory system
        b. coordinating related stimuli from two or more information sources
        c. recognizing sequence in spatial and temporal stimuli

2. Principles of teaching:
        a. Start with large differences and gradually decrease.
        b. Call direct attention to distinctive cues and essential features in stimuli.
        c. Provide direct practice in discriminating, coordinating and sequencing.

Level III: *Labeling.* The labeling level is one at which the individual attaches correct names, labels and simple definitions to objects and events. This level is a focus of learning from two years through eight years.

1. Major learning process:
    Memory: The process by which perceived stimuli are temporarily stored and rehearsed. It involves:
        a. temporarily storing an impression of stimuli
        b. rehearsing by repeating stimuli internally
2. Principles of teaching:
        a. Teach more than test.
        b. Provide direct modeling, rehearsal and drill.
        c. Reduce chances for error.
        d. Reduce emphasis on logical analysis and comprehension.

Level IV: *Understanding.* Understanding is the level at which the individual has a comprehension of concepts that is advanced enough to permit application of concepts and rules. This level is a focus of learning from nine years through adulthood.

1. Major learning process:
    Cognition: The process by which previously learned meanings are recognized as present, identified, and associated and new meanings are inferred. It involves:
        a. recognizing that meanings are present in relevant stimuli
        b. identifying the meanings that are present in relevant stimuli
        c. associating the meanings that are identified with other relevant meanings
        d. inferring new meanings that go beyond those identified in or associated with relevant stimuli

   2. Principles of teaching:
       a. Reduce or increase thinking time.
       b. Present the complex before the simple.
       c. Develop the logical steps in the thinking process.
       d. Develop a logical structure within which information can be
          organized.

Level V: *Habit:* The habit level is one at which the individual is able to respond
       appropriately and at will and performance is relatively effortless. Atten-
       tion to specific sensory stimuli is minimal, speed and consistency are
       intact. This level is a focus of learning from eleven years through
       adulthood.

   1. Major learning process:
       Encoding: The process by which internal meanings are recalled and
       organized for the purpose of communicating and responses are
       monitored. It involves:
       a. recalling the internal stimuli (ideas, words, movements) that
          will communicate the intended meaning
       b. organizing the internal stimuli (ideas, words, movements) in a
          sequence that will communicate the intended meaning
       c. monitoring responses to determine whether they are correct
   2. Principles of teaching:
       a. Inform the student of the nature of the learning problem and the
          proposed solution.
       b. Change the situation and the sensory feedback system.
       c. Help the student unlearn old habits by moving back to earlier
          levels of response.

References

Abikoff, H. Cognitive training interventions in children: review of a new approach. *Journal of Learning Disabilities*, 1979, *12*, 123-135.

Alley, G., & Deshler, D. *Teaching the learning disabled adolescent: Strategies and methods*. Denver: Love, 1979.

Anastasi, A. *Psychological testing*. (4th ed.). New York: MacMillan, 1976.

Appel, M.H., & Goldberg, L.S. (Eds.). *Topics in cognitive development, Vol. I. equilibration: theory, research, and application*. New York: Plenum Press, 1977.

Appleton-Century-Crofts. *Behavior modification–teaching language to autistic children*. Tarrytown, N.Y.: Prentice-Hall Media, distributor, 1972.

Argulewicz, E.N., Mealor, D.J., & Richmond, B.O. Creative abilities of learning disabled children. *Journal of Learning Disabilities*, 1979, *12*, 21-24.

Aten, J., & Davis, J. Disturbances in the perception of auditory sequence in children with minimal cerebral dysfunction. *Journal of Speech and Hearing Research*, 1968, *11*, 236-245.

Atkinson, R.C., & Shiffrin, R.M. The control of short-term memory. *Scientific American*, 1971, *225*, 82-90.

Atkinson, R.C., & Shiffrin, R.M. Human memory: a proposed system and its control processes. In K.W. Spence & J.T. Spence (Eds.), *The psychology of learning and motivation* (Vol. 2). New York: Academic Press, 1968, 89-137.

Ayers, A.J. Sensorimotor foundations of academic ability. In W.M. Cruickshank & D.P. Hallahan, *Perceptual and learning disabilities in children*. (Vol. 2). *Research and theory*. Syracuse, N.Y.: Syracuse University Press, 1975, 137-162.

Bachara, G.H. Empathy in learning disabled children. *Perceptual and Motor Skills*, 1976, *43*, 541-542.

Baddeley, A.D. *The psychology of memory*. New York: Basic Books, 1976.

Badian, N.A. Auditory-visual integration, auditory memory, and reading in retarded and adequate readers. *Journal of Learning Disabilities*, 1977, *10*, 108-114.

Baker, H.J., & Leland, B. *Detroit Tests of Learning Aptitude*. Indianapolis: Bobbs-Merrill, 1959.

Bauer, R.H. Memory processes in children with learning disabilities: evidence for deficient rehearsal. *Journal of Experimental Child Psychology*, 1977, *24*, 415-430.

Becker, L.D., Bender, N.N., & Morrison, G. Measuring impulsivity-reflection: a critical review. *Journal of Learning Disabilities*, 1978, *11*, 626-632.

213

Beery, K.E., & Buktenica, N.A. *Developmental Test of Visual-Motor Integration*. Chicago: Follett, 1967.

Belmont, I., & Belmont, L. Stability or change in reading achievement over time: developmental and educational implications. *Journal of Learning Disabilities*, 1978, *11*, 80-88.

Birch, H.G., & Belmont, L. Auditory-visual integration in normal and retarded readers. *American Journal of Orthopsychiatry*, 1964, *34*, 852-861.

Blalock, J.W. *A study of conceptualization and related abilities in learning disabled and normal preschool children*. Unpublished doctoral dissertation. Evanston, Ill.: Northwestern University, 1977.

Bloom, L., & Lahey, M. *Language development and language disorders*. New York: John Wiley and Sons, 1978.

Bornstein, P.H., & Quevillon, R.P. The effects of a self-instructional package on overactive preschool boys. In B.B. Lahey, *Behavior therapy with hyperactive and learning disabled children*. New York: Oxford University Press, 1979.

Bovet, M.C. Learning research within Piagetian lines. *Topics in learning and learning disabilities*, 1981, *1*, 1-9.

Bringuier, J. *Conversations with Jean Piaget*. Chicago: University of Chicago Press, 1980.

Bruner, J. *The process of education*. New York: Vintage Press, 1963.

Bryan, T. An observational analysis of classroom behaviors of children with learning disabilities. *Journal of Learning Disabilities*, 1974, *7*, 26-34.

Bryan, T. Learning disabled children's comprehension of nonverbal communication. *Journal of Learning Disabilities*, 1977, *10*, 501-506.

Bryan, T.H., & Bryan, J.H. *Understanding learning disabilities* (2nd ed.). Sherman Oaks, Calif.: Alfred, 1978.

Bryan, T.S., & Wheeler, R. Perception of learning disabled children: The eye of the observer. *Journal of Learning Disabilities*, 1972, *5*, 484-488.

Buzan, T. *Use both sides of your brain*. New York: E.P. Dutton, 1976.

Buzan, T., & Dixon, T. *The evolving brain*. New York: Holt, Rinehart, and Winston.

Carroll, J.B. *Language and thought*. Englewood Cliffs, N.J.: Prentice-Hall, 1964.

Case, R. Mental strategies, mental capacity, and instruction: A neo-Piagetian investigation. *Journal of Experimental Child Psychology*, 1974, *18*, 382-397.

Ceci, S.J., Lea, S.E.G., & Ringstrom, M.D. Coding characteristics of normal and learning-disabled 10-year-olds: Evidence for modality-specific pathways to the cognitive system. *Journal of Experimental Psychology: Human Learning and Memory*, 1980, *6*, 785-797.

Ceci, S.J., Ringstrom, M., & Lea, S.E.G. Do language-learning disabled children (L/LDs) have impaired memories? In search of underlying processes. *Journal of Learning Disabilities*, 1981, *14*, 159-162, 173.

Chalfant, J.C., & King, F.S. An approach to operationalizing the definition of learning disabilities. *Journal of Learning Disabilities*, 1976, *9*, 228-243.

Chalfant, J.C., & Scheffelin, M.A. *Central processing dysfunctions in children: A review of research*. Washington, D.C.: U.S. Government Printing Office, 1969.

Chall, J. *Learning to read: The great debate*. New York: McGraw-Hill, 1967.

Chi, M.T.H. Short-term memory limitations in children: capacity or processing deficits? *Memory and Cognition*, 1976, *4*, 559-572.

Clements, S.D. *Minimal brain dysfunction in children*. Washington, D.C.: U.S. Department of Health, Education, and Welfare, 1966.

Cohen, R.L., & Netley, C. Cognitive deficits, learning disabilities, and WISC Verbal-Performance consistency. *Developmental Psychology*, 1978, *14*, 624-634.

Cole, M., & Maltzman, I. (Eds.). *A handbook of contemporary Soviet psychology*. New York: Basic Books, 1969.

Craik, F.I.M., & Lockhart, R.S. Levels of processing: A framework for memory research. *Journal of Verbal Learning and Verbal Behavior*, 1972, *11*, 671-684.

Cruickshank, W.M. *Learning disabilities in home, school and community*. Syracuse, N.Y.: Syracuse University Press, 1977a.

Cruickshank, W.M. Myths and realities in learning disabilities. *Journal of Learning Disabilities*, 1977b, *10*, 51-58.

Cruickshank, W.M., & Hallahan, D.P. (Eds.). *Perceptual and learning disabilities in children. Vol. 1. Psychoeducational practices*. Syracuse, N.Y.: Syracuse University Press, 1975a.

Cruickshank, W.M., & Hallahan, D.P. (Eds.). *Perceptual and learning disabilities in children. Vol. 2. Research and Theory*. Syracuse, N.Y.: Syracuse University Press, 1975b.

Cullinan, D., Epstein, M.H., Lloyd, J., & Noel, M. Development of cognitive tempo in learning disabled and normal children. *Learning Disability Quarterly*, 1980, *3*, 46-53.

Cullinan, D., Epstein, M.H., & Silver, L. Modification of impulsive tempo in learning disabled pupils. *Journal of Abnormal Child Psychology*, 1977, *5*, 437-444.

DeBono, E. *New think*. New York: Basic Books, 1968.

Denckla, M.B. Research needs in learning disabilities: A neurologist's point of view. *Journal of Learning Disabilities*, 1973, *6*, 441-450.

DeRuiter, J.A., & Wansart, W.L. *Problem-solving strategies and cognitive training in learning disabled and normal adolescents*. Unpublished research report. Greeley, Col.: University of Northern Colorado Research Bureau, 1981.

Deshler, D.D., Ferrell, W.R., & Kass, C.E. Error monitoring of schoolwork by learning disabled adolescents. *Journal of Learning Disabilities*, 1978, *11*, 401-412.

Diaz, J.E. *Sentence facilitation in paired-associate learning by educationally handicapped and normal children*. Unpublished doctoral dissertation. Los Angeles: University of Southern California, 1976.

Dickinson, D.J. The direct assessment: An alternative to psychometric testing. *Journal of Learning Disabilities*, 1980, *13*, 472-476.

Dolan, A.B., & Matheny, A.P. A distinctive growth cure for a group of children with academic learning problems. *Journal of Learning Disabilities*, 1978, *11*, 490-494.

Douglas, V.I. Perceptual and cognitive factors as determinants of learning disabilities: a review chapter with special emphasis on attentional factors. In R.M. Knights & D.J. Bakker (Eds.), *The neuropsychology of learning disorders*. Baltimore: University Park Press, 1976.

Doyle, R.B., Anderson, R.P. & Halcomb, C.G. Attention deficits and the effects of visual distraction. *Journal of Learning Disabilities*, 1976, *9*, 48-54.

Dykman, R.A., Ackerman, P.T., Clements, S.D., & Peters, J.E. Specific learning disabilities: An attentional deficit syndrome. In H.R. Myklebust (Ed.), *Progress in learning disabilities*. Vol. 2. New York: Grune and Stratton, 1971.

Entwisle, D., Forsyth, D., & Muuss, R. The syntactic-paradigmatic shift in children's word association. *Journal of Verbal Learning and Verbal Behavior*, 1964, *3*, 19-20.

Epstein, M.H., Cullinan, D., & Sternberg, L. Impulsive cognitive tempo in severe and mild learning disabled children. *Psychology in the Schools*, 1977, *14*, 290-294.

Estes, W.K. *Learning theory and mental development*. New York: Academic Press, 1970.

Farnham-Diggory, S. *Learning disabilities: A psychological perspective*. Cambridge, Mass.: Harvard University Press, 1978.

Fincham, F. Conservation and cognitive role-taking ability in learning disabled boys. *Journal of Learning Disabilities*, 1979, *12*, 25-31.

Fletcher, J.M., & Satz, P. Unitary deficit hypothesis of reading disabilities: Has Vellutino led us astray? *Journal of Learning Disabilities*, 1979, *12*, 155-159.

Fletcher, J.M., & Satz, P. Has Vellutino led us astray? A rejoiner to a reply. *Journal of Learning Disabilities*, 1979, *12*, 168-171.

Frankel, F., Tymchuk, A.J., & Simmons, J.Q. Operant analysis and intervention with autistic children: Implications of current research. In E.R. Ritvo, B.J. Freeman, E.M. Ornitz & P.E. Tanguay (Eds.), *Autism: Diagnosis, current research and management*. New York: Spectrum Publications, 1976.

Frierson, E.C., & Barbe, W.B. *Educating children with learning disabilities: Selected readings*. New York: Appleton-Century-Crofts, 1967.

Frostig, M., Lefever, W., & Whittlesey, J.R. *Marianne Frostig Developmental Test of Visual Perception*. Palo Alto, Calif.: Consulting Psychologists Press, 1964.

Furth, H. *Piaget and knowledge*. Englewood Cliffs, N.J.: Prentice-Hall, 1969.

Gaddes, W.H. *Learning disabilities and brain function: A neuropsychological approach*. New York: Springer-Verlag, 1980.

German, D.J.N. Word-finding skills in children with learning disabilities. *Journal of Learning Disabilities*, 1979, *12*, 176-181.

Gibson, E.J., & Levin, H. *The psychology of reading*. Cambridge, Mass.: The MIT Press, 1975.

Gold, R.F. Constitutional growth delay and learning problems. *Journal of Learning Disabilities*, 1978, *11*, 427-429.

Gollin, E., & Saravo, A. A development analysis of learning. In J. Hellmuth (Ed.), *Cognitive studies*. (Vol. 1). New York: Brunner/Mazel, 1970.

Goodglass, H., Klein, B., Carey, P., & Jones, K. Specific semantic word categories in aphasia. *Cortex*, 1966, *2*, 74-89.

Gorman, R.M. *Discovering Piaget: A guide for teachers*. Columbus, Ohio: Merrill, 1972.

Greene, Judith. *Thinking and language*. London: Methuen, 1975.

Gruber, H.E., & Voneche, J.J. (Eds.). *The essential Piaget*. New York: Basic Books, 1977.

Guthrie, J.T., & Seifert, M. Education for children with reading disabilities. In H.R. Myklebust (Ed.), *Progress in learning disabilities*. (Vol. 4). New York: Grune and Stratton, 1978.

Guthrie, J.T., & Tyler, S.J. Psycholinguistic processing in reading and listening among good and poor readers. *Journal of Reading Behavior*, 1976, *8*, 415-426.

Guyer, B.L., & Friedman, M.P. Hemispheric processing and cognitive styles in learning-disabled and normal children. *Child Development*, 1975, *46*, 658-668.

Hagen, J.W., Hargrave, S., & Ross, W. Prompting and rehearsal in short-term memory. *Child Development*, 1973, *44*, 201-204.

Hagen, J.W., & Kail, R.V. The role of attention in perceptual and cognitive development. In W.M. Cruickshank & D.P. Hallahan (Eds.), *Perceptual and learning disabilities in children. Vol. 2. Research and theory*. Syracuse, N.Y.: Syracuse University Press, 1975.

Haines, D.J., & Torgesen, J.K. The effects of incentives on rehearsal and short-term memory in children with reading problems. *Learning Disability Quarterly*, 1979, *2* (No. 2), 48-55.

Hallahan, D.P. Comparative research studies on the psychological characteristics of learning disabled children. In W.M. Cruickshank & D.P. Hallahan (Eds.), *Perceptual and learning disabilities in children. Vol. 1. Psychoeducational practices.* Syracuse, N.Y.: Syracuse University Press, 1975a.

Hallahan, D.P. Distractibility in the learning disabled child. In W.M. Cruickshank & D.P. Hallahan (Eds.), *Perceptual and learning disabilities in children. Vol. 2. Research and theory.* Syracuse, N.Y.: Syracuse University Press, 1975b.

Hallahan, D.P., Gajar, A.H., Cohen, S.B., & Tarver, S.G. Selective attention and locus of control in learning disabled and normal children. *Journal of Learning Disabilities,* 1978, *11,* 231-236.

Hallahan, D.P., Tarver, S.G., Kauffman, J.M., & Graybeal, N.L. A comparison of the effects of reinforcement and response cost on the selective attention of learning disabled children. *Journal of Learning Disabilities,* 1978, *11,* 430-438.

Hammill, D. Training visual perceptual processes. *Journal of Learning Disabilities,* 1972, *5,* 552-559.

Hammill, D., & Larsen, S. Relationship of selected auditory perceptual skills and reading ability. *Journal of Learning Disabilities,* 1971, *4,* 40-46.

Haring, N.G., & Bateman, B. *Teaching the learning disabled child.* Englewood Cliffs, N.J.: Prentice-Hall, 1977.

Heath, E.J., & Early, G.H. Intramodal and intermodal functioning of normal and LD children. *Academic Therapy,* 1973, *9,* 133-149.

Hellmuth, J. (Ed.). *Cognitive studies* (Vol. 1). New York: Brunner/Mazel, 1970.

Hermann, K. *Reading disability.* Springfield, Ill.: Thomas, 1959.

Herndon, J. *How to survive in your native land.* New York: Simon and Schuster, 1971.

Hinshelwood, J. *Congenital word-blindness.* London: Lewis, 1917.

Hofstadter, D.R. *Gödel, Escher, Bach: An eternal golden braid.* New York: Basic Books, 1979.

Horner, G.C. *Hyperactive and non-hyperactive children's self-determined levels of stimulation.* Unpublished doctoral dissertation. Kansas City: University of Missouri, 1977.

Hresko, W.P., & Reid, D.K. Five faces of cognition: Theoretical influences on approaches to learning disabilities. *Learning Disability Quarterly,* 1981, *4,* 238-243.

Hunter, S.H., Russell, H.L., Russell, E.D., & Zimmerman, R.L. Control of fingertip temperature increases via biofeedback in learning-disabled and normal children. *Perceptual and Motor Skills,* 1976, *43,* 743-755.

Illich, I. *De-schooling society.* New York: Harper and Row, 1971.

Inhelder, B., & Chipman, H. *Piaget and his school: A reader in developmental psychology.* New York: Springer-Verlag, 1976.

Isaacs, N. *A brief introduction to Piaget.* New York: Schocken, 1960.

John, E.R., Karmel, B.Z., Corning, W.C., Easton, P., Brown, D., Ahn, H., John, M., Harmony, T., Prichep, L., Toro, A., Gerson, I., Bartlett, F., Thatcher, R., Kaye, H., Valdes, P., & Schwartz, E. Neurometrics. *Science,* 1977, *196,* 1393-1410.

Johnson, D., & Myklebust, H.R. *Learning disabilities: Educational principles and practices.* New York: Grune and Stratton, 1967.

Kagan, J., & Kogan, N. Individual variation in cognitive processes. In P.H. Mussen (Ed.), *Carmichael's manual of child psychology.* (3rd. ed., Vol. 1). New York: John Wiley, 1970.

Kass, C.E. Educational management of writing deficits. In J.V. Irwin & M. Marge (Eds.), *Principles of childhood language disabilities.* Englewood Cliffs, N.J.: Prentice-Hall, 1972.

Kass, C.E. Personal communication, 1970.

Kass, C.E. Identification of learning disability (dyssymbolia). *Journal of Learning Disabilities,* 1977, *10,* 425-432.

Keith, R.M. Do disorders of perception occur? *Developmental Medicine and Child Neurology*, 1977, *19*, 821-825.

Keogh, B.K., & Margolis, J. Learn to labor and to wait: attentional problems of children with learning disorders. *Journal of Learning Disabilities*, 1976, *9*, 276-286.

Kephart, N.C. *The slow learner in the classroom* (2nd ed.). Columbus, Ohio: Merrill, 1971.

Kephart, N.C. Developmental sequences. In S.G. Sapir & A.C. Nitzburg (Eds.), *Children with learning problems: Readings in a developmental-interaction approach*. New York: Brunner/Mazel, 1973.

Kershner, J.R. Visual-spatial organization and reading: Support for a cognitive-developmental interpretation. *Journal of Learning Disabilities*, 1975, *8*, 30-36.

Kershner, J.R. Cerebral dominance in disabled readers, good readers, and gifted children: Search for a valid model. *Child Development*, 1977, *48*, 61-67.

Kidder, H.C. *Auditory fusion and response latency among learning disabled, reading disabled, and normal children*. Unpublished doctoral dissertation. Wichita: Wichita State University, 1977.

Kingsley, P.R., & Hagen, J.W. Induced versus spontaneous rehearsal in short-term memory in nursery school children. *Developmental Psychology*, 1969, *1*, 40-46.

Kirk, S.A. *Educating exceptional children*. Boston: Houghton Mifflin, 1972.

Kirk, S.A., Kliebhan, J.M., & Lerner, J.W. *Teaching reading to slow and disabled learners*. Boston: Houghton Mifflin, 1978.

Kirk, S.A., McCarthy, J.J., & Kirk, W.D. *Illinois Test of Psycholinguistic Abilities*. Urbana, Ill.: University of Illinois Press, 1968.

Klees, M., & Lebrun, A. Analysis of the figurative and operative processes of thought of 40 dyslexic children. *Journal of Learning Disabilities*, 1972, *5*, 389-396.

Klein-Koningsberg, E.E. *Semantic integration in normal and learning disabled children*. Unpublished doctoral dissertation. New York: City University of New York, 1977.

Knights, R.M., & Bakker, D.J. (Eds.). *The Neuropsychology of learning disorders*. Baltimore: University Park Press, 1976.

Kohl, H. *Reading, how to*. New York: Bantam Books, 1974.

Kohlers, P.A. Pattern-analyzing disability in poor readers. *Developmental Psychology*, 1975, *11*, 282-290.

Koppell, S. Testing the attentional deficit notion. *Journal of Learning Disabilities*, 1979, *12*, 43-48.

Lahey, B.B. *Behavior therapy with hyperactive and learning disabled children*. New York: Oxford University Press, 1979.

LaPointe, C.M. Token Test performances by learning disabled and achieving adolescents. *British Journal of Disorders of Communication*, 1976, *11*, 121-133.

Lefton, L.A., Lahey, B.B., & Stagg, D.I. Eye movements in reading disabled and normal children: A study of systems and strategies. *Journal of Learning Disabilities*, 1978, *11*, 549-558.

Lewis, M. The development of attention and perception in the infant and young child. In W.M. Cruickshank, & D.P. Hallahan (Eds.), *Perceptual and learning disabilities in children. Vol. 2. Research and theory*. Syracuse, N.Y.: Syracuse University Press, 1975.

Lidz, C.S. Criterion referenced assessment. The new bandwagon? *Exceptional Children*, 1979, *46*, 131-132.

Liles, B.Z., Shulman, M.D., & Bartlett, S. Judgments of grammaticality by normal and language-disordered children. *Journal of Speech and Hearing Disorders*, 1977, *42*, 199-209.

Lilly, M.S., & Kelleher, J. Modality strengths and aptitude-treatment interaction. *Journal of Special Education*, 1973, *7*, 5-13.

Lovegrove, W.J., Bowling, A., Badcock, D., & Blackwood, M. Specific reading disability: Differences in contrast sensitivity as a function of spatial frequency. *Science*, 1980, *210*, 439-440.

Luria, A.R. Speech development and the formation of mental processes. In M. Cole & I. Maltzman (Eds.), *A handbook of contemporary Soviet psychology*. New York: Basic Books, 1969.

Luria, A.R. *Cognitive development: Its cultural and social foundations*. Cambridge, Mass.: Harvard University Press, 1976.

Luria, A.R. *Higher cortical functions in man*. (2nd. ed.) New York: Basic Books, 1980.

Mackworth, J.F. Some models of reading process: learners and skilled readers. *Reading Research Quarterly*, 1972, *7*, 701-733.

Maier, A.S. The effect of focusing on the cognitive processes of learning disabled children. *Journal of Learning Disabilities*, 1980, *13*, 143-147.

Maier, H.W. *Three theories of child development*. (3rd. ed.) New York: Harper and Row, 1978.

Mann, L., Goodman, L., & Wiederholt, J.L. (Eds.). *Teaching the learning-disabled adolescent*. Boston: Houghton Mifflin, 1978.

Mann, P.H., & Suiter, P. *Handbook in diagnostic teaching: A learning disabilities approach*. Boston: Allyn and Bacon, 1974.

Margolis, H. Auditory perceptual test performance and the reflection-impulsivity dimension. *Journal of Learning Disabilities*, 1977, *10*, 164-172.

Mayron, L.W. Ecological factors in learning disabilities. *Journal of Learning Disabilities*, 1978, *11*, 495-505.

Mayron, L.W. Allergy, learning, and behavior problems. *Journal of Learning Disabilities*, 1979, *12*, 32-42.

McCroskey, R.L., & Kidder, H.C. Auditory fusion among learning disabled, reading disabled, and normal children. *Journal of Learning Disabilities*, 1980, *13*, 69-76.

McIntyre, C.W., Murray, M.E., Cronin, C.M., & Blackwell, S.L. Span of apprehension in learning disabled boys. *Journal of Learning Disabilities*, 1978, *11*, 468-475.

McKinney, J.D., & Haskins, R. Cognitive training and the development of problem-solving strategies. *Exceptional Education Quarterly*, 1980, *1*, 41-51.

McKinney, J.D., Haskins, R., & Moore, M.G. *Problem solving strategies in reflective and impulsive children*. (Final Report, National Institute of Education, Project No. 3-0344). Washington, D.C.: U.S. Dept. of HEW, 1977.

McSpadden, J.V., & Strain, P.S. Memory thresholds and overload effects between learning disabled and achieving pupils. *Exceptional Children*, 1977, *44*, 35-37.

Meichenbaum, D. Cognitive-functional approach to cognitive factors as determinants of learning disabilities. In R.M. Knights & D.J. Bakker (Eds.), *The Neuropsychology of Learning Disorders*. Baltimore: University Park Press, 1976.

Meichenbaum, D. *Cognitive-behavior modification*. New York: Plenum Press, 1977.

Mercer, C.D., Forgnone, C., & Wolking, W.D. Definitions of learning disabilities used in the United States. *Journal of Learning Disabilities*, 1976, *9*, 376-386.

Merluzzi, T.V., Glass, C.R., & Genest, M. *Cognitive assessment*. New York: Guilford Press, 1981.

Messer, S.B. Reflection-impulsivity: A review. *Psychological Bulletin*, 1976, *83*, 1026-1052.

Miller, G.A., Galanter, E., & Pribram, K.H. *Plans and the structure of behavior*. New York: Holt, 1960.

Miller, M., Brecht, R.D., & Richey, D.D. Cognitive deficits in reading comprehension (a call for research). *Journal of Learning Disabilities*, 1978, *11*, 576-579.

Miller, M., & Rohr, M.E. Verbal mediation for perceptual deficits in learning disabilities: a review and suggestions. *Journal of Learning Disabilities*, 1980, *13*, 319-321.

Morrison, F.J., Giordani, B., & Nacy, J. Reading disability: An information-processing analysis. *Science*, 1977, *196*, 77-79.

Moses, N. Using Piagetian principles to guide instruction of the learning disabled. *Topics in Learning and Learning Disabilities*, 1981, *1*, 11-19.

Myklebust, H.R. *Development and disorders of written language: Vol. 1. Picture Story Language Test*. New York: Grune and Stratton, 1965.

Myklebust, H.R. (Ed.). *Progress in learning disabilities* (Vol. 2). New York: Grune and Stratton, 1971.

Myklebust, H.R. *Development and disorders of written language. Vol. 2. Studies of normal and exceptional children*. New York: Grune and Stratton, 1973.

Myklebust, H.R. *Progress in learning disabilities* (Vol. 4). New York: Grune and Stratton, 1978.

Neisser, U. *Cognitive psychology*. Englewood Cliffs, N.J.: Prentice-Hall, 1967.

Nelson, H.E., & Warrington, E.K. Developmental spelling retardation and its relation to other cognitive abilities. *British Journal of Psychology*, 1974, *65*, 265-274.

Newcomer, P., Hare, B., Hammill, D., & McGettigan, J. Construct validity of the ITPA. *Exceptional Children*, 1974, *40*, 509-510.

Norman, D.A. Post-Freudian slips. *Psychology Today*, 1980, *13* (11), 42-50.

Obrzut, J.E. Dichotic listening and bisensory memory skills in qualitatively diverse dyslexic readers. *Journal of Learning Disabilities*, 1979, *12*, 304-314.

Orton, S.T. Word-blindness in school children. *Archives of Neurology and Psychiatry*, 1925, *14*, 528-615.

Osgood, C.E. A behavioristic analysis of perception and language as cognitive phenomena. In J.S. Bruner (Ed.), *Contemporary approaches to cognition*. Cambridge, Mass.: Harvard University Press, 1957a.

Osgood, C.E. Motivational dynamics of language behavior. In M.R. Jones (Ed.), *Nebraska symposium on motivation*. Lincoln: University of Nebraska Press, 1957b.

Owen, J.A. *Storage, retrieval and organizational processes in normal and learning disabled third graders*. Unpublished doctoral dissertation, Atlanta: Georgia State University, 1976.

Peters, J.E., Romine, J.S., & Dykman, R.A. A special neurological examination of children with learning disabilities. *Developmental Medicine and Child Neurology*, 1975, *17*, 63-78.

Piaget, J. Equilibration and the development of structures. In J.M. Tanner & B. Inhelder (Eds.), *Discussions on child development* (Vol. 4). New York: International University Press, 1960.

Piaget, J. The general problems of the psychobiological development of the child. In J.M. Tanner & B. Inhelder (Eds.), *Discussions on child development* (Vol. 4). New York: International University Press, 1960.

Piaget, J. Development and learning. *Journal of Research in Science Teaching*, 1964, *2*, 176-186.

Piaget, J. *Six psychological studies*. New York: Random House, 1967.

Piaget, J. The growth of logical thinking from childhood to adolescence. In H.E. Gruber & J.J. Vonèche (Eds.), *The essential Piaget*. New York: Basic Books, 1977a.

Piaget, J. Science of education and the psychology of the child. In H.E. Gruber & J.J. Vonèche (Eds.), *The essential Piaget*. New York: Basic Books, 1977b.

Piaget, J. Equilibration processes in the psychobiological development of the child. In H.E. Gruber & J.J. Vonèche (Eds.), *The essential Piaget*. New York: Basic Books, 1977c.

Piaget, J., Grize, J., Szeminska, H., & Bang, V. *Epistemology and the psychology of functions.* Boston: Reidell, 1977.

Piatteli-Palmarini, M. *Language and learning: The debate between Jean Piaget and Noam Chomsky.* Cambridge, Mass.: Harvard University Press, 1980.

Pick, H.L., & Pick, A.D. Sensory and perceptual development. In P.H. Mussen (Ed.), *Carmichael's manual of child psychology* (Vol. 1). New York: John Wiley and Sons, 1970.

Pines, M. *The brain changers: Scientists and the new mind control.* New York: The New American Library, 1973.

Pirsig, R. *Zen and the art of motorcycle maintenance.* New York: William Morrow, 1974.

Poggio, J.P., & Salkind, N.J. A review and appraisal of instruments assessing hyperactivity in children. *Learning Disability Quarterly,* 1979, *2,* 9-22.

Poppen, R., Stark, V., Eisenson, J., Forrest, T., & Wertheim, G. Visual sequencing performances of aphasic children. *Journal of Speech and Hearing Research,* 1969, *12,* 288-300.

Powers, W.T. *Behavior: The control of perception.* Chicago: Aldine, 1973.

Prawat, R.S., & Kerasotes, D. Basic memory processes in reading. *Merrill-Palmer Quarterly,* 1978, *24,* 181-188.

Quay, H.C. Special education: Assumptions, techniques, and evaluative criteria. *Exceptional Children,* 1973, *40,* 165-170.

Rapp, D.J. Does diet affect hyperactivity? *Journal of Learning Disabilities,* 1978, *11,* 383-389.

Rees, N.S. Auditory processing factors in language disorders: The view from Procrustes' bed. *Journal of Speech and Hearing Disorders,* 1973, *38,* 304-315.

Reese, H.W. *Basic learning processes in childhood.* New York: Holt, Rinehart, Winston, 1976.

Renshaw, D.C. *The hyperactive child.* Chicago: Nelson-Hall, 1974.

Richie, D.J., & Aten, J.L. Auditory retention of nonverbal and verbal sequential stimuli in children with reading disabilities. *Journal of Learning Disabilities,* 1976, *9,* 312-318.

Robson, G.M. *Problem solving strategies in learning disabled and normal achieving children.* Unpublished doctoral dissertation. Los Angeles: University of California and California State University, 1977.

Rose, A.M., & Fernandes, K. *An information-processing approach to performance assessment: I. Experimental investigation of an information processing performance battery.* Washington, D.C.: American Institutes for Research, 1977.

Rosenthal, R.H., & Allen, T.W. An examination of attention, arousal, and learning dysfunctions of hyperkinetic children. *Psychological Bulletin,* 1978, *85,* 689-715.

Rourke, B.P. Brain-behavior relationships in children with learning disabilities. A research program. *American Psychologist,* 1975, *30,* 911-920.

Rudel, R.G., & Denckla, M.B. Relationship of IQ and reading score to visual, spatial, and temporal matching tasks. *Journal of Learning Disabilities,* 1976, *9,* 169-178.

Rugel, R.P., & Mitchell, A. Characteristics of familial and nonfamilial disabled readers. *Journal of Learning Disabilities,* 1977, *10,* 308-313.

Sabatino, D.A. (Ed.). *Learning disabilities handbook: A technical guide to program development.* DeKalb, Ill.: Northern Illinois University Press, 1976.

Salvia, J., & Ysseldyke, J.E. *Assessment in special and remedial education.* (2nd. ed.). Boston: Houghton Mifflin, 1981.

Samples, B. Mind cycles and learning. *Phi Delta Kappan,* 1977, *58,* 688-692.

Sapir, S.G., & Nitzburg, A.C. (Eds.). *Children with learning problems: Readings in a developmental-interaction approach.* New York: Brunner/Mazel, 1973.

Sapir, S.G., & Wilson, B. *A professional's guide to working with the learning disabled child.* New York: Brunner/Mazel, 1978.

Sattler, J.M. *Assessment of children's intelligence.* (revised reprint) Philadelphia: Saunders, 1974.

Schevill, H.S. Tactile learning and reading failure. In H.R. Myklebust (Ed.), *Progress in learning disabilities.* (Vol. 4). New York: Grune and Stratton, 1978.

Selz, M.J. *A neuropsychological model of learning disability: Classification of brain function in 9-14 year-old children.* Unpublished doctoral dissertation. Seattle: University of Washington, 1977.

Selz, M., & Reitan, R.M. Rules for neuropsychological diagnosis: Classification of brain function in older children. *Journal of Consulting and Clinical Psychology,* 1979, *47,* 258-264.

Senf, G.M. A perspective on the definition of LD. *Journal of Learning Disabilities,* 1977, *10,* 537-539.

Shea, R.A. *A comparison of the role of language and cognitive style variables in regular class and learning disabled student's recall of orally presented stories.* Unpublished doctoral dissertation. Los Angeles: University of Southern California, 1977.

Sies, L.F. (Ed.). *Aphasia theory and therapy: Selected lectures and papers of Hildred Schuell.* Baltimore: University Park Press, 1974.

Snyder, L.S. Communicative and cognitive abilities and disabilities in the sensorimotor period. *Merrill-Palmer Quarterly,* 1978, *24,* 161-180.

Sobotka, K.R., Black, F.W., Hill, S.D., & Porter, R.J. Some psychological correlates of developmental dyslexia. *Journal of Learning Disabilities,* 1977, *10,* 363-369.

Solomons, G. Guidelines on the use and medical effects of psychostimulant drugs in therapy. *Journal of Learning Disabilities,* 1971, *4,* 420-475.

Sommerhoff, G. *Logic of the living brain.* New York: John Wiley and Sons, 1974.

Spiker, C.C. Performance on a difficult discrimination following pretraining with distinctive stimuli. *Child Development,* 1959, *30,* 513-521.

Staats, A.W. *Learning, language, and cognition.* New York: Holt, Rinehart, and Winston, 1968.

Steinkamp, M.W. Relationships between environmental distractions and task performance of hyperactive and normal children. *Journal of Learning Disabilities,* 1980, *13,* 209-214.

Stellern, J., & Vasa, S.F. *A primer of diagnostic-prescriptive teaching and programming.* Laramie, WY: Center for Research, University of Wyoming, 1973.

Sternberg, R.J. *Intelligence, information processing, and analogical reasoning: The componential analysis of human abilities.* Hillsdale, N.J.: Lawrence Erlbaum Associates, 1977.

Sternberg, R.J. Developmental patterns in the encoding and combination of logical connectives. *Journal of Experimental Child Psychology,* 1979a, *28,* 469-498.

Sternberg, R.J. The nature of mental abilities. *American Psychologist,* 1979b, *34,* 214-230.

Swanson, H.L. Auditory recall of conceptually, phonetically, and linguistically similar words by normal and learning disabled children. *Journal of Special Education,* 1979, *13,* 63-67.

Swanson, H.L. Auditory and visual vigilance in normal and learning disabled readers. *Learning Disability Quarterly,* 1980, *3,* 71-78.

Sykes, D., Douglas, V. & Morgenstern, G. Sustained attention in hyperactive children. *Journal of Child Psychology and Psychiatry,* 1973, *14,* 213-220.

Tallal, P. Perceptual and linguistic factors in the language impairment of developmental dysphasics: An experimental investigation with the Token Test. *Cortex,* 1975, *11,* 196-205.

Tarver, S.G., & Dawson, M.M. Modality preference and the teaching of reading: A review. *Journal of Learning Disabilities,* 1978, *11,* 5-17.

Tarver, S.G., Ellsworth, P.S., & Rounds, D.J. Figural and verbal creativity in learning disabled and nondisabled children. *Learning Disability Quarterly,* 1980, *3*(3), 11-18.

Tarver, S.G., & Hallahan, D.P. Attention deficits in children with learning disabilities: A review. *Journal of Learning Disabilities,* 1974, *7,* 560-569.

Tarver, S.G., Hallahan, D.P., Cohen, S.B., & Kauffman, J.M. The development of visual selective attention and verbal rehearsal in learning disabled boys. *Journal of Learning Disabilities,* 1977, *10,* 491-500.

Tarver, S.G., Hallahan, D.P., Kauffman, J.M., & Ball, D.W. Verbal rehearsal and selective attention in children with learning disabilities: A developmental lag. *Journal of Experimental Child Psychology,* 1976, *22,* 375-385.

Torgesen, J.K. The role of nonspecific factors in the task performance of learning disabled children: A theoretical assessment. *Journal of Learning Disabilities,* 1977, *10,* 27-34.

Torgesen, J.K. Performance of reading disabled children on serial memory tasks: A selected review of recent research. *Reading Research Quarterly,* 1978-79, *12,* 57-84.

Torgesen, J.K. Factors related to poor performance on memory tasks in reading disabled children. *Learning Disability Quarterly,* 1979a, *2* (No. 3), 17-23.

Torgesen, J.K. What shall we do with psychological processes? *Journal of Learning Disabilities,* 1979b, *12,* 514-521.

Torgesen, J.K. Conceptual and educational implications of the use of efficient task strategies by learning disabled children. *Journal of Learning Disabilities,* 1980, *13,* 364-371.

Torgesen, J.K., & Houck, D.G. Processing deficiencies of learning-disabled children who perform poorly on the digit span test. *Journal of Educational Psychology,* 1980, *72,* 141-160.

Torgesen, J.K., Murphy, H.A., & Ivey, C. The influence of an orienting task on the memory performance of children with reading problems. *Journal of Learning Disabilities,* 1979, *12,* 396-401.

Vellutino, F.R. The validity of perceptual deficit explanations of reading disability: A reply to Fletcher and Satz. *Journal of Learning Disabilities,* 1979, *12,* 160-167.

Vellutino, F.R., Steger, B.M., Moyer, S.C., Harding, C.J., & Niles, J.A. Has the perceptual deficit hypothesis led us astray? *Journal of Learning Disabilities,* 1977, *10,* 375-385.

Vogel, S.A. Morphological abilities in normal and dyslexic children. *Journal of Learning Disabilities,* 1977, *10,* 35-43.

Wallace, G., & Larsen, S.C. *Educational assessment of learning problems: Testing for teaching.* Boston: Allyn and Bacon, 1978.

Wallbrown, F.H., Blaha, J., Huelsman, C.B. Jr., & Wallbrown, J.D. A further test of Myklebust's cognitive structure hypothesis for reading disabled children. *Psychology in the Schools,* 1975, *12,* 176-181.

Wallbrown, F.H., Blaha, J., Wherry, R.J., & Counts, D.H. An empirical test of Myklebust's cognitive structure hypothesis for 70 reading-disabled children. *Journal of Consulting and Clinical Psychology,* 1974, *42,* 211-218.

Wechsler, D. *Wechsler Intelligence Scale for Children–Revised.* New York: Psychological Corporation, 1974.

Weithorn, C.J., & Kagen, E. Training first graders of high-activity level to improve performance through verbal self-direction. *Journal of Learning Disabilities,* 1979, *12,* 82-88.

Wepman, J.M. The perceptual basis for learning. In E.C. Frierson & W.B. Barbe (Eds.), *Educating children with learning disabilities: Selected readings.* New York: Appleton-Century-Crofts, 1967.

Wepman, J.M. Auditory perception and imperception. In W.M. Cruickshank & D.P. Hallahan (Eds.), *Perceptual and learning disabilities in children. Vol. 2. Research and theory.* Syracuse, N.Y.: Syracuse University Press, 1975.

Whalen, C.K., & Henker, B. Psychostimulants and children: A review and analysis. *Psychologicat Bulletin,* 1976, *83,* 1113-1130.

Wiig, E.H. Speech presented at Colorado Association for Children with Learning Disabilities— Colorado Division for Children with Learning Disabilities Conference. Denver, Colo.: 1978.

Wiig, E.H., Lapointe, C., & Semel, E.M. Relationships among language processing and production abilities of learning disabled adolescents. *Journal of Learning Disabilities,* 1977, *10,* 292-299.

Wiig, E.H., & Semel, E.M. Comprehension of linguistic concepts requiring logical operations by learning-disabled children. *Journal of Speech and Hearing Research,* 1973, *16,* 627-636.

Wiig, E.H., & Semel, E.M. Productive language abilities in learning disabled adolescents. *Journal of Learning Disabilities,* 1975, *8,* 578-586.

Wiig, E.H., & Semel, E.M. *Language disabilities in children and adolescents.* Columbus, Ohio: Merrill, 1976.

Wilson, B.J. Free recall and subjective organization in performance of learning disabled children. *Psychological Reports,* 1977, *40,* 117-118.

Wissink, J.F., Kass, C.E., & Ferrell, W.R. A Bayesian approach to the identification of children with learning disabilities. *Journal of Learning Disabilities,* 1975, *8,* 158-166.

Wolf, S.R. *Selective attention, impulsivity and locus-of-control among upper elementary learning disabled children and their normally achieving peers: A comparison.* Unpublished doctoral dissertation. Austin: University of Texas at Austin, 1979.

Ysseldyke, J.E. Remediation of ability deficits: Some major questions. In L. Mann, L. Goodman, & J.L. Wiederholt (Eds.), *Teaching the learning disabled adolescent.* Boston: Houghton Mifflin, 1978.

Zentall, S.S., Zentall, T.R., & Barack, R.C. Distraction as a function of within-task stimulation for hyperactive and normal children. *Journal of Learning Disabilities,* 1978, *11,* 540-548.

Index

225

active, 168
assessment of, 26-27
deficient, 15-16
overview of, 24-27
vs. performance products, 154
specific, 27-57
study of, 116
Learning tasks, 112, 119
Lea, S.E.G., 78, 171
Lebrun, A., 15
Left cerebral hemisphere, 25
Lefton, L.A., 29
Letter reversals, 68
Levels
  I. *See* Awareness level
  II. *See* Differentiation level
  III. *See* Labeling
  IV. *See* Understanding
  V. *See* Habit
  of activity, 33, 34, 164
  of response. *See* Response levels
Levels-processes approach, 122
Levin, H., 29, 39, 41, 51, 165, 166
Lidz, C.S., 112
Liles, B.Z., 48, 56
Limits on acuity, 79
Linkletter, Art, 6
Logical strategies, 18, 88, 130, 172
Logical thinking, 85, 87, 137
Long-term memory, 43, 45, 53, 54, 161
Lower level thinking, 107
Luria, A.R., 14, 191

M

Manipulation
  environmental, 68
  stimulus, 165
Mann, P.H., 132
Margolis, J., 29, 30, 163
Matching judgments, 38
Materials selection, 152-153
Mathematical concept comprehension, 47
Mathematical structure analysis, 10

Maturation, 80
McCroskey, R.L., 39
McIntyre, C.W., 43, 46
Mealor, D.J., 51
Meaning, 69, 173
  associated, 49-51
  association of, 47
  complex, 70
  identification of, 47, 49
  inferring of, 51, 89
  personal, 57
  recognition of, 47, 48
  semantic-associative, 43
Measurement
  See also Assessment; Evaluation; Testing
  of abilities, 80
  of attention, 31
  of discrimination, 37
  of information processing, 26
  instruments for, 31
Mechanical strategies, 18, 87, 130, 169
Mediation, 14, 70, 106
Medical model of learning disability, 147
Meichenbaum, D., 115, 116, 131, 173, 190
Memorization, 18, 69, 70
Memory, 19, 27, 39, 43-47, 48, 57, 65, 128, 147, 210
  and behavior, 46-47
  capacity of, 43
  components of, 43, 47
  deficits in, 46
  defined, 15
  levels of storage in, 43
  long-term, 43, 45, 53, 54, 161
  models of, 43
  problems in, 41, 42
  process of, 46
  rote, 18, 69, 70
  short-term, 44, 45, 125, 147
  slots in, 44
  span of, 39, 43
  storage in, 3, 43-44, 47, 53
  tasks in, 83

About the Authors

JAMES A. DERUITER is Associate Professor of Special Education and Chairman of the Department of Special Education at the University of Northern Colorado, Greeley, Colorado. He completed his Bachelor of Arts in Secondary Education with a major in History and a minor in Psychology at Calvin College in Grand Rapids, Michigan. His Masters of Arts in Special Education is from Western Michigan University, Kalamazoo, Michigan. He completed his Ph.D. in Special Education at the University of Arizona in Tucson. He has experience as a regular classroom teacher, as a teacher of emotionally disturbed and learning disabled children in public school and residential settings, and as a clinical specialist in learning disabilities. His current professional interests include research related to the structures model of learning disabilities, in addition to university teaching and consulting in public school learning disability programs.

WILLIAM L. WANSART is completing doctoral studies in special education at the University of Northern Colorado, Greeley, Colorado. He completed his Bachelor of Science in Education with a major in Learning and Behavioral Disorders at the State University College at Buffalo, Buffalo, New York. His Masters of Arts is in Special Education: Learning Disabilities from the University of Northern Colorado, Greeley, Colorado. He has experience as a teacher of mentally retarded, emotionally disturbed, and learning disabled students in public schools. His current professional interests include research related to the structures model of learning disabilities, research related to the application of Piagetian theory to learning disabilities, and working with prospective teachers of the learning disabled.